Visits to Workhouses

The view from the inside

Peter Higginbotham

Introduction and illustrations © 2019 Peter Higginbotham / workhouses.org.uk
All Rights Reserved.
Published by the Workhouse Press.

Contents

Introduction..5

Glossary 20

Brighton, Sussex (1834) 22

Hawarden, Flintshire (1834)...25

Wallingford, Berkshire (1835).......................................26

Bulcamp, Suffolk (1835) 27

Blean, Kent (1838)..29

Nottingham, Nottinghamshire (1840)..................................32

Wandsworth & Clapham, London (1841) 36

North Dublin, Ireland (1844)..38

Manchester (Swinton), Lancashire (1850).............................41

Stepney (Wapping), London (1860) 48

St Martin in the Fields, London (1865) 54

Lewisham, London (1865)...58

Lambeth, London (1866) 62

Romford and Billericay, Essex (1866) 72

Basingstoke, Hampshire (1867).......................................74

Farnham, Surrey (1867)..83

Hursley, Hampshire (1867) 89

Leek, Staffordshire (1867)..97

Chorlton, Lancashire (1871)...110

Keighley, West Yorkshire (1887).....................................118

Macclesfield, Cheshire (1888).......................................124

St Pancras, London (1889) 133

St Pancras (Streatham), London (1889)...............................138

St Marylebone, London (1889)..143

St Marylebone Infirmary, London (1889) 152

Islington, London (1889)..159

Shoreditch, London (1889)...166

Lambeth, London (1890) 173

Chorlton, Lancashire (1890)..179

Liverpool, Lancashire (1890) 185

Cirencester, Gloucestershire (1890) 193

Gloucester, Gloucestershire (1890) 196

Swindon, Wiltshire (1890)...198

Newhaven, Sussex (1890) 201

Haverfordwest, Pembrokeshire (1894)...204

Reading, Berkshire (1894)..208

South Dublin, Ireland (1895)..213

Cootehill, County Cavan (1895)..219

Ecclesall Bierlow, West Yorkshire (1896) 224

Sheffield, West Yorkshire (1896)..232

Oundle, Northamptonshire (1896)...237

Haslingden, Lancashire (1898)...246

Whitechapel, London (1902) 251

Dewsbury, West Yorkshire (1904) 256

Tynemouth, Durham (1909) 261

Guildford, Surrey (1909) 263

Coventry, Warwickshire (1909) 266

Bradford, West Yorkshire (1909) 269

Birmingham, Warwickshire (1909) 270

Leith, Midlothian (1909) 272

Headington and Oxford, Oxfordshire (1931) 274

Bibliography 277

Notes and Sources...278

Location Index 280

Introduction

The Origins of the Workhouse

Henry VIII's dissolution of the monasteries and other religious houses in the 1530s removed what had been a major part of support for the nation's poor. Over the following decades, a succession of legislative experiments increasingly transferred the onus of supporting the helpless and destitute onto the public purse. A coalescence of these measures, in the form of the 1601 Poor Relief Act, placed this responsibility on the parish and its vestry committee.

Under the Act, parishes raised money through a local property tax, known as the poor rate. The poor rate was mostly distributed in the form of 'out-relief'— handouts in the form of cash or bread, or as one-off payments for items such as clothing. The able-bodied were expected to work in return for such support, with the poor rate being used to buy stocks of materials such as wool or flax for claimants to spin or weave in their own home or in daytime workshops. The poor rate could also be used to provide accommodation for the 'impotent' poor, such as the elderly and the chronic sick, who were unable to cope even with the help of a handout.

The 1600s witnessed the gradual appearance of establishments that became known as workhouses — premises that combined the functions of housing the impotent poor and where able-bodied destitute could work in return for their board and lodging.

The Workhouse Test

At the start of the eighteenth century, there was increasing interest in what became known as the workhouse 'test'. Parishes realised offered claimants only the workhouse instead of out-relief, their number could be greatly reduced. Only the truly needy would contemplate entry into a workhouse, which thus provided a test of their destitution. At around the same time, the onerous business of running workhouses was increasingly handed over to private contractors, who received payment from the parish based on the number of inmates in residence. The contactor also kept any income derived from the inmates' labour. Running a workhouse could be a profitable business, with competitive tendering for the contract sometimes taking place. In 1723, these ideas were formalised in what became known as the Workhouse Test Act, which also allowed small parishes to share the use of a workhouse.

The saving to a parish's ratepayers that could result from operating the workhouse test, and the use of private contractors, resulted in a workhouse boom in the eighteenth century. In a national survey in the 1770s, around one in seven parishes in England and Wales had a workhouse, with almost two thousand in operation.[1] Of course, if one in seven parishes had a workhouse, then six in seven were using only out-relief, which was always the dominant method of supporting the poor.

Multi-Parish Poor Relief

Although the 1723 Act allowed parishes to share a workhouse, other options emerged to allow parishes to unite in all aspects of poor relief operation. In 1696, Bristol obtained a Local Act of Parliament to allow the city's eighteen parishes to combine for this purpose and form an incorporation managed by a board of guardians. Bristol's example was followed by a number of towns and cities, including Exeter, Hull, Norwich, Oxford, Manchester, Birmingham, Sunderland and Brighton.

From the 1750s, Local Act incorporations were formed in a number of rural areas, often based on historical county 'hundreds'. Most of these rural incorporations were in East Anglia, with a few others in Shropshire and elsewhere. Like their civic counterparts, rural incorporations invariably included a large workhouse in the provision for their poor, often known as a House of Industry.

Promoting a Local Act was a costly business, and any change in its terms requiring a whole new Act to be obtained. In 1782, a simpler and more flexible mechanism was introduced through Gilbert's Act, which allowed groups or 'unions' of parishes to operate a shared system of poor relief, including a common workhouse. The workhouse was to be only for the old, the sick and infirm, and orphan children. Gilbert Unions were controlled by a board of guardians, elected by the ratepayers in each member parish and appointed by local magistrates.

The Rising Cost of Poor Relief

The national cost of poor relief escalated at the start of the nineteenth century, more than quadrupling from £2.0M in 1784 to £9.3M in 1818.[2] Claimant numbers similarly rose from about 400,000 in 1784 to about 1.6M in 1818.[3] The reasons for the spiralling cost including such factors as the distress caused by the Napoleonic wars, the subsidising of labourers' wages from the poor rate, the enclosure of common land and increasing rural unemployment. It was also claimed by some that there was a growing belief among the poor that if they didn't want to work, the parish would look after them. Many parish workhouses were said to be laxly run, offering no deterrent to entry, while parish officers criticised as incompetent or corrupt. The rise in costs was not, however, simply due to growth in the overall population which over the same period rose by a much smaller proportion, from around eight million to just under twelve million.

The New Poor Law

In 1832, the government appointed a Royal Commission to conduct a major review of the administration of poor relief.[4] Its recommendations resulted in the 1834 Poor Law Amendment Act, which overhauled the existing parish-based system.

The country was divided up into new administrative areas, known as Poor Law Unions. A union typically comprised twenty or thirty parishes around a market town, though some very populous parishes, particularly in London, were constituted as single Poor Law Parishes. Unions were administered locally by a board of guardians, elected annually by the ratepayers in each member parish. Each union was required to provide workhouse accommodation, either a large new building or modification of existing premises, to serve the whole area. The new workhouses were to be strictly run and to provide a regime that was less comfortable than the situation of even the lowliest independent labourer. Finally, the workhouse test was revived. For able-bodied men and their families, the workhouse would be the only form of poor relief on offer.

The new system was supervised by a new body, the Poor Law Commissioners (PLC), based in London's Somerset House. Assistant Commissioners were employed to oversee the introduction of the new system in each part of the country and to monitor its ongoing operation.

Resistance to the New System

The roll-out of New Poor Law was met with some resistance in parts of London and a few localised protests in Kent and Bedfordshire. However, opposition was much more serious in the north of England, particularly in the manufacturing areas of East Lancashire and West Yorkshire. Mass demonstrations were organised and in towns such as Bradford, Keighley, Huddersfield, Rochdale and Oldham, opposition was frequently violent, with a number of riots ending in the intervention of police and even mounted cavalry. Obstruction often also came from boards of guardians who adopted tactics of non-co-operation with the PLC, such as the guardians' non-attendance at board meetings, failing to appoint a clerk, or in endlessly postponing discussion of workhouse provision. There was also considerable opposition to the new system in central Wales, where a number of unions such as Rhayader held out against construction of a new workhouse until the 1870s.

New Workhouse Designs

Around half of the new unions erected a purpose-built workhouse, while the remainder adapted existing premises, sometimes distributing inmates across several sites. Very few new workhouses were initially erected in London as many of the capital's parishes already utilized large premises which could be adapted for the new system.

Some early union workhouse designs were derived from prison architecture of the period, with accommodation wings radiating from a central supervisory hub in the shape of a cross or a 'Y'. The space between the wings was used to form exercise yards.

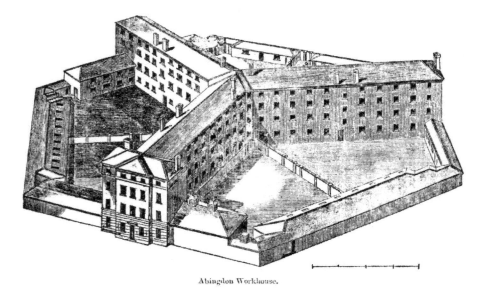

Abingdon Workhouse.

The radial design of the workhouse at Abingdon, Berkshire, erected in 1835.

In the 1840s, the corridor-plan design became popular with a separate entrance block, linear main block, and hospital block all running parallel to one another. The main block generally had a central corridor along its length with rooms off to each side, unlike the earlier which usually comprised a series of connected rooms. The main block had the administrative functions at its centre, often surmounted by a tower, and with kitchens and dining hall to the rear, creating a building that was T-shaped. Many of
these were in London and in the north of England, which had initially held out against erecting new workhouses.

From the 1870s, pavilion-plan designs placed inmates of a particular category or condition in separate blocks linked by covered walkways. Facilities such as receiving wards, offices and stores, and dining hall and kitchens would occupy further blocks.

The Workhouse Regime

Conditions in the new union workhouses were intended to be unattractive. On entry to the institution, new arrivals were given a bath and traded their own clothes for workhouse clothing. They were also given a medical examination and underwent a short period of quarantine before entering the main building.

Inmates were classified by age (aged and infirm, able-bodied, child) and gender, with each group housed in a separate part of the building. For the most part, there was no contact between each group until they left the workhouse. Thus, a family of father, mother, boy and girl, would be segregated during their stay. Children under the age of 7 could, with permission, live in the women's quarters. One or other of the parents could request a supervised daily 'interview' with a child. In practice, Sunday afternoon was the time when less formal meetings took place, though again, only with one parent at a time. From 1847, married couples over the age of 60 could request to share a separate bedroom, though relatively little such accommodation was provided, guardians often claiming that elderly couples were usually glad to be living apart.

Workhouse food in the 1830s was plain and repetitive, the typical diet consisting of bread and gruel for breakfast, and bread and cheese for both dinner and supper, with dinner replaced on two or three days a week with meat and vegetables, soup, or suet pudding and treacle. There were small concessions for the elderly who could trade in their breakfast gruel for a weekly ration of tea, sugar and butter. However, workhouse fare did gradually improve over the years. A major change came in 1900 when each workhouse was allowed to create its own weekly menu from a range of about fifty dishes approved for the purpose. These included such treats as Irish stew, pasties, fish pie, and roly-poly pudding.

The women's dining-hall at St Pancras workhouse, 1897.

Workhouse inmates were expected to work according to their ability. For women, this usually involved providing the domestic labour for the institution — laundry work, cleaning, kitchen work, and sewing. In many workhouses, the women made and repaired their own clothing. Work for able-bodied men included tasks such as stone-breaking, pumping water, chopping wood, and picking oakum — teasing apart old ropes into their raw fibres which could then be used for mat-making etc.

Inmates could depart from the workhouse whenever they wanted. However, leaving the premises without permission while wearing workhouse clothing, could lead to a charge of stealing workhouse property. A few hours notice for discharge had to given.

Medical Care

Prior to the 1870s, medical care in the workhouse was usually poor. Although a qualified doctor was employed, he was usually overworked and underpaid — any medicines he prescribed came out of his own salary. Workhouse infirmaries were often cramped and badly ventilated, with different conditions, such as medical and surgical cases mixed together. Nursing was usually done by elderly female inmates who couldn't read or write and who were often drunk, either from the daily ration of beer they were given for acting as nurses, or from filching some of the alcoholic beverages that were often prescribed for patients.

In the 1850s- 60s, a growing campaign for improvements in the medical care in London's workhouse infirmaries, culminating in the *Lancet*'s series of often shocking site visits reports, resulted in major changes. From 1867, the capital's workhouse infirmaries were required to be under separate management from the workhouse and, wherever possible, on a separate site. New buildings were erected and, thanks in great part to the efforts of Florence Nightingale, paid trained nurses increasingly became the norm. The changes in London gradually percolated out to the rest of the country, but progress was sometimes slow to happen, as reflected in by the workhouse site reports published the *British Medical Journal* in the mid-1890s.

From the 1870s, the poor outside the workhouse were increasingly able to access its infirmary without having first to be a workhouse inmate. In

The new Holborn union infirmary at Archway, opened in 1879.

many places, the workhouse infirmary acted as the local hospital for the poor, becoming a model for the Britain's future National Health Service, providing care that was free at the point of delivery.

Children in the Workhouse

In the era of the parish workhouse, and in the early years of the New Poor Law, children were just one part of the general workhouse population. The 1834 Act required that workhouse children receive at least three hours of basic education a day plus instruction to fit them for service. Most workhouses employed their own teachers to carry this out within the institution. From the early 1840s, however, the PLC encouraged unions to set up separate children's accommodation away from what was seen as the 'taint' of the workhouse, ideally serving several unions in a district. A residential school at Norwood, privately run by Mr Aubin, was developed in collaboration with an Assistant Poor Law Commissioner, James Kay-Shuttleworth, becoming a model for the PLC's efforts.

In the mid-1840s, the Poor Law authorities in Liverpool, Manchester and Leeds set up separate schools. Following a devastating cholera outbreak at another privately-run children's establishment at Tooting, run by Mr Drouet, the PLC established three School Districts in London, covering ten of the capital's thirty unions. Over 2000 children could be accommodated in the three schools set up by these Districts.

By the 1870s, such large institutions, disparagingly referred to as 'barrack' schools, were the subject of increasing criticism as being too impersonal, expensive to run, and a breeding grounds for infectious diseases such as ophthalmia and ringworm.

An alternative type of accommodation appeared in the form of the cottage homes system. Originally pioneered in France and Germany, cottage homes housed their inmates in family-style groups, typically of around twenty children, under the supervision of a house mother. Cottage homes developments were often set in a rural location, with the homes placed around a green or along a street. The 'village' usually included a school, infirmary, church, workshops, and sometimes a swimming bath.

Cottage homes, in their turn, began to receive criticism as not preparing their children for future life in the real word, typically working in a town or city. In the 1890s, the Sheffield Union began to house its children in what became known as scattered homes. These retained the family-group

The Poplar Union's cottage homes at Hutton, Essex, circa 1905.

principle, but placed the homes around the suburbs of a town or city, with the children attending local schools and joining in other local activities.

It was not unusual for a union, over time, to move from one form of children's accommodation to another, or operate a mix of various types.

The Casual Ward

Prior to 1837, workhouses were only obliged to receive individuals who were legally 'settled' in their area. However, following some widely publicised deaths on their doorsteps of passing travellers who had been ineligible for admission, workhouses began to provide temporary overnight shelter for any destitute person. The accommodation provided for this purpose was officially known as the casual ward, though became known among tramps and vagrants as the 'spike'. In London and some other large towns, casual wards were sometimes erected away from the main workhouse. The usual arrangement, though, was for the casual ward to be placed at the edge of the main workhouse site, often with its own separate access gate.

Casual wards were sometimes superintended by the workhouse porter, perhaps with his wife attending the female casuals. Some spikes were in the charge of a 'Tramp Major', usually a former tramp himself, and informally employed by the workhouse.

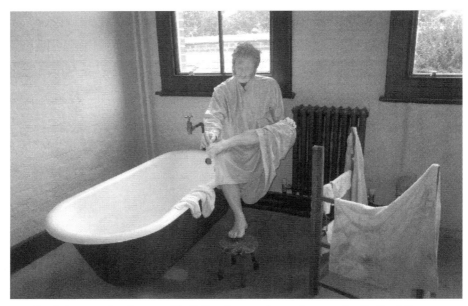

Bathtime at the former Guildford casual ward, now the Spike Museum.

At opening time, usually 5 or 6pm, new arrivals would be admitted and searched, with any money, tobacco or alcohol confiscated. Tramps often hid such articles in a nearby hedge or wall before entering the spike, although these items were often in danger of being removed by local children. Entrants were required to strip and bathe — in water that might already have been used by a number of others. They were then issued with one or more blankets and a workhouse nightshirt, with their own clothes being dried and fumigated or disinfected. Each was given a supper, typically 8oz of bread and a pint of 'skilly' (gruel) before being locked up for the night at 7p.m. until 6 or 7a.m. the next morning when a breakfast of bread and gruel would be served.

Until the 1870s, the norm was for casual wards to have communal association dormitories where the inmates slept on the bare floor or in low-slung hammocks. After that date, casual wards were increasingly constructed as blocks of individual cells.

Casuals were required to work for up to four hours before being released. For male casuals, stone breaking and oakum picking were widely employed. For females, labour tasks included oakum picking and domestic work such as scrubbing floors.

From 1882, casuals were detained for two nights, with the full day in between spent performing work. They were then released at 9 in the morning after the second night. The new scheme allowed more time to search for work or to travel to another workhouse. From 1871, return to the casual ward of the same union was not allowed within thirty days, the whole of London counting as a single union for this purpose.

In some counties, the police could issue casuals with a 'way-ticket', which aimed to keep them on a particular route and provide midday bread and cheese at designated places along the way. Arriving at a workhouse without a ticket could result in an extra day of work being imposed.

Evolution of the Workhouse

It is all too easy to picture the workhouse as being frozen in time, perhaps in a scene from *Oliver Twist*. However, the workhouse changed enormously in the century or so between the 1830s and 1930s. The buildings improved, the food improved, medical care improved, and the provision for children improved. Increasingly, specialised accommodation was being provided for specific groups of inmates. This included the cottage homes for the elderly erected by unions such Bradford, Salford and Wandsworth; the tuberculosis sanatoria established by the Bradford, Gateshead and Merthyr Tydfil; and the Langho epileptic colony jointly operated by the Manchester and Chorlton Unions.

The 1834 Act had primarily focused on making the workhouse a deterrent for the able-bodied poor, whereas by the 1870s the great majority of its inmates were the elderly, the chronic sick, the intellectually impaired, single mothers, and children. Gradually, the workhouse regime adjusted to its role as a refuge for much wider range of individuals who were not able-bodied.

By the 1890s, elderly inmates frequently had supplies of books and newspapers, outings organised to the countryside or seaside, entertainments provided by local groups, weekly rations of tobacco or snuff, and the possibility of going out to visit friends. In 1925, a wireless set was installed at the Leeds workhouse, while several patients in the infirmary had their own crystal radio sets.[5] At Abingdon, in Berkshire, some workhouse inmates even had weekly trips to a local cinema.[6]

The 1905 Royal Commission

In 1905, growing pressure for reform of the poor relief system led led to the appointment of a Royal Commission on the Poor Laws, which carried out the most extensive review of the subject since the one that had led to the 1834 Act. Over the next four years, the Commission collected a vast amount of evidence, including reports of visits to over 300 institutions across the British Isles.

The Commission was famously divided in its conclusions and its recommendations were published as separate Majority and Minority Reports. However, there were areas of broad agreement: the abolition of Boards of Guardians, with administration moving to the county level to allow workhouses to be replaced by more specialised institutions; better administration and targeting of outdoor relief, with greater involvement of voluntary agencies; the removal of children from workhouses; and the provision of old age pensions, health insurance and unemployment support.

Although the Commission's work did not result in any new legislation, it marked the beginning of reforms in workhouse administration. In 1913, a major update of the regulations governing the operation of workhouses and associated establishments gave boards of guardians greater autonomy in matters such as the classification of inmates, their daily timetable and dietary, bathing regulations, and the prohibition of particular articles being brought into the workhouse. Employment of a trained nurse was now obligatory in all workhouse infirmaries. Infants below the age of 18 months were to be medically examined at least once a fortnight. Proper medical records were to be kept and inmates assisting in sick wards were always to be supervised by an officer. And from April 1915, no healthy child was to reside in a workhouse for more than six weeks.

The End of the Workhouse

On 1 April 1930, the boards of guardians, who had administered the poor relief system for almost a century, were abolished and their responsibilities were taken over by county borough councils. Poor relief then became known as Public Assistance, with the majority of workhouses being rebranded as Public Assistance Institutions (PAIs). Some of the larger urban institutions with well developed medical facilities were divided in two, with the hospital section 'appropriated' for use as a municipal hospital, the remainder of the site continuing to be used for housing the poor. Some former workhouses sites were found to be unsuitable for further use and were turned into warehouses, offices, housing, or otherwise disposed of.

Under council control, most PAIs saw little change. The establishments largely continued in operation as they had prior to 1930, with the same buildings, same staff and same inmates although the able-bodied were now excluded from admission. Initially, many casual wards remained open, but their numbers steadily declined during the 1930s and 40s.

The real end for the workhouse came in 1948 with the inauguration of the new National Health Service. Many PAIs joined the new service as general or geriatric hospitals. Others, mostly the smaller and more rural ones, were retained by councils for use as old people's homes.

Ireland

The 1838 Irish Poor Relief Act introduced the workhouse system to the whole of Ireland along broadly similar lines to that in England and Wales, with the country divided into 130 poor law unions (increased to 163 following the famine of 1845-9). Most Irish workhouses were based on a design by English architect George Wilkinson, which could be scaled up or down to house from 400 to 1600 inmates.

During Ireland's War of Independence (1919-21) and Civil War (1922-23) many Irish workhouses were occupied by troops, leaving them damaged or destroyed. In the newly created Irish Free State (now the Republic of Ireland) the workhouse system was wound up but in Northern Ireland it continued operating until 1948.

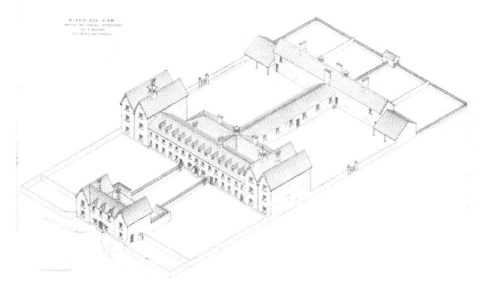

The 800-inmate version of George Wilkinson's Irish workhouse design.

17

Scotland

Scotland's parish-based poor relief system was always independent of that in the rest of Britain, with a preference towards the giving of out-relief rather than through institutional care. The 1845 Scottish Poor Law Act introduced a new system that was overseen by a central Board of Supervision and administered locally by annually appointed Parochial Boards who could raise funds voluntarily or by adopting a rating system. Poor relief could be given as cash or in kind. In addition, larger parishes, or 'combinations' of small parishes, could set up a poorhouse to shelter the sick or destitute but not the able-bodied. Around seventy poorhouses were eventually established.

The former Sutherland Combination Poorhouse at Bonar Bridge.

Visits to Workhouses

The rest of his book includes more than fifty first-hand descriptions of visits to workhouses and their associated accommodation for the sick, the elderly, children, and vagrants. Published between 1834 and 1931, these accounts were written by a wide variety of individuals including administrators, journalists, inspectors, campaigners, 'social explorers', vacationers, and the merely curious.

Some visitors had a specific agenda, usually with a view to a critical evaluation the institution, for example, of the quality of its medical care. In cases such as the reports by *The Lancet* in the 1860s, or the *British*

Medical Journal in the 1890s, the authors aim to present an objective and systematic description of the institution and the often unsatisfactory conditions they discovered. Their reports typically include such matters as staff and inmate numbers, the state of the accommodation and other facilities, and the character and competence of the officers. We may also hear the authors' views on various matters, e.g. 'abuses' such as the use of male nurses at Reading workhouse.

Visitors of a more literary persuasion, such as Charles Dickens, and others who contributed to his journals, often focus on the 'characters' they encountered, giving us an insight into their backgrounds and the way they speak. Journalists may try and present us with a visual image of the workhouse, such as the colours and materials of the inmates' clothing.

More informal accounts may throw up small but interesting details, such as how the inmates' potatoes were prepared and served at the North Dublin workhouse, or that as early as 1890 the Chorlton union workhouse at Withington had a telephone connection to central Manchester, or that on the tableware used in the St Marylebone workhouse infirmary, that for the patients had a blue badge while that for the nurses had a red one.

Although the workhouse is often portrayed as an unremittingly grim institution, it was not without its lighter moments, such as when the inmates of the Haslingden workhouse were introduced to the phonograph. Even out and out comedy occasionally makes an appearance, as when the man recording the details of entrants to the casual ward at Romford, Essex, was presented with the Welsh place name 'Llanfairfechan' — resorting instead to entering it as 'Barking'.

Whatever their reason for putting pen to paper, those who visited workhouses and recorded their impressions have left us with a valuable and often unexpectedly revealing source of information that has greatly enriched our knowledge of the institution.

Many of the accounts are extracts from longer works as detailed in the Notes and Sources section, and may have been further abridged.

Some authors did not identify the institution they were writing about, but it has been possible to locate it from other information they included The note preceding each entry indicates where this has been done.

Further information on all the establishments mentioned in this book can be found at www.workhouses.org.uk

Glossary

Brabazon Scheme
A scheme instigated in 1880 by Lady Brabazon to provide interesting and useful occupations such as knitting, embroidery or lace-making for non-able-bodied workhouse inmates.

Casual Ward
Part of a workhouse, usually located near the entrance, or occasionally at a separate site, providing one or two nights lodging for tramps, vagrants or other passing travellers. Inmates were required to perform a prescribed amount of work, typically stone breaking, oakum picking, wood chopping, cleaning etc.

Foul Wards
An alternative name for **lock wards**.

House of Industry
An alternative name for the workhouse, particularly one operated by a group of parishes prior to 1834.

The 'Itch'
An informal name for scabies — a medical condition caused by a lice-like parasite burrowing under the skin and resulting in severe itching. It was often contracted through sharing a bed with an infected individual. Workhouses sometimes had specially designated 'itch wards' for such cases.

Laundry
A room or outbuilding for the drying, ironing etc. of items coming from the **washhouse**.

Lavatory
Usually indicates a room where people washed rather than referring to a toilet or water-closet.

Lock Wards
Accommodation for inmates with venereal diseases.

Oakum Picking
A work task often given to workhouse inmates where short lengths of 'junk' — old hemp ropes from ships etc. — were untwisted into their raw fibres which were known as oakum. The oakum could be sold for mat-making and other uses.

Out-relief	Poor relief given outside the workhouse, in cash or kind.
Pannikin	A small metal cup or pan.
Phthisis	Tuberculosis of the lungs — a common condition amongst the poor in Victorian times. By the start of the twentieth century, workhouses increasingly had special provision for sufferers.
Poorhouse	An alternative name for the workhouse, especially in Scotland, but may denote an establishment where labour is not demanded.
Skilly	A thin oatmeal soup or gruel.
Spike	A tramps' name for a workhouse casual ward. Theories abound as to the origins of the name.
Stone-breaking	A task often give to able-bodied male inmates in which large lumps of stone were broken un into small pieces. Sometimes a metal grid was used to ensure the pieces were small enough. Broken stone could be sold for road-making.
Stoving	The decontamination of clothing in a heated cabinet, sometimes using steam or sulphur fumes.
Toke/Tommy	Tramps' names for bread.
Tramp Major	A person, often a tramp or former tramp, sometimes employed in a casual ward to supervise new admissions, the preparation of food etc.
Union	A group of parishes sharing a single poor relief administration. After 1834, also informally used to refer to a union's workhouse.
Wardsman/woman	A workhouse inmate appointed to carry out certain tasks in their ward, such as summoning assistance if needed during the night.
Washhouse	A room or outbuilding for the washing of dirty clothes, linens etc. People washed in a **lavatory**.

Brighton, Sussex (1834)

> The 1832 Royal Commission on the Poor Laws, published in 1834, recorded a visit by Assistant Commissioner C.H. Maclean to the Brighton workhouse, then located on Church Hill.[7] The inmates had one of the most generous workhouse diets in the country.[8]

In the Brighton workhouse I found 336 inmates of the following ages and sexes:

	Under 10	10-18	18-30	30-50	Above 50
Male	46	57	9	15	54
Female	28	31	24	26	46
Total	74	88	33	41	100

The Governor has a salary of £70, the Surgeon for attendance and medicine £60, the Matron £42, the Schoolmistress £12, the Schoolmaster £7. 10s.

Divine service is performed by the vicar of Brighton every Sunday morning previous to the service of the parish church, and the sick are regularly attended by the curate. The boys and girls go to church twice every Sunday. The children are either orphans, illegitimate or deserted, but by far the greater number of the latter class; orphans, 24; illegitimate, 22; deserted by their parents, 51.

The sexes are kept completely separate, except in the case of some old married people who are permitted to have rooms to themselves, and these are detached from the main building.

There are near seven acres of land cultivated as a garden, and part of the produce is sold to the inhabitants of Brighton.

A manufactory of whiting is also carried on, the raw material for which is dug upon the premises; also a manufactory of sacks, bed-sacking, ropes, lines, twine and door mats. The shoes and clothes worn by the whole of the inmates are made in the house; and also many which are given to the out-door poor by the orders of the directors and guardians. The cutting of wood into small bundles for fire-wood has recently been commenced.

There is a blacksmith's and a carpenter's shop on the premises, in which all the implements and tools used by the out-door paupers are repaired and new ones made; coffins for deceased paupers, who are buried at the expense of the parish, are made in the house.

Some of the girls are occupied in plaiting straw bonnets and hats, a few of which are sold, but the greater part are appropriated to the use of the inmates. The hours for working are from six o'clock to six o'clock in summer, and from daylight to dark in winter; one hour being allowed for breakfast, and one for dinner.

The boys are divided into two classes; the first class consisting of the greater boys who have made some proficiency in their education; these are allowed one hour in the afternoon for instruction. The second class is subdivided into two divisions each receiving three hours of instruction per day. The whole of the children, are engaged in some description of employment, which they leave off to attend school, and to which they return after school hours.

Two days in each week are set apart for the instruction of the girls by the schoolmaster, principally in writing and figures; at other times they are taught by a female inmate.

An infirmary, detached from the main building of the workhouse, has been recently erected, and is capable of accommodating 50 sick persons. The whole of the labour of erecting this building was performed by able-bodied paupers, in lieu of granting them the usual parish relief.

Provisions, &c. are contracted for every three months by the directors and guardians, who issue advertisements for tenders.

No one is allowed to leave the house without the permission of the governor; but there is no strong place in which to confine a refractory or turbulent pauper.

It is the custom of the workhouse to permit the adult paupers to leave the house by themselves on Sundays, for the purpose of attending divine service. This privilege is greatly abused, and is the cause of more drunkenness and disorderly conduct on the sabbath-day than during the whole week. On Sunday, the 10th of September, Charles Bentley, a single man, who had been an inmate of the house about six weeks, left the house after the dinner hour, under the pretext of going to church; he returned about half-past five o'clock, perfectly drunk and very disorderly. The governor placed him in a room by himself, where he broke the window, table, and several other articles of furniture. A police officer was sent for, and he was conveyed to the watch-house; next day he was taken before the bench of magistrates, and committed to the house of correction at

Lewes for 21 days. The governor told me, that has often heard paupers, when thus conducting themselves, boast that it would "only be for 21 days to the house of correction."

Brighton Workhouse Diet Table.

BREAKFAST

Women:—One pint of tea, with bread and butter.

Men, boys and girls:—Bread and gruel (of flour and oatmeal) except some old men, who are allowed a pint of tea, with bread and butter.

DINNER

Monday:—Pease soup, herbs, &c. with bread; men and women a pint of table-beer; boys about half a pint.

Tuesday:—Beef and mutton puddings, with vegetables; the beer, &c., same as Monday.

Wednesday:—Boiled beef and mutton (sometimes pork with. it), hard puddings, bread, vegetables, &c.; beer same as before.

Thursday:—Mutton and beef-suet puddings; beer same as before.

Friday:—Beef and mutton puddings, with vegetables; beer as before.

Saturday:—Irish stew-meat, potatoes, herbs, &c.; beer same as before.

Sunday:—Boiled beef and mutton (sometimes pork with it), hard puddings, bread; vegetables, &c.; beer as before.

SUPPER:

Women:—One pint of tea, with bread and butter or cheese.

Men and boys:—Bread and butter or cheese; men, one pint of beer or tea each; boys, about half a pint.

Girls and small children: — Bread and butter; drink, milk and water.

No specific quantity of food is weighed or delivered to any of the inmates, but all who are able are required to sit down to the table where the provisions are served out to them. The governor carves for the men and boys, and the matron for the women and girls.

Mutton broth is made every day, besides the above diet, for persons whose cases require it; and about eight pounds of meat roasted, baked, or made into pies, with an extra rice, or sonic other pudding, for persons to whom the surgeons may think proper to order a different description of diet than that used by the rest of the inmates. Strong beer, wine and spirits are also given, as the medical gentlemen may deem necessary.

Hawarden, Flintshire (1834)

The 1832 Royal Commission's report included a visit to Hawarden parish workhouse by Assistant Commissioner Stephen Walcott.[9]

The building will accommodate about 90 persons. It was formerly a mansion, and was converted to its present purpose in March 1830. The official establishment consists of governor and matron, at a yearly salary, for both, of £40, and a surgeon, who receives £30 per annum for attending sick pauper parishioners, whether in or out of the house. In consequence of the contiguity of the church and national school, a separate chaplain and schoolmaster are not thought necessary. The principal regulations to prevent residence in the house being a matter of desire or indifference to the poor are, the prohibition of spirituous liquors, separation of the sexes by night, regularity in hours, and forced employment. The latter, as regards the able-bodied, consists in the cultivation of part of the land by means of spade husbandry; but the work is not by the piece. The governor, however, states that he personally superintends the labourers; and as the number has always been small, probably he can do so with effect. Those who are incapable of laborious employment are set to pick oakum, and spin. The allowance of food is in no case proportioned to the work performed. The breakfasts and suppers consist of milk gruel, with seven ounces of wheaten bread for the men, (half an ounce less for the women,) and the dinners, of meat in some shape five times a week, with half-a-pint of beer to each daily. On Sundays the adults are restricted to six ounces of dressed meat at dinner; but there is no limit in quantity on the other days. A distinction is made in the treatment of the impotent and able-bodied, in favour of the former; those above 50, who have been accustomed to use tobacco or snuff, are each allowed weekly, half an ounce of the one or the other; and if females, a little tea and sugar is added, with a little butter, should their age exceed 70. The sleeping apartments of the sexes are effectually divided; but in the day, although a distinct room is appropriated to each sex, there is no separation beyond what the individuals themselves may chose to maintain, the communication between the sitting-rooms being quite free, and the premises common to all for exercise. Pregnant single women, and mothers of illegitimate children, sleep by themselves, but associate in the day time with the other females, to the manifest injury of the young and virtuous, since, besides the risk of contamination, the circumstance of observing no difference made in the treatment of the profligate and the chaste, must tend to weaken in their minds the distinction between virtue and vice. Every one is required, if capable, to attend Divine service on Sunday; and the children are sent to the national school for six or seven hours daily.

The aged and infirm, orphans, deserted children, bastards, pregnant single women, and able-bodied single men, are the classes usually sent to the house; married men and their children but seldom.

Wallingford, Berkshire (1835)

> After the passing of the 1834 Poor Law Amendment Act, Assistant Poor Law Commissioners began touring the country to implement its measures. One of these, Richard Hall, was clearly unimpressed by the existing state of affairs in Wallingford — a former Gilbert Union.[10]

I found that the guardians were annually appointed, and did nothing — in fact, they were ignorant that they had any official duty to perform beyond keeping the workhouse in repair; the overseers paid the poor, and all the abuses consequent upon that method of giving relief, flourished in the union just as out of it. The workhouse was divided into apartments, each furnished and tenanted by a family, by whom it was evidently regarded as their freehold; one woman had resided there for eleven years, and brought up a family of nine children; a shoemaker who had been an inmate seven years, told me that he earned his own living, and indignantly asserted, that he was entirely independent of the parish; in some rooms were young people just beginning life, having been lately married; in others three or four unmarried mothers, or those who were on the point of becoming so; in some were the sick, or those whose age and infirmities showed that they were on the verge of dissolution; 47 children were variously deposited throughout the building; one room only was vacant; on my asking the cause of this, I was informed that it was reserved for some preachers of the Methodist persuasion, who attended twice a week to hold a preaching, and a prayer meeting; those of the inmates who desired it were made members of the congregation, upon the weekly payment of one penny. There was not the slightest attempt at classification; old and young, male and female, sick and sound, were left to mingle at will; the discipline that could be maintained amounted to nothing; a man (who was parish beadle) and his wife, themselves just removed above pauperism, were dignified with the titles of governor and matron; or, as the woman more properly described their situation, they were paid 12s. per week "to set things straight, and keep all quiet:" the means resorted to, in order to effect the latter of these desirable objects, were novel and summary; when a pauper, in consequence of indulgence during the day at the beer shop (for be it remembered, by day there was not the slightest infringement on their liberty), was noisy and troublesome at night, the governor left his bed and turned him out of doors! It appeared that on a vacancy occurring in this parochial lodging-house, a sort of scramble ensued between the united parishes, each being anxious to secure a rent-free tenement to some pauper who was a burden to it. Such an establishment could not possibly answer anyone good end: It only served to enhance and disseminate mischief.

Bulcamp, Suffolk (1835)

Assistant Poor Law Commissioner, Charles Mott, described the eye-opening state of affairs that he discovered at the old Bulcamp workhouse, originally opened in 1766 to serve the Blything Hundred in Suffolk. In 1835, the site became Blything union workhouse.[11] Later home to Blythburgh and District Hospital, the building still exists, now in private residential use.

In the house of industry at Bulcamp, belonging to the Blything hundred, the most strange customs have obtained, and the paupers are indulged in a manner that render their situations far superior to that of the honest independent labourer.

A regularly licensed shop has for years been fitted up and allowed to be kept by a female pauper in the house of industry for the convenience of the other paupers. The exciseman attends periodically to "take stock" the same as at any tradesman's shop or warehouse; and the last time I visited the house application was made to me, on behalf of this old pauper shopkeeper, as to the future prospects of her trade. The season had arrived at which it was customary to renew the licenses for the sale of her tobacco, tea, &c. I recommended, however, at the risk of lessening the revenue, that the old lady should relinquish business and retire, as her trade was not likely to be so good under the new arrangements.

The house is surrounded by a small farm belonging to the hundred. There are ten milch cows kept, and the paupers are supplied with the milk and best fresh butter; and I was informed that the guardians had repeatedly declared that they could not get such butter at their own tables as the paupers were supplied with in the Bulcamp house of industry.

The want of classification and separation of the sexes is here exhibited in a frightful degree. Mr. Willson, the governor, who is a respectable man, complained much of it, and related some disgusting effects of the system.

The following facts will serve to illustrate the encouragement held out to married couples who are disposed to become paupers:— Many years since, two men of the names of Munn and Girling, with their wives and families, were admitted into this establishment. Several of their children were born and reared up in the workhouse until they attained the age of thirteen years, when they were apprenticed by the corporation. After serving their time, the sons married, and in their turn came with their wives to the workhouse. They were soon encircled by a rising family, who, — having attained the proper age, were, as their parents had been before them, apprenticed by the directors and guardians of the corporation. These children, at the expiration of their apprenticeship, likewise married, again became paupers, claimed their right of admission into their former asylum, the workhouse, were received, and are now living together, by the usage of the establishment.

Thus there are at this time, three generations of these paupers in the house of industry, and the same results are expected from the recently-married couples as from their ancestors, namely, a perpetuation of the stock of pauper families.

I received much information upon the subject of early marriages from various officers of this incorporation. I was informed that early marriages are very frequent, and that parties have been known to go directly from church to the workhouse, where, having gained admission, they are placed just in the society which suits them, the male paupers and their wives being allowed to mix indiscriminately together in the day time, and at night a separate sleeping apartment allotted to each couple — a degree of luxury and comfort is enjoyed to which the honest and industrious labourer is a total stranger. This custom, however, is not confined to Suffolk, for on visiting one of the large incorporated hundred houses in Norfolk, I observed several of the doors of the rooms appropriated for married couples were nailed up; and on inquiring of the governor, I found that they had been occupied by able-bodied men and their wives and families, who had gone out harvesting, and that they had nailed the doors of their rooms up in order that no other persons should inhabit them during their absence.

To such an extent was this marriage system at one time carried in the hundred of Blything, that ten or twelve cases of pauper young men marrying young women, also paupers, and directly claiming their right to relief, occurred close upon the heels of each other. The visiting guardian took upon himself the responsibility of publishing to the inmates, that if any more marriages occurred among the paupers, they would be prohibited from sleeping together. This had the desired effect of checking the practice as long as the prohibition was enforced.

Blean, Kent (1838)

The following account of the Blean Union workhouse, opened in 1835, comes from a letter written by George Trifle to Miss Lydia Laring, of Somerset.[12] En route to the institution, the author fell into the company of an applicant for the post of clerk to the Guardians, for which interviews were being held that day.

A VISIT TO THE BLEAN UNION WORKHOUSE.

Our conversation continued until we came within sight of the workhouse. There it is, said he; that's the place we're going to. How many persons have entered there, and will yet enter to-day, with high misplaced hopes, to meet only with disappointment.

Truly, I replied. What a cold desolate place it looks; its very appearance chills me. One would scarcely think it possible hope could ever enter the doors of that building.

We were soon within-side the massy doors, and entered a door way on our right hand; we then proceeded along a short passage, and went into a spacious room at the extreme end. This they told us was the Board-room. A long table down the middle was partially covered with books and papers. The Guardians had not all arrived, consequently the candidates were suffered to remain in the room. When we arrived we found one of the Guardians declaiming against a report that had gone abroad, and was highly disadvantageous to the Board. The following are the best particulars I was able to collect, but I do not vouch their accuracy.

A few weeks since, a woman far advanced in pregnancy was admitted into the House, and in consequence of refusing to work was condemned to the black hole, as a just punishment for the offence. During her confinement she was said to have been delivered of twins, and the three bodies were found frozen to death about a week afterwards. This report, like many others relating to the treatment of paupers in the different Unions, was found to be wholly false. I cannot distinctly state whether anything relating to the case was entered in the minute book. As several of the other Guardians had now arrived, we were directed to go up stairs, when it turned out that, instead of 143, there were only 16 candidates. Every countenance betrayed confidence of success, but all denied any such expectations.

The letters of the different candidates were soon called for to lay before the Board. My old friend strutted up consequentially and delivered his with the others, then returning to me, he winked his eye and whispered:— There, my friend, we shall see what they will do; but mind, I don't expect to get it.

In a short time the Governor came in to know if any of us would like to go round the wards with the visitors and himself, upon which most of us got up and followed him. But before I mention the paupers, let me endeavour to give you idea of the building itself. Facing the room door in which we then were, is a large bow window, from which I shall make my observations:— The building leaves a large open square in the interior; a wall down the middle separates the male from the female paupers; opposite the window are some low buildings, probably stables, with the back of which one end of the separation wall joins. These buildings are at a sufficient distance to leave a small open space or yard, on the right hand of which is a door leading to the male paupers, and on the left side a corresponding door leading to the female paupers. There were only ground and first floors; the latter were approached by stone steps, leading on to a gallery composed of the same materials, with an iron railing round, and on to which the doors opened. Our first visit was to the kitchen. Not only here, but throughout the whole building, the greatest cleanliness prevailed. I have little to say respecting the paupers; was very agreeably surprised to observe the mode of treatment adopted towards them. They presented generally a healthy and satisfied appearance. The men were mostly engaged in picking oakum, which is afterwards sold to boatmen. But too much praise cannot be given to the Guardians for the manner in which they treat the children. The latter, when we entered, were engaged at their lessons; the books selected were all religious. Their healthy and happy countenances presented the most cheerful appearance. One young gentleman asked where the black hole was; but some one called out, Does he expect to find a ghost there? Now, whether he really expected to find a ghost, or the three frozen bodies, I am unable to say, but he looked very timid, and the question was not again put. I did not observe the person who called out, otherwise I would describe him to you, possibly you might have recognised him from your general knowledge of the people in these parts.

When we returned to the room up stairs our patience was sorely tried (for even I took an interest the matter) in waiting for the decision of the guardians. Some sat gazing upon the ceiling, probably endeavouring to decipher a few magical symbols visible them alone; others were looking at their boots, and turned their feet in every direction likely to afford them an advantageous view of those articles. The heat of the room having communicated itself to the windows and occasioned a thick mist to settle thereon, the young gentleman who made the inquiries about the black-hole displayed his ability by drawing a profile with his fore-finger on of the panes of glass, which afterwards drew forth a few remarks at his expense.

The silence was not destined to be of long continuance; it was broken by some person in the room calling out, "a Quaker's meeting!" upon which another remarked to the aforesaid young gentleman, that birds were never seen to fly over the Union building. At that instant a large raven flew close to the outside of the wall, croaking and flapping its wings. The successful candidate was absent from the room at the moment — the circumstance was ominous; and on the announcement of the choice of the guardians, after a full and deliberate discussion on the merits of each gentleman's testimonials, I found that my pedestrian companion had been unsuccessful!

Nottingham, Nottinghamshire (1840)

> The following description of a visit to the Nottingham union workhouse was included by historian and social reformer, James Orange, in his classic work *The History of Nottingham*.[13]

Under the New Poor Law Bill, which passed in 1834, the poor in the workhouses of St. Peter and St. Nicholas were removed into that of St. Mary, which is now constituted the workhouse for the union of the three parishes.

The regulations of the workhouse are as follow:— 1. The women are separated from the men, except some couples of 60 years of age and upwards, who are allowed to live together in the male part of the building. The day rooms are unlocked at five o'clock in the morning in summer, and six in winter: One low dark room, of very inadequate dimensions, constitutes their *eating apartment* and *chapel*. Here the adults assemble at half-past six, a.m., for reading the scriptures and prayer, which is performed by the governor; after which breakfast is served about seven, which consists of milk porridge, thickened with fine flower, a pint and a half each; but there is no limit insisted on, so that each person takes as much as he pleases to call for, and the same with the women. We may observe, the breakfasts are always of the same kind, milk porridge, and suppers the same, and we must admit that both in taste and appearance it is superior to that generally made in private houses. Old persons of sixty years and upwards are allowed tea instead of milk porridge, both morning and night, if they choose it, and so are sickly persons, or others who cannot take porridge, if they apply, to the governor. Each man has seven ounces of bread in the morning, and six ounces the women; the same quantities are delivered to them for supper at night. The porridge for breakfast and supper is served up in quart cans, and it is very gratifying to witness the indulgence granted to some old people, who are allowed to have their tea served in earthenware, not liking to have it in the tin cans. After the adults have taken breakfast, they rise; to make way for the children; the able-bodied young men then go to their labour, grinding at the mills, at which they work and rest alternately twenty minutes, and the young women go to the washhouse and laundry, and the old people withdraw to their appropriate rooms. The children are taught to give thanks and ask a blessing on their food, which is sung by the whole of them in metrical verse. There is no limit attempted to be imposed on a child's appetite; but all are served with until they have had enough. Before breakfast they walk out two and two for an hour, in the fields, accompanied by the nurse, before entering the school; the same excellent regulation is observed towards the girls. We had very much pleasure in witnessing the order and regularity with which the three parish schools are conducted, and the attainments of the children in writing and accounts; and needlework among the girls was very creditable, demonstrating the industry and talent bestowed on the pupils by their teachers. The infant school under the management of Miss Redgate, is particularly interesting. The number of boys and girls is fluctuating, but 230, is about the average; in the infant school, about 70. Dinner is served at twelve to the adults, and because of the inadequacy of the eating apartment, the hungry children are obliged to wait till the elders have done, and after a proper time for recreation or play, the former return to their labour, and the latter to school.

Supper at half-past five o'clock for the children, which consists of an unlimited supply of bread and milk porridge, as at breakfast. After these are withdrawn to play, the adults come and take their places, when, as in the morning, there is reading the scripture and prayer, before supper, after which they amuse themselves in their proper apartments, and at eight o'clock the day rooms are locked up for the night. Then those whose business it is, clean the day rooms ready for the morning.

In the dietary of the house, we have specified the hours at which their three daily meals are taken, the quantity of bread each at breakfast and supper, and the unlimited supply of good wholesome porridge have been already described, we have therefore only to notice of what their dinners consist.

Sabbath-day: beef, seven ounces each for men, and six ounces each for women. No bread is allowed with this meal, but instead of weighing the potatoes, they have an unlimited supply.

Monday: Irish-stew made from the bones of the meat used on the previous day, with an additional quantity of fresh meat. No bread is allowed to this dinner, except what may have been reserved from a previous meal; instead of this being served to them by measure, the stew, which is good, is served without limit.

Tuesday: pudding, made of suet and fine flower, mixed with water; sixteen ounces for each man, and fourteen ounces each woman.

Wednesday: broth, in which carrots and other vegetables are boiled, to give It an agreeable flavour. Of this they have an unlimited supply, and an allowance of bread, seven ounces to a man six to a woman.

Thursday: this is a meat day again, served in the same manner and proportions as on Sabbath-days.

Friday: peas soup, of which there is no limit as to quantity, but as the peas are to serve the purpose, there is no allowance of bread except what they may have saved.

Saturday: broth and bread, in the same manner as on Wednesdays.

Religious Instruction; reading the scriptures and prayer, morning and night every day, and though no salaried chaplain has hitherto been appointed since the union was formed, yet the duties of the office have been uninterruptedly and efficiently supplied by the voluntary services of pious Christians, who perform two full services every sabbath; in the afternoon by dissenting ministers, and in the evening according to the formularies of the establishment, by a pious lay churchman. Well-conducted inmates are allowed to leave the house on Sunday mornings, to attend their respective places of worship; and in the afternoons of three or four days in the week, some of the aged persons are let out to visit, their friends, &c. There is a good library of books, religious, moral, and entertaining, for the use of the inmates who have the ability and are disposed to read.

Appearance. The cleanly and healthful appearance of the children is really delightful, which may be accounted for by the orderly discipline to which they are subjected; healthful exercises, plenty of wholesome food, warm clothing, particularly good shoes and stockings, in which respect they enjoy superior advantages to the generality of children of the poor. The appearance of the women is clean and becoming, and so is that of the men; and though they are generally well fleshed, there is a sickly paleness spread over the countenances of most of them, which probably originates in the crowded state of the house, and gives them the appearance of felon prisoners, undergoing a lengthened confinement in a cell, and look emaciated for want of fresh air.

That which more than any other thing interested us in this comfortless place, was the college of little cobblers. Here were ten of the bigger lads, with new leather aprons, sitting on the end of little shoemaker's stalls, learning the art and craft of shoe-making, some mending, and others making new shoes and laced boots for the various members of the establishment. Though none of them have been long engaged in acquiring that useful and necessary art, on examination, we found the work executed in the neatest manner, so as to induce the expectation that in time they will be able to execute these necessary and elegant articles in the first style of the art, and thus supply to the next generation one of the very few instances in which pauperism may issue in a blessing.

The food is prepared in a large kitchen, on the east side or the women's yard, and adjoins the governor's house, All the cooking is done by steam, which is very commendable, as it obviates the occurrence or any accident by fire, Under the kitchen are very deep spacious cellars, which constitute the boiler house and provision stores. North or the kitchen on the same side, are the wash-house and laundry, which are much too small for the business that is done in them, and must be injurious to the health of those by whom it is performed. The rooms over these constitute the store-house for linen, which is always kept clean and aired. West of these, constituting the north end of the establishment, are the brewhouse, fever room, and hospital for the women; all that can be said in their favour is, they are exceedingly clean, but low, contracted, and gloomy receptacles, unfit for the abode of persons in health, much less of those who are bowed down beneath the pressure of disease. Adjoining the west end of these, in a southern direction, is the new and best parts of this heterogeneous mass of building, but it is comparatively small, and is divided into day and sleeping rooms for the women, and utterly inadequate for the numbers crowded in it. South of these is the hospital for the men, Here there is one good room over the office, but to attain the other two, another flight of steps has to be ascended, and you enter two attics, which are so low that a man must stoop as he passes under the beams or enters the doors. Here the languishing inmates lie in beds exposed to all the variable changes of weather, inseparable from such rooms. We will not attempt to describe the shameful hovels in which the men and boys are crowded together, but when we recollect these houses are the unavoidable legal receptacles of the poor of all classes, from helpless infancy to extreme old age, how important to the poor, how interesting to the public, to devise means of maintenance and, instruction calculated to issue in beneficial results, but how is this sought to be obtained?

In the Nottingham house are presented shameless profligates in intimate association with inexperienced and unsuspecting childhood; it is a family in which deserted infancy; destitute youth, pauper manhood, worn-out age, wasting sickness, mental imbecility, and bodily decrepitude, are all indiscriminately mingled together. No one hesitates as to the propriety of preserving lunatics and idiots from annoyance. It is not for one moment disputed that the aged should enjoy quiet, and the imbecile protection; that the healthful and able-bodied should be really employed or that the young should be instructed by example as well as precept, and by suitable training be prepared to become useful and independent (self supported) members of society. Yet, obvious and important as are these duties, to discharge them in this house appears impossible. We are told, and it has never been denied, that the aged have little or no quiet; the able, no adequate employment; the vicious are not effectually restrained; the idle are not made to work; and, worse than all, the young those on whose culture the future welfare of society is mainly dependant, are not trained in habits of industrious application; and moral instruction, so far from being enforced by example, is powerfully if not completely counteracted by the evil influence of vicious association.

This deplorable state of things is inseparable from a house so crowded and ill arranged, that effective supervision and extensive classification are equally impracticable and unknown.

The results, however disgraceful, are such as might be expected; young men alternating between a prison and the workhouse, and women of loose character inadequately restrained.

Wandsworth & Clapham, London (1841)

In 1841, *Chamber's Edinburgh Journal* published an account of the recently opened Wandsworth & Clapham union workhouse on St John's Hill, Battersea. The site later became St John's Hospital. The surviving buildings are now in residential use.

One day, while in London, I took the opportunity of driving a few miles west from Vauxhall, on the Wandsworth road, to visit the large workhouse of the Battersea district, lately erected, and in full operation under the new system. Occupying a somewhat elevated piece of ground, overlooking the rich and populous valley of the Thames, with Chelsea and the towers of Westminster in the distance, and closely environed with an extensive garden and shrubbery, the house enjoys a remarkably pleasant, and, I should think, salubrious situation; while the exterior, with its neat porter's lodge and railings, suggests much more the idea of is gentleman's residence than a receptacle for parish paupers. Conducted over the whole establishment by the house governor, I was surprised at the extent and variety of the details, all apparently on a well-digested scheme for preserving order and discipline, combined with as great comfort as any one could reasonably expect. Each class of inmates — men, women, boys, and girls — occupied its respective division of the house, with an appropriate airing-ground behind. In one apartment, I found about thirty elderly men picking oakum, a very light employment; and is another place there were some men, of greater strength, working a pump which propelled water to a cistern, at the summit of the building. One or two men were also working in the large garden of the establishment. Proceeding up stairs to the women's division, I entered a species of parlour or sitting-room, cheerfully lighted by windows overlooking the country around, and here were sitting, quietly reading or knitting, a dozen old women; while one of extreme age, a good specimen of the old English dame in humble life, being incapable of locomotion, was wheeled in an easy chair by a companion along the floor and lobby, and with as much enjoyment as a child in its chaise.

The spotless purity of the walls and floors, the numerous water-closets and washing-rooms, the laundry, kitchen, school apartments, and small houses in which travelling paupers and their families could be lodged gratuitously for a night — all gave token of careful management, and concern for the comfort of the inmates. In the kitchen was the perfume of meat in process of cookery — something very different from the brothy odour which assails the nostrils on entering an Edinburgh workhouse. From a bakehouse, adjoining the kitchen, there issued great baskets of wheaten loaves, steaming from the oven; and passing onwards to the cellar, I was introduced to the presence of a dozen barrels of ale and porter — Barclay and Perkins', if recollect rightly — and the contents of which seemed as excellent as any liquors of the kind I had ever tasted. Ale and porter in a workhouse was a new feature, for which I had not been prepared, seeing that the inmates of our Scotch pauper asylums are judiciously restrained from indulging in any thing stronger than buttermilk or small beer, and that only as a liquefaction to their poor morning and evening meal. The contents of the ale and porter barrels, I

37

was informed, were not administered generally, but only to old or infirm paupers by order of the medical attendant, and to those who wrought in the garden, or at more than usually severe labour. As every kind of stimulating liquor is proved to be valueless, except where nature would unavoidably sink without such artificial aid, the beer served out here and elsewhere to all except the positively infirm, may be pronounced so much money of the parishioners' thrown away. At all events, the expenditure on those commodities argues any thing but niggardliness in the guardians of the poor. At my departure from the establishment, I could not help testifying my approbation of the general appearance and management of the house.

North Dublin, Ireland (1844)

In 1844, German traveller J.G. Kohl described his visit to the North Dublin union workhouse.[14] The institution originated in the 1770s as a House of Industry to receive poor, helpless men and women, and for the committal of vagabonds, sturdy beggars and disorderly women judged fit for labour. It became a union workhouse in 1840. Small parts of the building's frontage survive on what is now Morning Star Avenue.

The food and clothing within an Irish workhouse is certainly better than the pauper could enjoy out of it, for of course the inmates of such a house are not allowed to go about half-naked and half-starved, the usual condition of the poor in Ireland. The food consists generally of potatoes, oatmeal, and milk, particularly buttermilk. Bread is given only to the children and the sick. The diet tables and other regulations of public institutions are of interest to the inquiring traveller, for they often afford him a convenient insight into the manner of life of a whole nation. When, therefore, I detail to my readers the fare of a pauper in an Irish workhouse, I give them a picture of the style of living of the great mass of the Irish people, of those at least among them who have it in their power to eat their daily fill.

As among most classes in Ireland and England, the day is divided into three acts or meals, breakfast, lunch, and dinner. By the last is not to be understood the noonday meal, but the chief meal of the day. The lunch is participated in only by the children and invalids. The healthy and full-grown are excluded from it. The hours at which these meals are taken are later than with us in Germany. Nine o'clock is the hour for breakfast, and four in the afternoon for dinner. The breakfast, as in most parts of Ireland, among those who have the means of decent maintenance, consists of new milk and stirabout, a kind of porridge of oatmeal; the dinner is composed of potatoes and buttermilk. The children, for their lunch, receive bread and milk. On Sundays, holidays, and on every Thursday, a little brose, or soup, is given, in addition to the customary diet. An adult receives seven ounces of oatmeal and half a pint of new milk for breakfast, and four pounds of potatoes and a pint of buttermilk for dinner. The board of an adult is calculated to cost one shilling and fourpence three-farthings weekly. That of the children is more expensive, on account of the bread, and the more liberal supply of milk. The most costly of all is the board of the children under two years old, who cost one shilling and sixpence three-farthings a week, for which they receive one pint of new milk and a pound of bread daily. There is therefore a potato diet for adults, a bread diet for children, a rice and meat diet for the sick, and lastly, a fever diet for the class of patients always most numerous in an Irish workhouse.

I was astonished by the appearance of the potato-kettle at this house. No less than 1670 pounds of potatoes are boiled at once. This enormous quantity is all divided into portions of three and a half and four pounds, and each portion is enclosed in a small net. All these nets are laid together in a large basket, and this basket, with its nets and potatoes, is deposited in the boiler. When the potatoes are supposed to have been sufficiently boiled, the basket is wound up again by a machinery, constructed for the purpose, and the poor are then marched up in military order, when each receives his net and marches away with it.

In the school, belonging to this house, the Chinese-Russian calculating board, or numerical frame, had already been introduced, but only a fortnight before my arrival.

Most of the people were employed picking oakum, the occupation assigned to the inmates of most of the prisons and workhouses of England, who are thus made to prepare lint for the wounds of the British men of war. This article is indispensable in the dockyards, where it is used for calking ships. Hundreds of thousands of hands are daily occupied in the workhouses, and houses of correction, in untwining old rope ends for this purpose.

One of the most interesting parts of the establishment is the old clothes store, in which the variegated rags that the paupers bring with them are carefully preserved, to be returned to them on their departure. A pauper, on entering the house, receives in exchange for his motley drapery, the grey uniform of the house, with N.D.U.W.H. (North Dublin Union Workhouse) embroidered upon it in large letters. His liberty rags, together with hat, stockings, shoes, &c., are first carefully fumigated, and then, having been folded together, are marked with the name of their owner, and deposited in the old clothes store. The pauper may at any time have his discharge, by simply intimating a wish to that effect to the governor, but to allow him to take with him the clothes worn in the workhouse would never do, or many would enter one day and go away again the next, merely for the sake of a new suit of apparel. Their old rags are therefore restored to them, and their ingenuity is again taxed to discover the right entrance to their distorted sleeves. It happens almost every day that among the 2000 inmates of the house, one or other, weary of discipline and confinement, and longing for his former liberty, gives the governor notice to quit, and demands the restitution of his wardrobe. It so happened that, at the period of my visit, such an application had just been made, and the clothes store was, in consequence, open. All the theatres in Europe could not have matched, in point of variety, the wardrobe here displayed to me. It must cost the poor a painful struggle when they waver between the servile N.D.U.W.H. costume, and the ragged *sans-culotte* drapery of freedom. Most of them prefer the latter, with all the privations that accompany it.

If a man remains twelve months in the house, conducts himself well, and holds out the hope that he will in future maintain himself by his own exertions, a suit of clothes is given him, to help him forward on the new and thorny path of life on which he is about to enter.

Manchester (Swinton), Lancashire (1850)

> Manchester was one of the first unions to set up a separate institution to house pauper children away from the workhouse. The Swinton Schools, erected in 1843-5, could house over 1,100 children. This article appeared in 1850 in *Household Words*. Its uncredited authors were William Henry Wills and Philip Taylor.[15] Salford Civic Centre now stands on the site.

A DAY IN A PAUPER PALACE.

At the easy distance of five miles from the great Cotton Capital, on the road to the great Cotton Port, through shady lanes and across verdant meadows, is the village of Swinton. At its entrance, on a pleasing elevation, stands a building which is generally mistaken for a wealthy nobleman's residence. The structure is not only elegant but extensive; it is in the Tudor style of architecture, with a frontage of four-hundred and fifty feet. It is studded with more than a hundred windows, each tier so differing in shape and size from the others as to prevent monotonous uniformity. Two winding flights of steps in the centre lead to a handsome entrance hall, above which rise two lofty turrets to break the outline of the extensive roof. The depth of the edifice is great — its whole proportions massive. Pleasure-gardens and playgrounds surround it. In front an acre and a half of flower-beds and grass-plots are intersected by broad gravel-walks and a carriage-drive. Some more of the land is laid out for vegetables. Beyond is a meadow, and the whole domain is about twenty-two acres in extent; all in good, some in picturesque, cultivation.

The stranger gazing upon the splendid brick edifice, with its surrounding territory, is surprised when he is told that it is not the seat of an ancient Dukedom; but that it is a modern palace for pauper children. He is not surprised when he hears that it cost £60,000.

Having passed through the entrance hall, we chatted for a time with the chaplain, who is at the head of the establishment. From him we learnt that there are in the institution six hundred and thirty children, of whom three hundred and five are orphans, and one hundred and twenty-four deserted by their parents. Besides the chaplain there is a head master, a medical officer, a Roman Catholic priest, a governor and matron, six schoolmasters and four schoolmistresses, with a numerous staff of

Manchester's massive Swinton Schools in the early 1900s.

subordinate officials, male and female, including six nurses, and teachers of divers trades. The salaries and wages of the various officers and servants amount to about £1800 a year, exclusive of the cost of their board which the greater number enjoy also.

We went into the playground of the junior department, where more than a hundred and fifty children were assembled. Some were enjoying themselves in the sunshine, some were playing at marbles, others were frisking cheerfully. These children ranged from four to seven years of age. There are some as young as a year and a half in the school. The greater number were congregated at one end of the yard, earnestly watching the proceedings of the master who was giving fresh water to three starlings in cages that stood on the ground. One very young bird was enjoying an airing on the gravel. Two others were perched on a cask. The master informed us it was a part of his system to instruct his charges in kindness to animals by example. He found that the interest which the children took in the animals and in his proceedings towards them, was of service in impressing lessons of benevolence among them towards each other. The practical lessons taught by the master's personal attention to his feathered favourites, outweighed, he thought the theoretic inconsistency of confining birds in cages.

The play-ground is a training school in another particular. On two sides grew several currant trees, on which the fruit is allowed to ripen without any protection. Though some of the scholars are very young, there do not occur above two or three cases of unlawful plucking per annum. The appropriate punishment of delinquents is for them to sit and see the rest of their school-fellows enjoy, on a day appointed, a treat of fresh ripe fruit, whilst they are debarred from all participation.

The personal appearance of the pupils was not prepossessing. Close cropping the hair may be necessary at the first admission of a boy, but surely is not needed after children have been for some time trained in the establishment, in habits of cleanliness. The tailors of the establishment (its elder inmates), are evidently no respecters of personas. Measuring is utterly repudiated, and the style in vogue is the comic or incongruous. The backs of the boys seemed to be Dutch-built; their legs seemed cased after Turkish patterns; white the front view was of Falstaffian proportions, some of the trousers are too short for the legs, and some of the legs too short for the trousers. The girls are better dressed. Amongst them are some of prepossessing faces, intelligent appearance, and pleasing manners. Here and there may be discerned however, vacancy of look, and inaptness to learn. Among the boys, sometimes, occurs a face not quite clean enough, and a shirt collar that, seems to have suffered too long a divorce from the wash-tub.

During the time we spent in the playground, sundry chubby urchins came to the master with small articles which they had found; it being the practice to impress on each, that nothing found belongs to the finder unless, after due inquiry, no owner can be discovered. One brought something looking like liquorice; another produced a halfpenny, which the master appropriated. Perhaps, the master had dropped the halfpenny to test the honesty of some of his pupils. One little fellow was made happy by permission to keep a marble which lie had picked up.

The children obeyed the summons to school with pleasing alacrity. This is owing partly to the agreeable mode of tuition adopted, and in some measure to the fact that the lessons are not allowed to become tedious and oppressive. As soon as any parties give unequivocal signs of weariness, either there is some playful relaxation introduced, or such children are sent into the play-ground. On the present occasion, as soon as the master applied his mouth to a whistle, away trouped the children in glad groups to an ante-room. Here, arranged in five or six rows, boys and girls intermixed stood with eyes fixed on the master, awaiting his signals. At the word of command, each alternate row faced to the right, the others to the left, and filed off, accompanying their march with a suitable tune; their young voices blending in cheerful harmony, while they kept time by clapping their hands, and by an occasional enthusiastic stamp of the foot.

To enliven the routine of school duties, the master's cur takes part in them He is a humorous dog, with an expressive countenance, and a significant wag of the tail. In the intervals of lessons, his duty — which is also his pleasure — consists in jumping over the benches or threading the labyrinths of little legs under them. Now he darts with wild glee into a spelling class; now he rushes among an alphabet group, and snarls a playful 'r-r-r-r,' as if to teach the true pronunciation of the canine letter; now he climbs up behind a seated urchin, puts his forepaws on the favourite's shoulders, and, with a knowing look towards the master, recommends his friend for promotion to a monitorship.

It was surprising to find that the pupils took not the slightest notice of the antics of the master's dog. They heeded nothing but their lessons; but we learned that the dog was a part of the discipline. He accustomed the children to startling eccentricities and unexpected sounds; he presented a small, extraneous, but wholesome difficulty in the pursuit of Knowledge. He, and the currant bush, the pretty treasure-troves, and other contrivances, were intentional temptations which the children were trained to resist. We beg very pointedly to recommend the study of these facts to the attention of the inventors and advocates of the Pentonville Model system. They involve an important principle, — and a principle equally applicable to adults as to children. The morals of the young, or the penitence of the criminal, which result from a system depriving the pupil of every possible temptation to do otherwise than right, will assuredly lapse into vice when incentives to it are presented. Evil exists very plentifully in this world, and it must be recognised and dealt with; it is not by concealing it from the young but by teaching him to resist it that we do wise. It must at the same time be admitted that the principle can be carried too far; and if the master did intentionally drop the halfpenny, it was exactly there that he pushed his excellent principle too far.

The teaching of the juniors is conducted mainly *viva voce*; for the mass of them are under six years of age. The class was opened thus:

'What day is this?'

'Monday.'

'What sort of a day is it?'

'Very fine.'

'Why is it a fine day?'

'Because the sun shines, and it does not rain.'

'Is rain a bad thing, then?'

'No.'

'What is it useful for?'

'To make the flowers and the fruit grow.'

'Who sends rain and sunshine?'

'God.'

'What ought we to do in return for his goodness?'

'Praise him!'

'Let us praise him, then,' added the master. And the children, all together, repeated and then sung a part of the 149th Psalm. — A lesson on morals succeeded, which evidently interested the children. It was partly in the form of a tale told by the master. A gentleman who was kind to the poor, went to visit in gaol a boy imprisoned for crime. The restraint of the gaol, and the shame of the boy, were so described, as to impress the children with strong interest. Then the boy's crime was traced to disobedience, and the excellence of obedience to teachers and parents was shown. The fact that punishment comes out of, and follows our own actions was enforced by another little story.

By this time some of the very young children showed symptoms of lassitude. One fat little mortal had fallen asleep; and this class was consequently marshalled for dismissal, and as usual marched out singing, to play for a quarter of an hour.

A lesson in reading was now administered to a class of older children. For facilitating this achievement, generally so difficult, the master has introduced the phonic system, in some degree according to a mode of his own, by which means even the youngest children make remarkable progress. We need not discuss it here.

The scene the schoolroom, during the reading lesson, presented, was remarkable. Groups of four or five little fellows were gathered in various parts of the room before a reading-card, one acting as monitor; who was sometimes a girl. It was a pleasing sight to see half-a-dozen children seated or kneeling in a circle round the sane book, their heads almost meeting in the centre, in their earnestness to see and hear, while the monitor pointed quickly with the finger to the word which each in succession was to pronounce. All seemed alert, and the eyes of the monitors kindled with intelligence. Meanwhile the master wan busied in passing from one class to another, listening to the manner in which the pronunciation was caught, or the correctness with which the rapid combination of letters and syllables was made. Sometimes he stayed a few minutes with a class to give aid, then proceeded to another; and occasionally, on finding by a few trials, that a boy was quite familiar with the work of his class, he would remove him to another more advanced. These transfers were frequent.

In an adjoining room were assembled, under the care of the schoolmaster's wife, some of the more advanced scholars. One class in this room was particularly interesting — a class composed of the monitors who receive extra instruction in order to fit them for their duties.

After an interval the whole attended a class for general knowledge; in this the mutual instruction system was adopted. A pupil stood out on a platform — the observed of all observers — to be questioned and cross-questioned by his or her schoolfellow, like a witness in a difficult law case, until supplanted by a pupil who could answer better. A degree of piquancy was thus imparted to the proceeding, which caused the attention of the pupils not to flag for a moment. One girl, with red hair and bright eyes, weathered a storm of questions bravely. A sample of the queries put by these young inquisitors, will show the range of subjects necessary to be known about. What are the months of spring? What animal cuts down a tree, and where does it live? Which are the Cinque Ports? What planet is nearest the sun? What is the distance from Manchester to Lancaster? How high is St. Paul's Cathedral? What are the names of the common metals? What causes water to rise and become Clouds?

One urchin who could scarcely be seen over the head of another, and who was evidently of a meteorological turn of mind, bawled out in a peculiarly sedate and measured manner,

'What does the wind do?'

To have answered the question fully would have taken a day, but a single answer satisfied the querist, and was of a sanitary character.

'The wind,' replied the female Rufus, 'cools us in summer and blows away the bad air.' An agreeable enough answer as we sat in the middle of the schoolroom on a hot day, when the thermometer was seventy-one degrees in the shade, and a pleasant breeze stealing through the open windows occasionally fanned our warm cheeks. This concluded our visit to the junior department.

Meanwhile, the education of the elder children was proceeding in other parts of the building. The lessons of the senior sections are conducted in a much quieter manner than those of the junior classes; even in a way which some persons would consider tame and uninteresting. This quietude was, however, more than balanced by another department. As we passed to the elder boys' court-yard, the chaplain threw open the door of a room, where a small music class was practising the fife and the drum. The class consisted of eight youths, who had not learnt long, but performed the 'Troubadour' in creditable style. When they marched out, they headed about two hundred boys, who were drawn up in line; the music-master acting as drill-sergeant and commander-in-chief. After passing through some drill-exercises, they marched off, drums beating and colours flying, to dinner.

After dinner, we visited the workshops — a very active scene. The living tableaux were formed chiefly by young tailors and cobblers. A strict account is kept of all manufactured articles and of their cost; and we learnt that a boy's suit of fustian (labour included) costs 4s. 10½d.; a girl's petticoat 12¾d.; and that the average weekly cost of clothing worn by the children was estimated at 3½d. per head making 15s. 2d. for the wearing apparel of each child per year. This may be taken as a commentary on the 'slop work' prices to which public attention has been so forcibly drawn of late.

In all the industrial sections, the children are occupied alternately at their work and in school — labouring for one afternoon and next morning, and then attending their classes in school for the next afternoon and morning. This is a decided improvement on the Mettray system. In that agricultural colony the boys only attend school once a week, and work at handicrafts, or on the farm, during the other five. There is, however, something defective in the Swinton plan, as applicable to advanced pupils; perhaps they are not stimulated sufficiently; but it happens that no pupil-teacher had ever passed a government examination; although last year the grant of money, by the Committee of Privy Council for the educational departments of the Swinton school, amounted to £531. Those among the scholars who have gone into other lines of life, have generally conducted themselves well; and when absorbed into the masses of society, have become a help and a credit instead of a bane to it. Indeed, having been brought up at the Pauper Palace appears a safe certificate with the public, who are eager for the girls of this school as domestic servants. Both boys and girls, on leaving the institution, are furnished with two complete sets of clothes, and their subsequent behaviour is repeatedly inquired into.

Thus ended our visit to the 'Pauper Palace' As we issued from the iron gate into the open road we met a long line of the elder girls, accompanied by a master, returning from a walk which they had taken, after school hours and before supper, for the benefit of their health. The glad smile of recognition, and the cheerful salutation with which they greeted us as we bade them good evening, were a touch of that gentle nature which 'makes the whole world kin.' It refreshed us like a parting blessing from well-known friends.

Stepney (Wapping), London (1860)

Charles Dickens paid an incognito visit to the Wapping workhouse, one of three then run by the Stepney Union, after reading that a Thames Police Court Magistrate, Henry Selfe, had claimed that a 'monstrous state of things' existed there. Dickens' account of the establishment first appeared in his own periodical *All the Year Round* as part of a series entitled 'The Uncommercial Traveller'.[16] The workhouse was closed in 1863 but was re-opened and rented from 1867 to 1872 by the Poplar Union. St Patrick's Catholic Church now occupies the site.

I was going to Wapping, because an Eastern police magistrate had said, through the morning papers, that there was no classification at the Wapping workhouse for women, and that it was a disgrace and a shame, and divers other hard names, and because I wished to see how the fact really stood.

I made bold to ring at the workhouse gate, where I was wholly unexpected and quite unknown.

A very bright and nimble little matron, with a bunch of keys in her hand, responded to my request to see the House. I began to doubt whether the police magistrate was quite right in his facts, when I noticed her quick, active little figure and her intelligent eyes.

The Traveller (the matron intimated) should see the worst first. He was welcome to see everything. Such as it was, there it all was.

This was the only preparation for our entering "the Foul wards." They were in an old building squeezed away in a corner of a paved yard, quite detached from the more modern and spacious main body of the workhouse. They were in a building most monstrously behind the time — a mere series of garrets or lofts, with every inconvenient and objectionable circumstance in their construction, and only accessible by steep and narrow staircases, infamously ill-adapted for the passage up-stairs of the sick or down-stairs of the dead.

A-bed in these miserable rooms, here on bedsteads, there (for a change, as I understood it) on the floor, were women in every stage of distress and disease. None but those who have attentively observed such scenes, can conceive the extraordinary variety of expression still latent under the general monotony and uniformity of colour, attitude, and condition. The form a little coiled up and turned away, as though it had turned its back on this world for ever; the uninterested face at once lead-coloured and yellow, looking passively upward from the pillow; the haggard mouth a little dropped, the hand outside the coverlet, so dull and indifferent, so light, and yet so heavy; these were on every pallet; but when I stopped beside a bed, and said ever so slight a word to the figure lying there, the ghost of the old character came into the face, and made the Foul ward as various as the fair world. No one appeared to care to live, but no one complained; all who could speak, said that as much was done for them as could be done there, that the attendance was kind and patient, that their suffering was very heavy, but they had nothing to ask for. The wretched rooms were as clean and sweet as it is possible for such rooms to be; they would become a pest-house in a single week, if they were ill-kept.

I accompanied the brisk matron up another barbarous staircase, into a better kind of loft devoted to the idiotic and imbecile. There was at least Light in it, whereas the windows in the former wards had been like sides of school-boys' bird-cages. There was a strong grating over the fire here, and, holding a kind of state on either side of the hearth, separated by the breadth of this grating, were two old ladies in a condition of feeble dignity, which was surely the very last and lowest reduction of self-complacency to be found in this wonderful humanity of ours. They were evidently jealous of each other, and passed their whole time (as some people do, whose fires are not grated) in mentally disparaging each other, and contemptuously watching their neighbours. One of these parodies on provincial gentlewomen was extremely talkative, and expressed a strong desire to attend the service on Sundays, from which she represented herself to have derived the greatest interest and consolation when allowed that privilege. She gossiped so well, and looked altogether so cheery and harmless, that I began to think this a case for the Eastern magistrate, until I found that on the last occasion of her attending chapel she had secreted a small stick, and had caused some confusion in the responses by suddenly producing it and belabouring the congregation.

So, these two old ladies, separated by the breadth of the grating — otherwise they would fly at one another's caps — sat all day long, suspecting one another, and contemplating a world of fits. For everybody else in the room had fits, except the wards-woman; an elderly, able-bodied pauperess, with a large upper lip, and an air of repressing and saving her strength, as she stood with her hands folded before her, and her eyes slowly rolling, biding her time for catching or holding somebody. This civil personage (in whom I regretted to identify a reduced member of my honourable friend Mrs. Gamp's[17] family) said, "They has 'em continiwal, sir. They drops without no more notice than if they was coach-horses dropped from the moon, sir. And when one drops, another drops, and sometimes there'll be as many as four or five on 'em at once, dear me, a rolling and a tearin', bless you! — this young woman, now, has 'em dreadful bad."

She turned up this young woman's face with her hand as she said it. This young woman was seated on the floor, pondering in the foreground of the afflicted. There was nothing repellent either in her face or head. Many, apparently worse, varieties of epilepsy and hysteria were about her, but she was said to be the worst here. When I had spoken to her a little, she still sat with her face turned up, pondering, and a gleam of the mid-day sun shone in upon her.

— Whether this young woman, and the rest of these so sorely troubled, as they sit or lie pondering in their confused dull way, ever get mental glimpses among the motes in the sunlight, of healthy people and healthy things? Whether this young woman, brooding like this in the summer season, ever thinks that somewhere there are trees and flowers, even mountains and the great sea? Whether, not to go so far, this young woman ever has any dim revelation of that young woman — that young woman who is not here and never will come here; who is courted, and caressed, and loved, and has a husband, and bears children, and lives in a home, and who never knows what it is to have this lashing and tearing coming upon her? And whether this young woman, God help her, gives herself up then and drops like a coach-horse from the moon?

I hardly knew whether the voices of infant children, penetrating into so hopeless a place, made a sound that was pleasant or painful to me. It was something to be reminded that the weary world was not all aweary, and was ever renewing itself; but, this young woman was a child not long ago, and a child not long hence might be such as she. Howbeit, the active step and eye of the vigilant matron conducted me past the two provincial gentlewomen (whose dignity was ruffled by the children), and into the adjacent nursery.

There were many babies here, and more than one handsome young mother. There were ugly young mothers also, and sullen young mothers, and callous young mothers. But, the babies had not appropriated to themselves any bad expression yet, and might have been, for anything that appeared to the contrary in their soft faces, Princes Imperial, and Princesses Royal. I had the pleasure of giving a poetical commission to the baker's man to make a cake with all despatch and toss it into the oven for one red-headed young pauper and myself, and felt much the better for it. Without that refreshment, I doubt if I should have been in a condition for "the Refractories," towards whom my quick little matron — for whose adaptation to her office I had by this time conceived a genuine respect — drew me next, and marshalled me the way that I was going.

The Refractories were picking oakum, in a small room giving on a yard. They sat in line on a form, with their backs to a window; before them, a table, and their work. The oldest Refractory was, say twenty; youngest Refractory, say sixteen. I have never yet ascertained in the course of my uncommercial travels, why a Refractory habit should affect the tonsils and uvula; but, I have always observed that Refractories of both sexes and every grade, between a Ragged School and the Old Bailey, have one voice, in which the tonsils and uvula gain a diseased ascendency.

"Five pound indeed! I hain't a going fur to pick five pound," said the Chief of the Refractories, keeping time to herself with her head and chin. "More than enough to pick what we picks now, in sich a place as this, and on wot we gets here!"

(This was in acknowledgment of a delicate intimation that the amount of work was likely to be increased. It certainly was not heavy then, for one Refractory had already done her day's task — it was barely two o'clock — and was sitting behind it, with a head exactly matching it.)

"A pretty Ouse this is, matron, ain't it?" said Refractory Two, "where a pleeseman's called in, if a gal says a word!"

"And wen you're sent to prison for nothink or less!" said the Chief, tugging at her oakum as if it were the matron's hair. "But any place is better than this; that's one thing, and be thankful!"

A laugh of Refractories led by Oakum Head with folded arms — who originated nothing, but who was in command of the skirmishers outside the conversation.

"If any place is better than this," said my brisk guide, in the calmest manner, "it is a pity you left a good place when you had one."

"Ho, no, I didn't, matron," returned the Chief, with another pull at her oakum, and a very expressive look at the enemy's forehead. "Don't say that, matron, cos it's lies!"

Oakum Head brought up the skirmishers again, skirmished, and retired.

"And *I* warn't a going," exclaimed Refractory Two, "though I was in one place for as long as four year — *I* warn't a going fur to stop in a place that warn't fit for me — there! And where the family warn't 'spectable characters — there! And where I fortunately or hunfort'nately, found that the people warn't what they pretended to make theirselves out to be — there! And where it wasn't their faults, by chalks, if I warn't made bad and ruinated — Hah!"

During this speech, Oakum Head had again made a diversion with the skirmishers, and had again withdrawn.

The Uncommercial Traveller ventured to remark that he supposed Chief Refractory and Number One, to be the two young women who had been taken before the magistrate?

"Yes!" said the Chief, "we har! and the wonder is, that a pleeseman an't 'ad in now, and we took off agen. You can't open your lips here, without a pleeseman."

Number Two laughed (very uvularly), and the skirmishers followed suit.

"I'm sure I'd be thankful," protested the Chief, looking sideways at the Uncommercial, "if I could be got into a place, or got abroad. I'm sick and tired of this precious Ouse, I am, with reason."

So would be, and so was, Number Two. So would be, and so was, Oakum Head. So would be, and so were, Skirmishers.

The Uncommercial took the liberty of hinting that he hardly thought it probable that any lady or gentleman in want of a likely young domestic of retiring manners, would be tempted into the engagement of either of the two leading Refractories, on her own presentation of herself as per sample.

"It ain't no good being nothink else here," said the Chief.

The Uncommercial thought it might be worth trying.

"Oh no it ain't," said the Chief.

"Not a bit of good," said Number Two.

"And I'm sure I'd be very thankful to be got into a place, or got abroad," said the Chief.

"And so should I," said Number Two. "Truly thankful, I should."

Oakum Head then rose, and announced as an entirely new idea, the mention of which profound novelty might be naturally expected to startle her unprepared hearers, that she would be very thankful to be got into a place, or got abroad. And, as if she had then said, "Chorus, ladies!" all the Skirmishers struck up to the same purpose. We left them, thereupon, and began a long walk among the women who were simply old and infirm; but whenever, in the course of this same walk, I looked out of any high window that commanded the yard, I saw Oakum Head and all the other Refractories looking out at their low window for me, and never failing to catch me, the moment I showed my head.

And what was very curious, was, that these dim old women had one company notion which was the fashion of the place. Every old woman who became aware of a visitor and was not in bed hobbled over a form into her accustomed seat, and became one of a line of dim old women confronting another line of dim old women across a narrow table. There was no obligation whatever upon them to range themselves in this way; it was their manner of "receiving." As a rule, they made no attempt to talk to one another, or to look at the visitor, or to look at anything, but sat silently working their mouths, like a sort of poor old Cows. In some of these wards, it was good to see a few green plants; in others, an isolated Refractory acting as nurse, who did well enough in that capacity, when separated from her compeers; every one of these wards, day room, night room, or both combined, was scrupulously clean and fresh. I have seen as many such places as most travellers in my line, and I never saw one such, better kept.

Among the bedridden there was great patience, great reliance on the books under the pillow, great faith in GOD. All cared for sympathy, but none much cared to be encouraged with hope of recovery; on the whole, I should say, it was considered rather a distinction to have a complication of disorders, and to be in a worse way than the rest. From some of the windows, the river could be seen with all its life and movement; the day was bright, but I came upon no one who was looking out.

In one large ward, sitting by the fire in arm-chairs of distinction, like the President and Vice of the good company, were two old women, upwards of ninety years of age. The younger of the two, just turned ninety, was deaf, but not very, and could easily be made to hear. In her early time she had nursed a child, who was now another old woman, more infirm than herself, inhabiting the very same chamber. She perfectly understood this when the matron told it, and, with sundry nods and motions of her forefinger, pointed out the woman in question. The elder of this pair, ninety-three, seated before an illustrated newspaper (but not reading it), was a bright-eyed old soul, really not deaf, wonderfully preserved, and amazingly conversational.

The object of my journey was accomplished when the nimble matron had no more to show me. As I shook hands with her at the gate, I told her that I thought justice had not used her very well, and that the wise men of the East were not infallible.

St Martin in the Fields, London (1865)

In the *Lancet*'s survey of London workhouse infirmaries in 1865-6, one of the worst that they visited was that of St Martin in the Fields.[18] The building was demolished in 1871 to make way for an extension to the National Gallery.

The whole workhouse, a gloomy prison-like structure, forms an irregularly four-sided enclosure, of which the infirmary proper occupies the south-side (immediately behind the National Gallery, from which it is separated only by a narrow court); or rather, the "sick wards" occupy two of the three stories which compose the buildings on this side of the workhouse area. The ground within the buildings is raised so much above the level of the surrounding streets that the ground-floor is converted into a basement on that aspect; and this elevation of the ground is due to the circumstance that the site is, in fact, an ancient and well-stocked *churchyard*. This being the case, it would hardly be believed, but is nevertheless true, that the basement floor, with this offensive abutment of churchyard earth blocking up its windows on one side, has been converted into surgical wards, the first floor not being used for infirmary purposes! After such an instance of carelessness in the location of the sick, one is not disposed to expect any great things of the accommodation in the wards themselves, and inspection fully confirms the anticipation. Not one of them is more than 8 ft. 6 in. in height, and the surgical wards are scarcely over 8 ft.; the allowance of cubic space per bed, on the average of the four sick wards, is only 428 ft. (little more than one-third of that prescribed for the construction of the military hospitals); and the gloomy darkness of the wards, especially those in the basement, is most objectionable. Nothing but the presence of windows on each side of the sick wards prevents them from being intolerably oppressive, for there is no proper system of subsidiary ventilation; and, of course, at those times when, from cold weather or other causes, the windows are obliged to be shut, the atmosphere becomes very offensive. Of the bedsteads and bedding the most that can be said is that they are not conspicuously below the average workhouse standard; but the beds are lumpy and comfortless, the means of washing are extremely deficient, and the waterclosets are decidedly bad.

The faults which are evident in the arrangement of the sick wards are repeated throughout the house. Like most of the metropolitan workhouses, St. Martin has a population which, without reckoning the nominal "sick," who are housed in the infirmary, really consists almost entirely of diseased or infirm persons who require more or less of medical attendance. Thus in June last, on the occasion of our first visit, out of a total population of 368, 114 were entered as "sick;" but there was a total of 256 names on the medical relief books as requiring extra diets, and besides these there were numerous other patients. In short, the condition of the inmates generally is such as demands particular attention to ventilation, and this is precisely the subject which is treated with the most reckless neglect. The lying-in-ward, the nursery, and the casual wards, may be selected as examples—the badness of the arrangements following a *crescendo* scale. The lying-in department is contained in a single ward on the third story of the main block of the workhouse. The room is awkwardly shaped, a large piece being taken out of its width, at the lower end, by a projection of the wall : but as there are seldom more than six inmates, it happens that there is a much more liberal allowance of cubic space than in most of the other wards. This advantage, however, is utterly neutralized by the fact that there are but two windows and one ventilator : the windows are blocked up by massive wooden screens, which the sapience of the guardians has devised in order to protect the modesty of the gentleman-paupers in the court-yard from possible demonstrations on the part of the unfortunate creatures who are expecting or recovering from their confinement; the one ventilator is a large square hole in the wall, leading into a shaft which goes out through the roof, and the only conceivable use of it is to pour a down-draught of cold air upon the luckless occupant of the labour bed, which is conveniently placed below it. At night, of course, the windows are snugly closed and the flap of the ventilator turned up, if it be anything like cold weather; and we observed that the nurse had, with careful forethought, *papered over* some meagre ventilating slits in the window panes which might still have permitted some trifling ventilation to go on. With the atmosphere thus produced, and with the additional infliction of being forced to hear the groans of any patient who may be actually in labour, the inmates of the St. Martin's lying-in ward endure a state of things which we suppose no man of the commonest sense or feeling could bear to inflict, unless he were a "guardian of the poor." It is a very different matter, however, when we come to consider the results of the neglect of ventilation in the nursery. The allowance of cubic space in this apartment is much less ample than in the lying-in ward, and the subsidiary arrangements for ventilation are of the same kind; the atmosphere is extremely foul. Into this room, a few months since, there accidentally came a woman bearing with her the infection of measles, and the result of this, in such a vitiated atmosphere, was a most disastrous outbreak of the disease, in which eight children died : the malady assumed a very virulent type, which must doubtless be referred to the sanitary deficiencies of the apartment. As for the tramp-wards, the only epithet which can be applied to them is — "abominable." The male tramp-ward, in particular, struck us with horrified disgust. We scarcely had a fair glance at it on the occasion of our first visit, being accompanied by the visiting committee (for whose edification, by the way, we suspect it had been furbished up in an unusual manner); but a few days since we revisited it, and the impression produced on our minds is that we have seldom seen such a villainous hole. It is situated completely underground, and is approached by an almost perpendicular flight of stone steps, leading to a grated iron door, through which one passes into an ill-smelling watercloset, which forms the antechamber of *messieurs* the tramps. The apartment at the moment of our entrance (about mid-day) was being ventilated and cleaned by a very nasty-looking warder. There is but *one window, closely grated*, to this apartment, in which some sixteen or twenty people sleep, and that is quite close up to the watercloset end. From the other part of the room, in which the beds (or shelves) for the tramps are situated, and in which the nasty-looking man was making feeble movements with a brush, there arose a concentrated vagrant-stink which fairly drove us out, not without threatenings of sickness. The bath-room, in which the "casuals" are facetiously supposed to wash before retiring to rest, is a still-more dungeon-like place; or rather it is like a *very* bad beer-cellar, through the obscurity of which one may dimly perceive a tin bath, while one's nose is assaulted by new and more dreadful stench. Both bath-room and sleeping-room were extremely dirty; and considering that the allowance of cubic space for each sleeper is but 294 feet under the most favourable circumstances, it is really a marvel that typhus does not spontaneously arise among the temporary inhabitants of this disreputable ward. If any of the tramps fall sick, they are taken up into a miserable ward in a one-storied building at the east end of the premises, and *closely adjoining the dead-house*, in which they are greatly over-crowded when the place happens to be full, and the bed-furniture of which is squalid and mean.

As might be expected in an establishment the managers of which are so neglectful of such important matters as ventilation and the supply of proper water-closets, the nursing arrangements are very insufficient. There is but one paid nurse, a very intelligent and active woman, who confesses that it is impossible for her, even with the most fatiguing exertions, to keep up a really efficient supervision of the house. Her apartment is placed next to the lying-in ward, and far away from the infirmary proper. There is a pauper day-nurse to each ward, and extra nurses are supplied for night duty. The master, who is a very active and conscientious officer, does his best to superintend the ward management generally; and he reports that, in his opinion, the pauper nurses, on the whole, do their duty fairly. But we saw great reason to doubt whether this is the case with regard to the administration of medicines, nor could this be expected, by those who know hospital requirements, from the character and appearance of these females. A good instance of their inefficiency is supplied by the way in which they manage, or rather neglect, the few imbecile patients in the house (who, by the way, are scattered through several different wards); these poor creatures have no suitable employment at all, and it is clear that the attendants of the wards in which they may happen to be have no notion of any such management as might tend to improve their mental state. It must be confessed, however, that the guardians are primarily to blame in this matter, since they have organized no arrangements calculated to be useful to their insane inmates, and seem to consider them as of no consequence.

The medical attendance on the sick appears to be performed in an exemplary manner by Mr. Skegg, the medical officer; far better, indeed, than the guardians have any right to expect, seeing that they give him only the miserable salary of £120 a year, and out of this sum require him to find drugs of all kinds, and to dispense them.

Our opinion is so decidedly in favour of immediate removal as the only efficient remedy for the evils of this infirmary we deem it useless to recapitulate all the defects.

Lewisham, London (1865)

Not all the London workhouse infirmaries visited by *The Lancet* were as bad as that of St Martin in the Fields. Although not without faults, such as its uncomfortably small beds, Lewisham's establishment was found to have many redeeming features. It was noted that the workhouse predominantly accommodated the elderly, infirm and sick and appears largely to have been performing the role of a pauper hospital.[19] The 1817 frontage of what is now University Hospital Lewisham still survives.

This workhouse is situated in the centre of the picturesque village of Lewisham, five miles south-east of London. It is a three-storied brick building of three blocks, and was erected in 1817. The centre has a south aspect, while the front of the house looks east; the parallel wing being in the rear, with a west face. The entire house represents three-fourths of a square, leaving a considerable space towards the south for airing ground,

58

and which, being paved, forms two good yards for males and females respectively. The original plan has been, however, marred by the erection of several low buildings on the south, and which more or less obstruct the free circulation of air through the entire structure. In the rear are well-cultivated kitchen-gardens, yards for work, laundry, and other purposes, including separate erections for infectious cases, and a dead-house.

The union consists of seven parishes, with a population of 65,757 persons. The house, which is the property of the parish, is rented by the union at an annual charge of £350, and was built for 300 inmates. The drainage is good; the water-supply (from a well in the yard) defective. On the occasion of our visit there were 160 in residence; and we were most obligingly shown over the house by Mr Want, the master, who appeared to us fully alive to his duties and responsibilities.

With the exception of the infection wards, four in number, in a detached building in the yard. there is no proper classification. Sick, infirm, and able-bodied — so-called at least, but we saw none in the entire house — were placed in close approximation. The sandwich fashion obtained, showing at least a complete want of organization and method.

The sick wards are seven in number: three for males, containing thirty-three beds, and allowing all average of 494 cubic feet per bed; and four for females, containing thirty-nine beds, and allowing an average of 489 cubic feet; besides four infection wards, containing twenty-two beds, with an average cubic space of 539 feet. There can be no doubt that, were these wards filled, the accommodation would be very deficient (though not seriously below the Poor-law Board's standard), and that the infectious cases in particular would be very badly off with only 539 cubic feet per bed. Practically this need not be of much consequence, as the house, which was built for 300, is never filled, and, at the time of our visit, contained, as we have stated, only 180 inmates; but in several wards the neglect of the most ordinary precautions made the atmosphere very foul. In many respects the wards are commendable. There is great attention paid to cleanliness of floors, walls, windows, &c.; there are pictures, texts, and suitable books in plenty; and the bed furniture is sufficient and good. But there is one cruel piece of neglect — viz., the excessive shortness of the iron bedsteads, which are only 5 ft. long by 2 ft. 5 in. wide! Towels, and the other appliances for washing the sick, are well arranged and well supplied.

In the presence of much that was deserving of praise in the style of management, we were surprised to find in several wards a total absence of water-closets, and to be told that the inmates bad to pass along an entire range of buildings to obtain the accommodation. [*We are glad to say that the guardians have, since our visit, removed this objection to a great extent, and made other valuable improvements at considerable cost, especially with regard to the baths, &c. Our labour has not been in vain!*] There was the same absence of lavatories and baths; indeed, no individual ward had its own exclusive closet, lavatory, or bath. There is but one, and that a movable, bath in the house, and no hot-water apparatus; so that a bath being wanted, water must be specially heated and carried to the ward in which it is required, and this to the annoyance and discomfort of the rest of the ward-patients.

The condition of the patients — chiefly persons advanced in life, and suffering from the diseases of old age — appeared very satisfactory; and when spoken to, many of them, in language as emphatic as truthful, expressed gratitude and thankfulness for what was done for them. We saw a good supply of macintoshes, and other appliances indicating more than usual regard for the comfort and well-being of the poor. Cards over the beds, giving name, age, disease, and treatment, have not yet reached this suburb; we trust, however, that the medical officer will accept our suggestion, and resort to them as a valuable help in hospital management.

The care — domestic, at least — of the sick (and we saw few in the house who could very properly be removed from this dependent category) is committed to the matron (the wife of the master), one paid nurse, and thirteen pauper helps. The whole of the latter appeared to us admirable objects of one's sympathy, but without exception disqualified, physically and morally, for the responsible duties of nursing the sick — fit rather to be nursed themselves; the paid nurse, after many years' faithful service, justly entitled to a pension; consequently, in our judgment, the only reliable aid left to carry out the directions of the medical officer is the matron, whose other duties as mistress of the house must consume her time and exhaust her energies. Hence it must follow that the sick and infirm are wanting in proper care and hospital appliances. We would therefore suggest the appointment of properly qualified and well-trained nurses to meet the wants of the different classes of sick and infirm; all of whom might act under the direction of the matron, herself guided by the medical officer.

The various kinds of food and the methods of cooking are in most instances good and commendable. We tasted both the beef and mutton, which were well dressed and wholesome; also the potatoes, bread, ale, and porter, all of which were really good; and the quantity served out to each individual was abundant. For the really sick, however; we would suggest *roast* meat occasionally, instead of boiled. To boil meat is to abstract a large amount of its nutritive qualities, and, unless the broth is drunk with the meat, the recipient is thus deprived of what really belongs to him. At very little additional cost roast meat might be given in turn with boiled. Beef-tea (and really good we found it), arrowroot, milk, and extra tea are given out when asked for, without need of a medical order: a practice which we commend very strongly, and which we should be glad to see introduced as a common practice into all our workhouse infirmaries.

The medical officer, Mr. Hugh Stott, who is also surgeon to the district of Lewisham, is expected to visit the house at least four times a week, and daily when summoned. He supplies, all the drugs except cod-liver oil and quinine, and compounds for both in-and-out-patients, receiving for the whole of these duties about £105. per annum. On the books we found about ninety patients in March, and sixty-seven in May. One case of scarlet fever was being treated in the infection wards, which are in many of their relations good. The number of midwifery cases in the house averages about eight in the year, which are attended by the paid nurse — nominally, however, by the medical officer, and for which he is paid at the rate of 10s. 6d. per case.

The inferences we arrived at respecting the medical officer are that he has almost, if not practically altogether, unlimited control over all the arrangements for the sick; that the guardians are really most liberal, and, if well managed, may be induced to do whatever is for the good of the inmates, guided by the medical officer. The latter gentleman can order a liberal diet, and any and every appliance that may be needed for the sick; and he can also ask for any change in the arrangements which his experience suggests as desirable, with a good prospect of obtaining his request. Consequently, if the most enlightened principles of hospital treatment which are now accepted in the profession are not carried out, we must suppose that the blame rests chiefly with the medical officer. It is true that his salary is utterly inadequate, and his whole position a false one; but this has nothing to do with the obligation to urge on the guardians improvements which are of vital importance to the sick.

As already stated, the type of diseases which prevail at Lewisham Union is chiefly characteristic of old age and declining powers: chronic cough, paralysis, and sore legs, with some few cases of phthisis, include nearly all. We carefully examined the medical records, and could find no trace of any epidemic. Formerly skin diseases prevailed in the house, when it was crowded with children; it was then remarked that all children who came into the house contracted a form of scabies, that treatment did little good, but that on sending the children away into the country the disease almost immediately disappeared. At present there are no children kept here, and the disease has never appeared in the adults.

The mortality of 1863 was 35; that of 1864 was 45 — a high death-rate, which, however, depends chiefly on the accidental circumstance that many inmates enter the house in a dying condition.

The details we have given justify, we believe, the position of Lewisham as capable, with certain important modifications, of developing into a really good and well-conducted hospital.

Lambeth, London (1866)

In January 1866, journalist James Greenwood, disguised as a tramp, spent a night in the casual ward of the Lambeth workhouse. His titillating account of the repugnant conditions he experienced and the rowdy behaviour of the other inmates caused a sensation after it was published in the *Pall Mall Gazette* under the pseudonym 'the Amateur Casual'.[20] His undercover investigation was subsequently emulated by many other 'social explorers'.

A NIGHT IN A WORKHOUSE.

I lifted the big knocker, and knocked; the door was promptly opened, and I entered. Just within, a comfortable-looking clerk sat at a comfortable desk, ledger before him. Indeed, the spacious hail in every way was as comfortable as cleanliness and great mats and plenty of gaslight could make it.

"What do you want?" asked the man who opened the door.

"I want a lodging."

"Go and stand before the desk," said the porter; and I obeyed.

"You are late," said the clerk.

"Am I, sir?"

"Yes. If you come in you'll have a bath, and you'll have to sleep in the shed."

"Very well, Sir."

"What's your name?"

"Joshua Mason, Sir."

"What are you?"

"An engraver." (This taredaddle I invented to account for the look of my hands.)

"Where did you sleep last night?"

"Hammersmith," I answered — as I hope to be forgiven!

"How many times have you been here?"

"Never before, Sir."

"Where do you mean to go when you are turned out in the morning?"

"Back to Hammersmith, Sir."

These humble answers being entered in a book, the clerk called to the porter, saying, "Take him through. You may as well take his bread with you."

Near the clerk stood a basket containing some pieces of bread of equal size. Taking one of these, and unhitching a bunch of keys from the wall, the porter led me through some passages all so scrupulously clean that my most serious misgivings were laid to rest. Then we passed into a dismal yard. Crossing this, my guide led me to a door, calling out, "Hillo! Daddy, I've brought you another." Whereupon Daddy opened to us, and let a little of his gaslight to stream into the dark where we stood.

"Come in," said Daddy, very hospitably. "There's enough of you to-night, anyhow! What made you so late?"

"I didn't like to come in earlier."

"Ah! that's a pity now, because you've missed your skilly (gruel). It's the first night of skilly, don't you know, under the new Act?"

"Just like my luck!" I muttered dolefully.

The porter went his way, and I followed Daddy into another apartment where were ranged three great baths, each one containing a liquid so disgustingly like weak mutton broth that my worst apprehensions crowded back.

"Come on, there's a dry place to stand on up at this end," said Daddy, kindly. "Take off your clothes, tie 'em up in your hank'sher, and I'll lock 'em up till the morning."

Accordingly, I took off my coat and waistcoat, and was about to tie them together when Daddy cried, "That ain't enough, I mean *everything.*" "Not my shirt, Sir, I suppose?" "Yes, shirt and all; but there, I'll lend you a shirt," said Daddy. Whatever you take in of your own will be nailed, you know. You might take in your boots, though — they'd be handy if you happened to want to leave the shed for anything; but don't blame me if you lose 'em."

With a fortitude for which I hope some day to be rewarded, I made up my bundle (boots and all), and the moment Daddy's face was turned away shut my eyes and plunged desperately into the mutton broth. I wish from the bottom of my heart my courage had been less hasty; for hearing the splash, Daddy looked round and said, "Lor, now! there was no occasion for that; you look a clean and decent sort of man. It's them filthy beggars" (only he used a word more specific than "filthy") "that want washing. Don't use that towel — here's a clean one! That's the sort! and now here's your shirt (handing me a blue striped one from a heap), and here's your ticket. Number 34 you are, and a ticket to match is tied to your bundle. Mind you don't lose it. They'll nail it from you if they get a chance. Put it under your head. This is your rug — take it with you."

"Where am I to sleep, please, sir?"

"I'll show you."

And so he did. With no other rag but the checked shirt to cover me, and with my rug over my shoulder, he accompanied me to the door at which I had entered, and, opening it, kept me standing with naked feet on the stone threshold, full in the draught of the frosty air, while he pointed out the way I should go. It was not a long way, but I would have given much not to have trodden it. It was open as the highway — with flagstones below and the stars overhead; and, as I said before, and cannot help saying again, a frosty wind was blowing.

"Straight across," said Daddy, to where you see the light shining through. "Go in there and turn to the left, and you'll find the beds in a heap. Take one of 'em and make yourself comfortable." And straight across I went, my naked feet seeming to cling to the stones as though they were burning hot instead of icy cold, till I reached the space through which the light was shining, and I entered in.

No language with which I am acquainted is capable of conveying an adequate conception of the spectacle I then encountered. Imagine a space of about thirty feet by thirty enclosed on three sides by a dingy whitewashed wall, and roofed with naked tiles which were furred with the damp and filth that reeked within. As for the fourth side of the shed, it was boarded in for (say) a third of its breadth; the remaining space being hung with flimsy canvas, in which was a gap two feet wide at top, widening to at least four feet at bottom. This far too airy shed was paved with stone, the flags so thickly encrusted with filth that I mistook it first for a floor of natural earth. Extending from one end of my bedroom to the other, in three rows, were certain iron "cranks" (of which I subsequently learnt the use), with their many arms raised in various attitudes, as the stiffened arms of men are on a battle-field. My bed-fellows lay among the cranks, distributed over the flagstones in a double row, on narrow bags scantily stuffed with hay. At one glance my appalled vision took in thirty of them — thirty men and boys stretched upon shallow pallets with but only six inches of comfortable hay between them and the stony floor. Those beds were placed close together, every occupant being provided with a rug like that which I was fain to hug across my shoulders. In not a few cases two gentlemen had clubbed beds and rugs and slept together. In one case, four gentlemen had so clubbed together. Many of my fellow casuals were awake — others asleep or pretending to sleep; and shocking as were the waking ones to look upon, they were quite pleasant when compared with the sleepers. For this reason: the practised and well-seasoned casual seems to have a peculiar way of putting himself to bed. He rolls himself in his rug, tucking himself in, head and feet, so that he is completely enveloped; and, lying quite still on his pallet, he looks precisely like a corpse covered because of its hideousness. Some were stretched out at full length; some lay nose and knees together; some with an arm or a leg showing crooked through the coverlet. It was like the result of a railway accident; these ghastly figures were awaiting the coroner.

From the moral point of view, however, the wakeful ones were more dreadful still. Towzled, dirty, villainous, they squatted up in their beds, and smoked foul pipes, and sang snatches of horrible songs, and bandied jokes so obscene as to be absolutely appalling. Eight or ten were so enjoying themselves — the majority with the check shirt on and the frowsy rug pulled about their legs; but two or three wore no shirts at all, squatting naked to the waist, their bodies fully exposed in the light of the single flaring jet of gas fixed high upon the wall.

My entrance excited very little attention. There was a horse-pail three parts full of water standing by a post in the middle of the shed, with a little tin pot beside it. Addressing me as "old pal", one of the naked ruffians begged me to "hand him a swig", as he was "werry nigh garspin." Such an appeal of course no "old pal" could withstand, and I gave him a pot full of water. He showed himself grateful for the attention. "I should lay over there if I was you," he said, pointing to the left side of the shed; "it's more out of the wind than this 'ere side is." I took the good-natured advice and (by this time shivering with the cold) stepped over the stones to where the beds or straw bags were heaped, and dragged one of them to the spot suggested by my naked comrade. But I had no more idea of how to arrange it than of making an apple-pudding; and a certain little discovery added much to my embarrassment. In the middle of the bed I had selected was a stain of blood bigger than a man's hand! I did not know what to do now. To lie on such a horrid thing seemed impossible; yet to carry back the bed and exchange it for another might betray a degree of fastidiousness repugnant to the feelings of my fellow lodgers and possibly excite suspicions that I was not what I seemed. Just in the nick of time in came that good man Daddy.

"What! not pitched yet?" he exclaimed; "here, I'll show you. Hallo! somebody's been a bleedin'! Never mind; let's turn him over. There you are you see! Now lay down, and cover your rug over you."

There was no help for it. It was too late to go back. Down I lay, and spread the rug over me. I should have mentioned that I brought in with me a cotton handkerchief, and this I tied round my head by way of a nightcap; but not daring to pull the rug as high as my face. Before I could in any way settle my mind to reflection, in came Daddy once more to do me a further kindness, and point out a stupid blunder I had committed.

"Why, you *are* a rummy chap!" said Daddy. "You forgot your bread! Lay hold. And look here, I've brought you another rug; it's perishing cold to-night." So saying, he spread the rug over my legs and went away.

It was about half-past nine when, having made myself as comfortable as circumstances permitted, I closed my eyes in the desperate hope that I might fall asleep, and so escape from the horrors with which I was surrounded. "At seven to-morrow morning the bell will ring," Daddy had informed me, "and then you will give up your ticket and get back your bundle." Between that time and the present full nine long hours had to wear away.

But I was speedily convinced that, at least for the present, sleep was impossible. The young fellow (one of the three who lay in one bed, with their feet to my head) whom my bread had refreshed, presently swore with frightful imprecations that he was now going to have a smoke; and immediately put his threat into execution. Thereupon his bedfellows sat up and lit their pipes too. But oh! if they had only smoked — if they had not taken such an unfortunate fancy to spit at the leg of a crank distant a few inches from my head, how much misery and apprehension would have been spared me! To make matters worse, they united with this American practice an Eastern one; as they smoked they related little autobiographical anecdotes — so abominable that three or four decent men who lay at the farther end of the shed were so provoked that they threatened, unless the talk abated in filthiness, to get up and stop it by main force. Instantly, the voice of every blackguard in the room was raised against the decent ones. They were accused of loathsome afflictions, stigmatized as "fighting men out of work", and invited to "a round" by boys young enough to be their grandsons. For several minutes there was such a storm of oaths, threats, and taunts — such a deluge of foul words raged in the room — that I could not help thinking of the fate of Sodom; as I did, several times during the night. Little by little the riot died out, without any the slightest interference on the part of the officers.

Soon afterwards the ruffian majority was strengthened by the arrival of a lanky boy of about fifteen, who evidently recognized many acquaintances, and was recognized by them as "Kay". He was a very remarkable-looking lad, and his appearance pleased me much. Short as his hair was cropped, it still looked soft and silky; he had large blue eyes set wide apart, and a mouth that would have been faultless but for its great width; and his voice was as soft and sweet as any woman's. Lightly as a woman, too, he picked his way over the stones towards the place where the beds lay, carefully hugging his cap beneath his arm.

"Tell us a 'rummy' story, Kay," said somebody: and Kay did. He told stories of so "rummy" a character that the decent men at the farther end of the room (some of whom had their little boys sleeping with them) must have lain in a sweat of horror as they listened. Indeed, when Kay broke into a "rummy" song with a roaring chorus, one of the decent men rose in his bed and swore that he would smash Kay's head if he didn't desist. But Kay sang on till he and his admirers were tired of the entertainment. "Now," said he, "let's have a swearing club! You'll all be in it."

The principle of this game seemed to rest on the impossibility of either of the young gentlemen making half-a-dozen observations without introducing a blasphemous or obscene word; and either the basis is a very sound one, or for the sake of keeping the "club" alive the members purposely made slips. The penalty for "swearing" was a punch on any part of the body, except a few which the club rules protected. The game was highly successful. Warming with the sport, and indifferent to punches, the members vied with each other in audacity, and in a few minutes Bedlam in its prime could scarcely have produced such a spectacle as was to be seen on the beds behind me. One rule of the club was that any word to be found in the Bible might be used with impunity, and if one member "punched" another for using such a word, the error was to be visited upon him with a double punching all round. This naturally led to much argument, for in vindicating the Bible as his authority, a member became sometimes so much heated as to launch into a flood of "real swearing", which brought the fists of the club upon his naked carcase as thick as hail.

These and other pastimes beguiled the time until, to my delight, the church chimes audibly tolled twelve. After this the noise gradually subsided, and it seemed as though everybody was going to sleep at last. I should have mentioned that during the story-telling and song-singing a few "casuals" had dropped in, but they were not habitués, and cuddled down with their rugs over their heads without a word to any one.

In a little while all was quiet — save for the flapping of the canvas curtain in the night breeze, the snoring, and the horrible, indescribable sound of impatient hands scratching skins that itched. There was another sound of very frequent occurrence, and that was the clanking of the tin pannikin against the water pail. Whether it is in the nature of workhouse bread or skilly to provoke thirst is more than my limited experience entitles me to say, but it may be truthfully asserted that once at least in the course of five minutes might be heard a rustling of straw, a pattering of feet, and then the noise of water-dipping; and then was to be seen at the pail the figure of a man (sometimes stark naked), gulping down the icy water as he stood upon the icy stones.

At half-past two, every one being asleep, or at least lying still, Daddy came in and counted us: one, two, three, four, and so on, in a whisper. Then, finding the pail empty (it was nearly full at half-past nine, when I entered), he considerately went and refilled it, and even took much trouble in searching for the tin pot which served as a drinking cup, and which the last comer had playfully thrown to the farther end of the shed. The pail refilled, Daddy returned, and was seen no more till morning.

It still wanted four hours and a half to seven o'clock — the hour of rising — and never before in my life did time appear to creep so slowly. Four o'clock, five o'clock, six o'clock chimed, and then I had news — most welcome — of the world without, and of the real beginning of day. Half a dozen factory bells announced that it was time for working men to go to labour; but my companions were not working men, and so snored on. A little while, and doors were heard to open and shut; yet a little while, and the voice of Daddy was audible in conversation with another early bird; and then I distinctly caught the word "bundles". Blessed sound! I longed for my bundle — for my pleasing brown coat — for my warm if unsightly "jersey" which I adopted as a judicious substitute for a waistcoat — for my corduroys and liberty.

"Clang!" went the workhouse clock. "Now, then! wake 'em up!" cried Daddy. I was already up — sitting up, that is — being anxious to witness the resurrection of the ghastly figures rolled in the rugs. But nobody but myself rose at the summons. They knew what it meant well enough, and in sleepy voices cursed the bell and wished it in several dreadful places; but they did not move until there came in at the hole in the canvas, two of the pauper inhabitants of the house, bearing bundles. "Thirty-two," "Twenty-eight!" they bawled, but not *my* number, which was thirty-four. Neither thirty-two nor twenty-eight, however, seemed eager to accept his good fortune in being first called. They were called upon several times before they would answer; and then they replied with a savage "Chuck it here, can't you!" "Not before you chucks over your shirt and ticket," the bundle-holder answered, whereupon "Twenty-eight" sat up, and, divesting himself of his borrowed shirt, flung it with his wooden ticket, and his bundle was flung back in return.

It was some time before bundle No. 34 turned up, so that I had fair opportunity to observe my neighbours. The decent men slipped into their rags as soon as they got them, but the blackguards were in no hurry. Some indulged in a morning pipe to prepare themselves for the fatigue of dressing, while others, loosening their bundles as they squatted naked, commenced an investigation for certain little animals which shall be nameless.

At last my turn came, and "chucking over" my shirt and ticket, I quickly attired myself in clothes which, ragged as they were, were cleaner than they looked. In less than two minutes I was out of the shed, and in the yard; where a few of the more decent poor fellows were crowding round a pail of water, and scrambling after something that might pass for a "wash" — finding their own soap, as far as I could observe, and drying their faces on any bit of rag they might happen to have about them, or on the canvas curtain of the shed.

By this time it was about half-past seven, and the majority of the casuals were up and dressed. I observed, however, that none of the younger boys were as yet up, and it presently appeared that there existed some rule against their dressing in the shed; for Daddy came out of the bath-room, where the bundles were deposited, and called out, "Now four boys!" and instantly four poor little wretches, some with their rugs trailing about their shoulders and some quite bare, came shivering over the stones and across the bleak yard, and were admitted to the bath-room to dress. "Now four more boys," cried Daddy; and so on.

When all were up and dressed, the boys carried the bed rugs into Daddy's room, and the pauper inmates made a heap of the "beds", stacking them against the wall. As before mentioned, the shed served the treble purpose of bed-chamber, workroom, and breakfast-room; it was impossible to get fairly at the cranks and set them going until the bedding was stowed away.

Breakfast before work, however, but it was a weary while to some of us before it made its appearance. For my own part, I had little appetite, but about me were a dozen poor wretches who obviously had a very great one: they had come in overnight too late for bread, and perhaps may not have broken fast since the morning of the previous day. Full three quarters of an hour of loitering and shivering, and then came the taskmaster: a soldierly-looking man, over six feet high, with quick grey eyes, in which "No trifling" appeared as distinctly as a notice against trespassing on a wayside board. He came in amongst us, and the gray eyes made out our number in a moment. "Out into the yard, all of you!" he cried; and we went out in a mob. There we shivered for some twenty minutes longer, and then a baker's man appeared with a great wooden tray piled up with just such slices of bread as we had received overnight. The tray was consigned to an able-bodied casual, who took his place with the taskmaster at the shed door, and then in single file we re-entered the shed, each man and boy receiving a slice as he passed in. Pitying, as I suppose, my unaccustomed look, Mr Taskmaster gave me a slice and a large piece over.

The bread devoured, a clamour for "skilly" began. The rumour had got abroad that this morning, and on all future mornings, there would be skilly at breakfast, and "Skilly! skilly!" resounded through the shed. No one had hinted that it was not forthcoming, but skilly seems to be thought an extraordinary concession. There was a loud "hooray!" when the longed for skilly appeared in two pails, in one of which floated a small tin saucepan, with a stick thrust into its handle, by way of a ladle. Yellow pint basins were provided for our use, and large iron spoons. "Range round the walls!" the taskmaster shouted. We obeyed with the utmost alacrity; and then what I should judge to be about three-fourths of a pint of gruel was handed to each of us as we stood. I was glad to get mine, because the basin that contained it was warm and my hands were numb with cold. I tasted a spoonful, as in duty bound, and wondered more than ever at the esteem in which it was held by my *confrères*. It was a weak decoction of oatmeal and water, bitter, and without even a pinch of salt to flavour — that I could discover. But it was hot; and on that account, perhaps, was so highly relished, that I had no difficulty in persuading one of the decent men to accept my share.

It was now past eight o'clock, and, as I knew that a certain quantity of labour had to be performed by each man before he was allowed to go his way, I was anxious to begin. The labour was to be "crank" labour. The "cranks" are a series of iron bars extending across the width of the shed, penetrating through the wall, and working a flour mill on the other side. Turning the "crank" is like turning a windlass. The task is not a severe one.

Four measures of corn (bushels they were called — but that is doubtful) have to be ground every morning by the night's batch of casuals. Close up by the ceiling hangs a bell connected with the machinery, and as each measure is ground the bell rings, so that the grinders may know how they are going on. But the grinders are as lazy as obscene. We were no sooner set to work than the taskmaster left us to our own sweet will, with nothing to restrain its exercise but an occasional visit from the miller, a weakly expostulating man. Once or twice he came in and said mildly, "Now then, my men, why *don't* you stick to it?" — and so went out again.

The result of this laxity of overseeing would have disgusted me at any time, and was intensely disgusting then. At least one half the gang kept their hands from the crank whenever the miller was absent, and betook themselves to their private amusements and pursuits. Some sprawled upon the beds and smoked; some engaged themselves and their friends in tailoring, and one turned hair-cutter for the benefit of a gentleman who, unlike Kay, had *not* just come out of prison. There were three tailors, two of them on the beds mending their own coats, and the other operating on a recumbent friend in the rearward part of his clothing. Where the needles came from I do not know; but for thread they used a strand of the oakum (evidently easy to deal with) which the boys were picking in the corners. Other loungers strolled about with their hands in their pockets, discussing the topics of the day, and playing practical jokes on the industrious few: a favourite joke being to take a bit of rag, anoint it with grease from the crank axles, and clap it unexpectedly over somebody's eye.

The consequence of all this was that the cranks went round at a very slow rate and now and then stopped altogether. Then the miller came in; the loungers rose from their couches, the tailors ceased stitching, the smokers dropped their pipes, and every fellow was at his post. The cranks spun round furiously again, the miller's expostulation being drowned amidst a shout of "Slap bang, here we are again!" or this extemporised chorus:

> We'll hang up the miller on a sour apple tree,
> We'll hang up the miller on a sour apple tree,
> We'll hang up the miller on a sour apple tree,
> And then go grinding on.
> Glory, glory, Hallelujah, &c., &c.

By such ditties the ruffians enlivened their short spell of work. Short indeed! The miller departed, and within a minute afterwards beds were reoccupied, pipes lit, and tailoring resumed. So the game continued — the honest fellows sweating at the cranks, and anxious to get the work done and go out to look for more profitable labour, and the paupers by profession taking matters quite easy. I am convinced that had the work been properly superintended the four measures of corn might have been ground in the space of an hour and a half. As it was, when the little bell tinkled for the fourth time, and the yard gate was opened and we were free to depart, the clock had struck eleven.

Romford and Billericay, Essex (1866)

> These two extracts, about the workhouse casual wards at Romford and Billericay, are from the periodical *All the Year Round*, and published not long after James Greenwood's visit to Lambeth.[21] The text was said to come from a letter from a man who had slept in the Lambeth casual ward on the same night as Greenwood.

TOLD BY A TRAMP.

One man said he was going to Romford as soon as he got out, and that as much skilly as you liked was given you there. I consented to go with him, as he wanted a companion, and we got to Romford about five o'clock in the afternoon. On the left-hand side, going into the town, stands the relieving-officer's house; a young man came out and gave us two tickets, scratched with a pen. We turned sharply round and up a narrow lane, and at the top sat down for a few minutes. A young woman came past, from work I should think, and my companion asked her what she had got in the basket she was carrying? She had some bread and cheese, the remains of her dinner, and gave it us willingly. The man at the gate would not admit us until six o'clock, and we lay down on the grass by the roadside, in company with several more. The man who took our names at Romford workhouse was an ignorant fellow, and a very slow writer, and some of the casuals gave him extra trouble. I thought I might as well try my hand, and gave him Owen Evans as my name, taking care to pronounce it "Howing Heavens." This produced endless bother, and was only capped by the name of the town I came from, which was Llanfairfeckan. He gave this latter word up, and put Barking instead. The casual ward has no bunks, but has a raised board with mattresses, blankets, and counterpanes, dirty enough. It is a very small place, and might hold seven or eight; but they managed to cram double that number in it this night. The man who takes care of this place is an old pauper, who has been at sea all his life. He had some soup and meat to sell at a penny a plateful; but I must confess the humiliating fact, that the whole of the occupants of the ward could not produce that sum, and old Daddy — they are all called Daddies — said, "Well, I nivver seed anything like it! Why, last summer there allers used to be a penny or two in the place; but now! why I can't get a farthing to scratch my nose with." One gentleman said that unfortunately he had left his money on the pianer in the droring-room; another said that he paid the whole of his money away for hincom-tax; while Dick said that the last time he was in quod he gave his tin to the governor for the Lancashire Distress Fund. All this "chaff" produced much laughter; and everybody went to sleep in the best humour. I should have been a little easier if I had been less crowded. In the morning you turn a crank from seven to eight, and then have breakfast, which is the thinnest of all thin skilly I ever saw. Two pailfuls were brought up among about fifteen or sixteen men, and all swallowed. One man had six or seven pints of it, and I hope he enjoyed it. I took a good share of it myself. After breakfast we did another hour at the crank, and were then free.

*   *   *

We got into Billericay at five o'clock, and went to a policeman for a ticket. This policeman was a long man, and a great bully, and made divers grand efforts to impress us with a sense of his importance; he took our names, height, colour of hair, eyes, &c., and gave us a ticket with as magnificent an air as if he was conferring upon us a pension. Billericay workhouse is a fine building with an imposing gateway. An old porter took our tickets, and having made a memorandum of them, conducted us to the casual ward, which was a small place, and smelt horribly. Some straw on a raised board was the bed, and the covering was a counterpane that might have been white once, but from long service it had grown grey or nearly black. Right opposite the bed, hung against the wall, was a figure of wood. This figure was clothed in carpet, and had the wrong or white side on one arm, one leg, and half the body, and the red or right side on the corresponding parts. It had a notice under it, that any person tearing up clothes in Billericay workhouse would be provided with a suit of the above description, and afterwards taken before a magistrate. The appearance of a person dressed in this way must be highly ludicrous, and I was given to understand by a pauper in the house that it had the desired effect, and that the guardians were rarely troubled by a "tear-up." The figure against the wall was as large as a man, and I remember being rather startled when I awoke in the morning by its appearance. All kinds of names were written on the whitewashed walls; among them a piece of poetry, which began:

And what do you think is Billericay law?
Why, lying till eleven in the dirty straw.

I forget the rest of it, but remember that it contained about a dozen lines, and that toward the latter end it was very abusive of the master of the workhouse. It was signed, "Bow-street." Scottie assured me that this gentleman's effusions were to be seen in most workhouses in the country, and that he had the honour of the great poet's personal acquaintance. True to the rhyme of "Bow-street," we were kept until eleven, and, what is surprising, had nothing to do but lie in bed. A piece of bread at night., and a similar piece in the morning, was all the food we got.

Basingstoke, Hampshire (1867)

This piece, another from *All the Year Round*, records a visit to what can be identified as the union workhouse at Basingstoke, then a small market town.[22] The uncredited author was James Parkinson. The workhouse later became Basing Road Hospital but the site is now occupied by the modern buildings of the Hampshire Clinic.

A COUNTRY WORKHOUSE.

Passing down Southampton-wards, the reader may remark a formal, gloomy building standing off the railway to the left. It has small narrow windows and high walls. Its shape is of the well-known windmill pattern, with the four wings for wards and the centre for the master's house. A younger brother of the Millbank Penitentiary, who has settled down to agricultural pursuits, with a surly regret for the turnkeys and warders, the handcuffs and punishment cells of the metropolitan head of the family, is what this building suggests most strongly as we pass it in the train. To ask at the station, a few miles further, what it is; to shorten our journey and sacrifice the remainder of our fare on learning it is a workhouse; to be seated in a frouzy fly and to be rolling past vast manufactories, the mere look of which should act as a powerful tonic, so full are they of iron; and to be in a large garden where a couple of labourers are at work, and where one of the latter, touching his hat, follows us into the house — all this is part of the set purpose with which our investigations commenced. Our route for the day had been to another workhouse in a different county; but seeing this one, with its barrack-prison-penitentiary air, we decided to inspect it, without at the time knowing its name, or neighbourhood, or guardian board. Its physiognomy was enough, and its internal character was fully in accordance with what we had seen written on its face.

A prison-like block at Basingstoke workhouse.

The red-faced gardener — who is a healthy, stalwart, loud-voiced, brisk-mannered fellow, who looks as if he could fell an ox, and who, on a nearer inspection, might be the foreman or overlooker of a factory in which manual labour is severe — turns out to be the master. A boisterous hearty man of five-and-forty, confident and strong, nothing will give him greater pleasure than to show us over the house. "He's a worker he is, and has been all his days; and he's been in the service of the Poor Law Board, man and boy, the best part of his life. A young-looking man, you think? Ah, but he was porter a many years before he was master, that's where it is, you see, and now he is looking forward to being 'superannuasiated,' if his employers will be so good. Always given satisfaction, and never had no complaints either from his guardians or from the Poor Law Board; always at it, you see, always busy — can't bear being idle; and there's always something to do about a house this size. Much help from the inmates? Well, he naturally gets what he can, but it's poor work with the class he's got to deal with. All got something the matter with 'em — old, or ill, or infirm, or imbecile — so that the plain truth is, it ain't possible to get a good day's work out of one of 'em." "Are there none of them able-bodied?" we ask. "It would be a positive treat to see an able-bodied man in this workhouse," the master assures us, with strong feeling, "for then there might be a chance of having one's directions regularly and properly carried out. As it is, he hopes we'll excuse it, if there's anything out of order. He tries his best to keep things straight, and he's always at it himself. His gentlemen, too, the guardians that is, are always ready to back him up, always wanting to do everything for the poor creatures, and to make 'em happy." If appearances did not belie this master more than is those faithful tell-tales' wont, he was a kind-hearted, well-meaning servant, anxious to do his duty, and with a wholesome reverence for "his gentlemen," and his pastors, masters, and superiors generally. He would have made an admirable boatswain, or drill-sergeant; an able member of the fire-brigade, a good gang-master or sub-contractor. His lungs, his gait, his bustling busy air, his love of order and discipline, his overflowing health, his abundant physical energy, marked him out for these or cognate employments. He was one of those vigorous creatures who seem like a tornado in a sick-room, and who, with the best and kindest intentions, would speak to a sinking invalid in a stentorian whisper, calculated to take the roof off St. Paul's, or, stronger testimony still, to be heard distinctly in St. Stephen's. That is when the sinking invalid is not a pauper. What the tone is in the latter case we shall have the means of judging presently; for though "our gentlemen" have hired a paid nurse from Netley, she confines her attention to the female infirmary ward, and holds it to be no part of her duty to attend upon sick or dying men. Need the master tell us he would prefer to have her help, though for that matter all the sick are well looked after, we may take his word.

The female infirmary contains four patients, and has a foot-warmer, a bed-pan, a plentiful supply of water, a sufficiency of towels, and fairly appointed beds. One of the water-beds is in London, being mended, but the other is in use; and from the poor girl who sits reading at the fire to the poor invalid who is pouting her life away in bed, these infirmary inmates seem decently housed and cared for. It is true the nurse's complaint that the windows could not be opened without, in wet weather, letting the rain pour in, nor in cold weather without giving all the inmates cold, might be avoided by the simple process of making them movable at the top; while her statement as to the foul smell arising from the closet close by, was a sufficiently grave reflection upon the management; but this infirmary, with its light cheerful aspect, its bright fire, and trained nursing, was so superior to what we saw subsequently, that we are anxious to look on the bright side, and to give full credit for the pains taken to supply the more obvious and pressing wants. We hint that with but four sick people to look after, the nurse must lead a somewhat leisurely life; and, feeling considerably puzzled as to the extent of the staff under our rigorous friend, the master, if the remainder of the house is looked after on the same liberal scale, we pass to the male infirmary.

Our puzzle is at an end. The female infirmary, which was built some years since as a fever hospital, is away from the main building, and its arrangements are as exceptional as its architecture. There, the windows admitted light as well as rain, and could be looked out of by the people inside. Here, they are ingeniously arranged to admit the minimum of light, and to make looking out impossible. The other arrangements are to match. The sick men die unnursed, or with such nursing as a shambling invalid pauper thinks proper to supply. This man cannot read, and, though one in whom our friend the master "has great confidence, or he wouldn't be allowed to be here," is as painfully unfit for duty as ignorant, shiftless incompetence can make him.

Take this room, with its melancholy semi-circle of white-smocked aged figures, crouching round the fire. They sit, each in his chair, motionless and silent, and blinking at the hot coals as if to learn from them the mystery of their drudging, cheerless lives. "Old age, gentlemen, old age and infirmities are what they're suffering from; and they've been good labourers in their day." They are all under medical treatment, as the row of bottles on the shelf opposite the fire testifies; and their beaten, worn look, their bovine, placid endurance of evil, as they moved their poor mouths helplessly to and fro, gave to the scriptural quotation in illuminated characters over the doorway, "Rest in the Lord, wait patiently for Him," a rather bitter significance. Illuminated writing, garish lettering, mock mediaeval scroll-work — all told their own story of gratified taste, and seemed terribly out of place here. "Given by one of the ladies who visits the house," explained the master, in his hearty quarter-deck manner; and the contrast between the drawing-room look of the text and the demeanour of the poor wretches it was meant to guide, was not the less striking for this fact. These old men were clean, and were mercifully permitted to wait by the fire in-doors, and not huddled into potato-shed or yard, as in the workhouse described last week. But they were so obviously waiting for death, sore moved in their utter indifference or ignorance from all sense of our presence, so oblivious of everything but the fire, that for sheer pity's sake we spoke to none of them. There they sat, each with the same distinctiveness of feature as a close observer may discover in a flock of sheep, to which in their uniform smocks they bore a strong generic resemblance. There is something awe-inspiring in humanity from which the spirit seems to be already winging its flight; and to rouse any of these poor creatures from their torpid trance with questions as to diet or treatment, was felt to be impossible. A semicircle of clay figures whose breathing arrangements continued somehow after life had fled, but who, for all rational purposes of existence, for comprehension of their own identity, or the identity of those formerly dearest to them; for feeling aught higher than a confused consciousness that the fire gave comfort and warmth; for hope, or love, or regrets; for any of the complex feelings which go to make up sentient humanity, seemed as dead as the oldest mummy or the earliest pre-Adamite.

We ask in low tones of the master as to their several ailments. "Mostly old age, of course," that ostentatiously able-bodied person replies, adding, with increased cheerfulness, "but here are their bottles, if you'd like to examine them, gentlemen." These are embrocations, to swallow which would be certain death; harmless mixtures, to be taken by spoonfuls every few hours; liniments and potions; drugs to act powerfully in one way upon the human system, and drugs having equal power in a precisely opposite direction — all labelled and ranged upon the shelf. We ask whose duty it is to see that these helpless people take the drugs prescribed for them, and are told the wardsman. This is the shambling broken-down fellow in dirty fustian, who fumbles at his greasy cap, and bows and smiles, and is blandly confident. "Oh yes, gentlemen, I'm very particular, very particular indeed, that they have their medicines at the right time. I allers gives it out to them myself, gentlemen — allers, and I'm never late with it, no, never. Here the medicine is, and there the inmates are, and they all has every drop the doctor sends — every drop." Here, as elsewhere, there is an eagerness to repudiate all desire to appropriate the medicines prescribed for others, as if not to drink off nauseous medicines surreptitiously were in itself a highly meritorious act of self-denial. The master supports the wardsman with unabated heartiness. "A respectable man, this; he wouldn't say anything but what's true, or do anything but what's right, and you surely take what he says, gentlemen — you may take what he says." At this time the canvas bundle nearest the fire gives a feeble bleat, as if for help; but on looking round we find the old pauper composing it to be still, moving his mouth to and fro like the rest, and to be blinking stolidly as ever at the fire. So our conversation is resumed, not without a nervous dread that "something may happen," as the phrase goes; that the last remnant of some life may slip away before we leave. "What is this medicine, and how often is it used?" asked my medical companion, holding up a bottle containing some five ounces of diluted sugar of lead. *"Well, sir, I can't read, so I can't say what it is; but they all know their own bottles, sir, and that prevents mistake!"* This is the guarantee formed by ratepayers, guardians, and the Poor Law Board! This the fitness of the "respectable man" for the most delicate and responsible of duties! It was impossible to suppress all tokens of the horror we felt; and the master, who became healthier and more vigorous every moment, added breezily, "But I'm generally about myself, you know, gentlemen — generally about; for I'm always at it, and nothing takes place without my knowing." The group, nodding, blinking, dozing, and silently chewing the cu at the fire, seemed so incapable of choice or thought; their chrysalis state was so utterly opposed to the exercise of any reasoning faculty — even to the comprehension of where they were, or what their life had been — that to suppose them capable of choice of medicine, or of doing aught than swallow mechanically whatever was put before them, seemed little short of madness. Useless, defenceless, impotent, and with nothing their own but the power of choice between them and the death which the drugs at their elbow would provide, the sacred injunction, "Rest in the Lord," and wait for death, in its ornamental lettering and semi-ecclesiastical dress, seemed little better than a mockery.

A few paces and we are in another ward, with a man dying of cancer in one corner, and two other patients in beds opposite him. It would be improper to detail in these columns the worst of the evils rampant here. It is sufficient to say these patients were untended, save by the shambling pauper who could not read, and that the evidence of neglect was more palpable than among the clean old people in the adjoining room. One of the men was up, and partly dressed; another gazed at us with fierce eyes from his bed; while the third, and cancerous one, neither spoke nor moved, but groaned heavily, as if in his acute pain. "They say I'm well, and I'm to go," said the man in the bed furthest from the door — a man with hollow cheeks and hungry eyes, which followed us irritably wherever we went — "but I'm fit for nought, and I can't stand for weakness. Complaints? I don't know what yer means by complaints. Complaining won't give me work, or make me fit for working, I reckon. Complaints? Come to lie where I do, with a man like that in the corner, sleeping in the same room with yer, and ye'll perhaps know what complaining means. Have I enough to eat? Am I well taken care of? Do I enjoy my food? Yes, yes, well enough — well enough. It isn't for the like of me to make a fuss. Lie here — lie here, that's all I ask yer, and yer won't want a book or a compass to teach yer how to be unhappy. What's the use of talking? Here I am, and here I've been, and here I've got to quit next Tuesday, thank God; though I know no more what's to become of me than a child unborn. Bin in this parish all my life, and my father before me; know my duty, and know it ain't for me to find particular fault. Lie here on yer back for three weeks — lie here on yer back, and then ye'll know more than yer'll get by poking about with a pencil and a little book, and asking questions about winders." A coarse man, in a high state of nervous irritability, this pauper resented the presence of strangers, and fidgeted dreadfully under the master's eye. The invalid in the chair could not stand up, and upon those two devolved all care of the dying plan, save when the "respectable man," who could not read, came in. In other words, each man lived or died without nursing or attendance. The paid nurse from Netley Hospital had her three or four women patients to look after in the other building, and spent her time in comparative idleness, while the men passed away in hospital lingeringly, if no accidents occurred, speedily when the knowledge of "their own bottles" failed them, and the shambling pauper's incompetence fulfilled itself. The windows of these sick wards, as well as those all over the house, were so contrived as to admit the light without enabling those inside to look out — an ingenious contrivance for increasing the dismalness and misery of pauper sickness meriting special notice. We hint that the room would be more cheerful if the windows came within reach of the eye, and are at once snuffed out by the master's superior knowledge and beaming health.

"Couldn't look out of window; bless you, sir, if the windows was made ever so low those men couldn't, sir," with a convincing smile. "I don't see the use of altering it myself. The old men had rather look into the fire, and these are confined to their beds or chairs, so no windows would be of much value, would they? Besides, if you once began altering you might go through the house, for all the windows are alike, as was the fashion for workhouses when this was built — about thirty years old, gentlemen, more or less; and there's very few windows you can see out of. It was considered a beauty in those days, and I'm not sure it would be wise to alter even now. There's no object in paupers looking out of window, that I can see. Light and cheerfulness? Oh! I assure you there's light enough for work, and my people ain't up to much work, either." "But for those who are past work," we plead. "You say, yourself, it would be 'a treat to see an able-bodied pauper' in your workhouse; would it not be proper, then, to give the old and worn-out such comfort as they might derive from changing their abode from a prison to an asylum?" Our master's rubicund face is puzzled as if with an insoluble problem, and his head shakes to and fro meditatively, as if suffering from too much beef on the brain. But the uniform kindness and consideration of the guardians consoles him, and he says, with the air of a man delivering a knockdown argument, "Our gentlemen haven't thought so, however, or I'm certain it would have been done."

Does it need any consideration, we ask, whether darkness should be preferred to light? But we address the wind, for the master has discovered a spot upon the white wall, and is busy removing it with his pocket-handkerchief as tenderly.as if the coarse size and whitewash were a child. I could fancy a clean hard-working labourer, who conformed to rules, obeyed the master, and kept down the work, having better times under our friend than he would be likely to know outside the workhouse walls. Labour, hard coarse labour, and keeping the place clean, are his passions. His notion of "a treat" is to catch some able-bodied paupers instead of the imbecile and helplessly infirm, who persist in drifting through the gates, and to turn them to active scrubbing and cleansing uses. His great plaint is that he can't keep represent duty to his narrow conscientious mind. The paupers are mere accessories, pawns on the chess-board, of quite subordinate interest to the prime function of keeping the house in order. A better or more industrious housekeeper, or a less sympathetic spirit for the weak and ailing, it would be hard to find. Not that there was a trace of intentional unkindness in his speech or manner. "Old man washing the floor is terrible deaf, and ain't much use, but he does his best. Young man at the fire ain't exactly off his head, but has fits dreadful bad, and hasn't been able to do a good day's work since he's bin in here. Men in the shed outside pumping, look better than the rest? Lord bless you, gentlemen," despondently, "there ain't one on 'em sound, if you come to examine 'em — not one on 'em you could count on for good work." So in the kitchens, sculleries, and outhouses. So in the other offices of this gloomy penal place. The women, with the exception of a few who were nursing young infants, imbecile, infirm, and given to fits. The men invalided or past work. The house has been studiously made to resemble a prison, and the gloomy vaults, in which cooking and dish-cleaning are carried on, would show with disadvantage against the catacombs of Kensal-green. Unlike our friends in Staffordshire, no pretence is made of nursing the sick and dying men, or of keeping the paid nurse within call. The functionary last named — who, if we may make bold to say so, might have been selected for the angularity of figure and sharp iciness of speech, which gave her a general shrewish resemblance to Miss Miggs[23] — appeared to be queen of the situation. The faults she pointed out in windows and approaches, and, above all, in the arrangements of her private apartments, were launched at the master with an "I-told-you-so" air, as personal grievances he ought to have redressed; while with an absurdly exaggerated estimate of our powers, her preliminary answer to every question was an attitude suggesting fatalistic submission, as if to tell us, with suppressed spitefulness, that she was ready, there and then, to look on while the master was being bowstrung or bastinadoed under our dread decree. Superfluous in her denunciation and repudiation of all that was faulty in her department, it was easy to see that while our energetic friend the master is overworked, the nurse has nothing to do. To look after four women patients, none of whom require close watching or attendance, and to be carefully placed in a building away from the workhouse, so that "calling up" or rendering extra assistance is impossible, while men are dying unnursed in a pest-house over the way, seems such a ridiculous perversion of common sense as well as common humanity, that we ask, weakly enough, whether the Poor Law inspector has not remarked upon it. "Very satisfactory," is that official's verdict, and "has been for years," the master proudly adds; so we can but conclude that poisoning off male paupers is the parochial set-off against having sick women nursed.

Farnham, Surrey (1867)

In 1867, following its reports on London workhouses. the medical journal *The Lancet* visited a number of provincial establishments. The extracts below come from its report on the Farnham workhouse, which the authors feared would prove 'sensational'.[24] The despotic former workhouse master referred to was James Sargeant, great-great-grandfather of the modern-day leader of the Britain's Labour Party, Jeremy Corbyn. Farnham Hospital now occupies the site but none of the workhouse buildings survive.

The Farnham Union Workhouse is a perfect marvel of bad construction for any purpose, whether of simple dwelling, or still more of the housing of sick persons. It consists, firstly, of a main building (an old-fashioned pile, which has apparently been a residence of the better class, and is now occupied by the master's apartments and certain offices, and by dormitories for the "able-bodied"); secondly, of an infirmary (two-storied), at the other extreme of the buildings; thirdly, of a two-storied block, devoted to so-called "fever wards;" fourthly, of a range of miserable one-storied buildings (running parallel to the fever wards, and forming, with them, the third and fourth sides of an incomplete quadrangle), which contain a nursery, a ward for infirm women, a laundry, and other offices; fifthly, of a block of buildings in the centre of the quadrangle, containing the dining-hall and, beneath it, the kitchen. Outside the buildings there is a considerable space of garden-ground, which is very properly applied to the production of vegetables for the consumption of the inmates.

To commence our description with the infirmary — the more immediate object of our inspection, — we may first speak of the female syphilitic wards. These are in a two-storied building, of which the upper room only was occupied at the time of our visit. We ascended to this by an open wooden staircase, which leads straight up from the lower ward, so that the air of the two rooms is mixed. There are seven syphilitic patients here, of whom three or four were the subjects of most severe affections. The room was extremely bare and gloomy; it was a "roof-ward," the dimensions being 36 ft. x 18 x 10 (*plus* the roof-space); so that the allowance of cubic space to the present number of inmates is as much as 1100 feet per head; but there have been many occasions in which the surgeon has been obliged to place twice as many patients in the ward. The lighting is by a very insufficient number of windows, but these are fortunately opposite each other, and the medical officer has fitted them with glass Venetian ventilating panes, fixed open. It happens not unfrequently, however, in cold or windy weather, that the patients complain, and then the panes are simply boarded up.

It was in this apartment that our attention was called to many features which are common to all the infirmary wards, and may be described once for all. The walls were bare and dirty, the bedsteads were narrow, the beds (except one water-bed, on which an almost moribund patient lay) were single mattresses, filled with chopped straw. There are only *two round towels per week* allowed for all purposes of ablution to this whole ward, and a proportionately niggardly allowance reigns through the house. The only watercloset is a dark and filthy place *outside the lower story.* And the only lavatory is a miserable room adjoining the watercloset, with a kind of cellulated slate manger (looking more like a urinal than a washing-place) at one side of it. There are no lockers or cupboards of any kind in this or any other ward; and the natural consequence is that all manner of miscellaneous articles of food, dress, and convenience are hidden under sheets or mattresses. The only drinking vessels are some coarse slop-basins of yellow crockery, which hold by turns the beef-tea, the tea, the porter, and any other drink that may be ordered for the sick. What struck us with most disgust, however, was the fact that in this ward, where two, if not three, patients lay mortally sick, there was no attendant nurse, not even a pauper; so that the patients, in any emergency, must rely on the bell to fetch them assistance. But *what* assistance? There is but one paid female nurse (a good and skilful woman, but not capable of ubiquity), aided by one broken-down male pauper, who has been five times tapped for dropsy, for all nursing purposes in the house whatever. There are no night nurses at all. Beyond a few pauper "helps" (for merely menial purposes), and a pauper keeper of the nursery, there is no supplement to the above-named staff.

In the body of the infirmary the arrangement both of male and female wards is very bad. The general plan in each case is this:— One larger ward, with from nine to fifteen patients; outside this a gloomy, little, so-called "day-room;" and then two or three little wards, with three beds each. The long ward is lighted by windows only on one side; the little wards by one window each. The connecting passage is narrow and inconvenient. The plan of out-door waterclosets is universal, except that there is one tolerably good in-door closet near the female wards. Nearly all these places are dirty; and as the guardians do not condescend to supply necessary paper, the drains frequently get choked with rags and other rubbish which the unlucky patients are forced to use. The drainage is into cesspools, and stinks abound from time to time.

Of the "fever wards" we shall not say much, because there were no fever cases in the house, although typhoid is at any time a possibility, owing to the state of the drainage of Farnham. The male and female wards are above each other, and communicate by an inside staircase. The only watercloset is one which must be reached through the open air, and by passing through the lower ward. The ventilation of the wards is most insufficient.

Passing across to the opposite side, we came to the nursery, and the ward for infirm women. Two more melancholy apartments we never saw. The former is a gloomy, damp, brick-floored room, with absolutely no furniture, except one low wooden bench, on which seven or eight little children were sitting in front of the fire. Most of these looked healthy enough; but we encountered three of their companions in one of the female infirmary wards (cowering together over a plate of nasty-looking, lukewarm mutton and potatoes), all of whom bad itch, and one of them porrigo.[25] The nursery-woman — an untidy but kind-hearted woman — complained bitterly that the children had no furniture in their room. They, visibly, had no toys, no amusement, and no education. It is true that some twelve months since the guardians subscribed for a sovereign's worth of toys; but only about two shillings' worth ever made their appearance in the nursery, and since these were broken no more are forthcoming.

The infirm women's day-room presented, if anything, a still more pitiable spectacle. Here were seven aged women, toothless and decrepid, crouching over the fire, and making believe to dine. The doctor kindly orders them a meat dinner every day. The actual dinner supplied consisted on the day of our visit of thick lumps of beef or bacon (not mutton, as ordered); and, as if to mock the poor old creatures in their efforts to dispose of these tough morsels, knives were served out to them, *but no forks*. It may be mentioned that all the meat is cut up in the dining-hall, and by the time the various rations for the sick and infirm arrive at their respective wards, they are in a condition of tepid greasiness which is well calculated to repress inordinate appetites.

Passing to the day-room for infirm old men, we found another gloomy room, barer and more cheerless than any prison cell of modern construction, in which some dozen old men were sitting on hard benches, with no occupation whatever. The only happy-looking persons amongst them were two fidgety imbeciles. One of these had such very dirty hands that we were induced to ask for an explanation of their state. "Oh!" said our informant, "he does all the dirty work of the house." Among the inmates of the room, we found one man, aged eighty, who was a hard-working, respectable fellow till late in life; then broke down, and came to depend upon his wife's exertions; then lost his wife, and was presented by his merciful Board of Guardians with out-door relief to the extent of 2s. 6d. a week and one loaf. Under this genial treatment he found himself rapidly approaching the vanishing-point; so he wisely came into the house, and avoided starvation. Another old man, for sixty-two years a ratepayer, and who has a rich and genteel nephew in Farnham, had come to the end of his working powers, and was allowed out-relief to the amount of 2s. a week and one loaf. He, too, preferred residence in the workhouse to the role of Ugolino.[26] It is a remarkable feature in the character of the late master of the workhouse (of whom more anon), that when the poor old fellows in this room once obtained some newspapers to while away their time with, he immediately took them away.

The dormitories for the so-called able-bodied (of whom about nine-tenths are infirm) are really good and spacious rooms, with nearly sufficient ventilation; but the inmates are locked in at night, without watercloset or any bell to call assistance. In answer to our expressed desire to see the able-bodied men, we were shown into a brick-floored room, in which there were precisely four persons, all of whom were diseased or infirm. In all the house we saw no really healthy people, except a few young women, mostly with babies, and a few young children.

One word more, and we have done with the mere description of what we *saw* at Farnham Workhouse. In one of the yards we observed what looked like two rabbit-hutches, on a rather large scale certainly, but with the ordinary furniture of frowsy straw, and fastened with huge padlocks. These are the male and female tramp-wards. The men are allowed no food at all, however weary or faint they may be. The women are allowed a piece of bread if they have children with them, not otherwise. One night, not long ago, a female tramp, known to be on the verge of confinement, was locked up all night in the female rabbit-hutch. When the porter unlocked the door at seven in the morning, the woman had been already four hours in labour.

We have hurried through the merely descriptive portion of our narrative, because the remainder of our limited space must necessarily be devoted to a historical *aperçu* of the management of this remarkable, and, we almost hope, unique workhouse. For fourteen years the virtual government of the place has been a despotism on the part of the late master, tempered, however, during the last four years by revolution on the part of the doctor. The master was a large man, with an imposing presence, a confident manner, and a faculty for talking down any mildly remonstrant guardian. Among other notable performances of this official we may cite an outbreak of indignant virtue on his part which led to awkward consequences. He chose to think that an epileptic inmate, who had remained in bed to repose himself after a severe fit, was unduly self-indulgent, and made him get up and go into the garden to ladle out manure from a cesspool. The lazy man perversely went into another fit, fell into the liquid sludge, was pulled out three parts drowned, and a few hours afterwards gave up his fits and his life together. Fortune, however, favoured the master; and he escaped the more serious consequences which might have been expected. On various occasions he threatened the doctor, who was always proposing some tiresome reform or other, with personal violence. He has finally succumbed to the stroke of fate, and resigned his office, in consequence of a Poor-law inquiry which was held because he (a widower with seven children) had seduced one of the female inmates. The present master and matron would seem to be decent and respectable persons, and they are now actively engaged in cleansing the house from top to bottom.

Of the medical officer, Dr. Powell, it is impossible to speak without sincere esteem. This worthy man, with a salary of £55 per annum, with some few extra fees for lunacy and midwifery cases (and the privilege of supplying and dispensing all drugs at his own cost), has fought a good and persistent tight against the evil traditions of the place. He has constantly remonstrated against the condition and management of the house, and at length, we believe, has won not merely the respect but the support of the better members of the board. Bare and cheerless as the wards still are, the patients are possessed of many comforts which they lacked when Dr. Powell first took office. For instance: it is a fact that even the scanty allowance of towels which are now provided were then altogether absent; so that the inmates, after washing or bathing (which they did in the chamber utensils), dried themselves *on the sheets of their beds*. The medical officer has also procured, by diligent and incessant asking, various articles, such as feet and stomach warmers, night-dresses, &c., which are a great alleviation to the discomforts of sickness. And although he has at present sixty patients (and often a great many more) to attend to, and has to provide and dispense all drugs, there is neither stinginess nor carelessness in the way he does his work; the medicines are good in quality, and properly dispensed in clearly labeled bottles. The one paid nurse, though preposterously overworked, really does appear to keep a general supervision over all the medicine taken. This good and zealous person eagerly assured us that she never allowed anyone to administer the medicines but herself. The wounds and sores which we saw on various patients were dressed with proper care.

Our most painful task is to say what we must say about the guardians. These gentlemen, we are informed, are some of them farmers, some of them clergymen, and some of them squires, and there are not wanting in their number men of genuinely kind hearts and intelligence above the average. And yet the fact is, that for years past they have tolerated a state of things in their workhouse which was like nothing but Pandemonium, simply because they chose to believe implicitly all the master told them, and ignore all complaints from other quarters. And should the guardians answer to our censures that, after all, it was natural for them to trust the master's judgment (since they believed him to be a respectable and faithful servant), we can reply at once with an instance which affords irrefragable proof that this excuse would be empty and insincere. It is a fact that they followed the master's advice not merely in matters as to which they might distrust their own judgment, but in committing the cruelty of locking up faint and weary travellers all night in a mere cage, without one morsel of food; and this although their medical officer repeatedly begged that at least a slice of bread might be given to these wanderers. And although the bareness and discomfort of the wards must have been patent to the most careless eye, the stinking closets obvious to the least sensitive nose, and the inadequacy of the nursing staff unmistakable to anyone above the capacity of an idiot, not one word of complaint about these vitally important matters can be found amongst the numerous records, in the Visitors' Book, of the guardians' visits of inspection. On the contrary, the perpetually recurring statement in those records is that "we found the wards clean, and everything very satisfactory," or something equivalent to this.

It is time we drew this report to a conclusion. What can we say — what can any reasonable person say — of the Farnham Workhouse but this: that the existence of such places is a reproach to England — a scandal and a curse to a country which calls itself civilised and Christian!

Hursley, Hampshire (1867)

Emulating the *Lancet*'s reports, Charles Dickens' journal *All the Year Round*, published two of its own 'probes' into provincial workhouses. In each case, the visitor is thought to be Joseph Charles Parkinson — journalist, civil servant, social reformer, and one of the magazine's regular contributors. Although not named in the text, the establishment described in this first article can be identified as the Hursley union workhouse in Hampshire.[27]

A WORKHOUSE PROBE.

A coal-cellar without coals; a punishment-cell for refractory criminals; a dreary black-hole, with grated windows, and cold damp floor and walls; a tank with the water let off, and the oldest fish-inhabitant departed — such is the Hampshire casual ward we are visiting to-day. It is very small. Its sole furniture is one bedstead, without clothes or wraps; and, though we are assured that a fire is lighted in it "sometimes," there is no evidence of any such genial contingency now. Its massive door is plentifully studded with the heavy iron nails which adorn the entrances to her Majesty's jails, and are supposed to strike terror into the hearts of evil-doers; and it is altogether as cold, comfortless, and penal a resting-place as the sternest disciplinarian could wish. If it does not do duty as village lock-up, the local authorities are extravagant; for a fitter place in which any obstreperously convivial Giles or Roger might shake off the hilarity of a Saturday night's carouse, and might become penitent, meek, and subdued, it would be hard to find. You step down into it direct from the road without intervening hall or corridor, and the approach to its one door is graced by a stagnant pool, the foetid smell from which offends the least sensitive nose. "We're not much troubled with tramps here, gentlemen;

they prefer going on to the town, four miles off," remarks the matron, with a smile. As we look down shudderingly, this wet and foggy autumn day, into the damp dark place, and fancy the key turned and ourselves locked in till morning, we fully appreciate the preference shown. Any sensible wayfarer, however footsore, hungry, and exhausted, would struggle on for another four miles to avoid spending the night in a dungeon, compared to which a police-cell is comfort, and a model prison luxury.

"No admittance to the workhouse, except on business, by order of the guardians," does not apply to us. Our open sesame is the inquiry we have on hand; for "we" are the *Lancet* Commission, which your servant, the present writer, has been permitted to accompany on its errand of humanity, and admission is cheerfully accorded, apparently by instinct, certainly without a question as to our credentials. A snug, cozy little union of four parishes, managed by a board, the chairman of which is the squire of the neighbourhood, with for a vice-chairman the squire's namesake and near relative; a union in which the workhouse is rented by the board of managers from the presiding member of that board (!) — a union where the clergyman of the parish is paid an annual sum, not for holding regular service as chaplain, but for occasionally visiting the twenty-one paupers now in the house; a little place where "wards" are cottage-rooms, and where the master and matron are collectively chief nurse, governor, superintendent, labour-master, mistress, and head-cook. Matters which would be abuses on a large scale are part of a system here, under which paupers are, perhaps, better cared for than in many an establishment whose pretensions are fourfold.

The "workhouse" consists of twelve little cottages, forming an enclosed quadrangle, in which there is practically no classification, and where some of the sanitary arrangements are as bad as ignorance and old-fashioned prejudice can make them. A cesspool which has "not been cleared out in the twelve years we've been here," lies under the windows of the lying-in and infectious wards; and the closets, which have been "inspected" twice a year, with great regularity, by the representative of the Poor Law Board, are as disgustingly unfit for human use as if they belonged to some savage kraal, where the commonest laws of decency and health were unknown. But in many of the inner domestic details in which kind and thoughtful interest makes people happy, the twenty-one men and women were well placed. You see it in the bright alacrity of the matron, in the cheerful readiness of her replies, in the snugness of some of the internal arrangements, and in the cleanliness and contentment of the small handful of paupers at home. The entrance to the master's house — which is simply one of the cottages furbished up and snugly furnished — is opposite the door of the dungeon in which tramps pay the penalty of their calling. The master is at church, but his wife will show us over the workhouse with the greatest pleasure. There is no pause, nor evasion, nor holding back; and, in two minutes from the time of our ringing the bell, we have passed through the private apartments, and are on the female side of the central yard. Such a little place to be a union workhouse! After a long experience of workhouses like towns, of long and dreary chambers in which a short-sighted person could easily mistake his own father if placed at the opposite end to himself, Mr. Wemmick's Walworth fortress,[28] with its Lilliputian drawbridge, moat, and guarded postern, irresistibly occur to us as we are shown over "wards" not much larger than bathing-machines, and "refectories" and "day-rooms" which would be undersized for a family of six. There is no communication through what we suppose we must call the house. The cottages are — save here and there, where two bedrooms have been thrown into one — almost as distinct as in the pre-New Poor Law period when they were built. Hearing with pleasure that the child-inmates are sent to the ordinary parish school, and not educated like pariahs apart, we pass into the first cottage on the women's side.

A little room, with what seemed to be the car of a balloon in wicker-work standing in one corner, and one small tin basin — of the size of the vessels in which "half portions" of soup are served at a club — filled with soapsuds, is shown us as the lavatory. On remarking that the latter article looked, if anything, a trifle small to be the washing vessel of the establishment, we were told of increased accommodation looming in the future; and that upon a board or sub-committee making up its mind and presenting a report, a larger basin and a more copious supply of towels would be granted. The balloon-car turns out to be a cradle, unoccupied at present, but in which four pauper babies can be rocked at once, two at each end — a comprehensive provision if the total population of the workhouse, twenty-one, all decrepid or disabled, be considered. Two women, one weak-minded and the other subject to fits, a child, and a bedridden old man, are the only inmates at home. The other paupers — including a couple of idiots and a young man of suicidal tendencies —

are with the master at church, for a great anniversary festival is being held, and the little knot of male worshippers, in clean white smock-frocks, seated to the right of the middle aisle, and the handful of poor women opposite them, are the workhouse's contribution to the celebration of the day. The child smiles upon us, and gazes up wonderingly, with grave black eyes, in which, by the way, there is not a trace of fear, as the matron precedes us into the room. It is another cottage apartment, with the two women just spoken of busily at work. They are all scrupulously clean, despite the size of the tin cup just hinted at; and here, as elsewhere, during our visit, we are disposed to declare the little place to be exceptional, and not to be judged by the rules it is essential to enforce in other establishments of its class. That it should, in spite of some grave defects, rise superior to circumstances, is doubtless due to the character and disposition of its governing board and their two delegates, the master and matron. The latter is as cheery and kind as a warm heart and good disposition could make her. The pauper child's smile of recognition and welcome, and the way her little hand closed familiarly upon our guide's gown, spoke volumes as to habitual kindnesses; while the demeanour of the two women — familiar and confident; though not wanting in respect — was a testimonial infinitely more convincing than a whole wilderness of votes of thanks and minutes of approval. After a question from one of the women on a point of household discipline has been answered, and the little girl's whispered petition smilingly granted, we pass to the kitchen, where boiled bacon, cabbages, and some added condiment, giving a deliciously appetising flavour, are swimming in the coppers we are invited to peer into. A most savoury and toothsome mixture it seems to be, and our railway journey from London, and moist drive subsequently from Barchester, has left us hungry enough to envy the paupers for whom it is preparing.

More cottage apartments, the down-stair rooms, with flooring of stone or brick; those up-stairs holding three or four beds, all well appointed, and each cottage containing two rooms. Chairs or benches, a rough table, and a cupboard used in common by the occupants, comprise the furniture. After traversing the yard, and going over every room of every cottage — finding, of course, a wonderful uniformity throughout — we come to the one bedridden old man. A room has been fitted up for him on the ground floor, and here he is lying cozily enough, but quite alone, with his feet to the door, and his limbs and body stretched out in an attitude which suggests rather painfully the time when lameness, and old age, and poverty will be over, and when he will be carried from his present resting-place for ever. Not that there was anything in the man himself, as distinguished from his attitude, to suggest aught but the keenest appreciation of life; for he started up in bed and bobbed his head to the Commission, as if he guessed the purport of the visit, and had been waiting these thirteen years to speak his autobiography. He was a hale, ruddy, vigorous old fellow, who had lost an eye, but whose voice showed no sign of infirmity. Nay, as we had understood before we visited him that he was very deaf, this vigour of voice led to a rather boisterous colloquy between one of our party and himself. "How do you find yourself, my man?" inquired our friend, in tones adapted to a patient whose infirmity aural surgeons had failed to relieve. "Noicely, thankee, zur, but oise lame, you know, oise lame!" shouted back the invalid, in accents fitted for the quarter-deck of a battle-ship in the heat of action; and so the conversation went on, each sorry for the other's deafness, and politely anxious to accommodate himself to it. For the old pauper was not satisfied with emulating the bellow of an exceptionally strong-lunged bull. He made a speaking-trumpet of his wrinkled hands; and, taking steady aim at his visitor's ear, repeated every assertion twice. "Yes, am well enough;" then more slowly, "Oi'm well enough" (pause), "bar the lameness — bar the lameness." He had been at full pitch for some minutes now, and though red in the face could still have cleared the busiest thoroughfare for a fire-engine's progress. "It was Mr. Mullings's horse, it was, yes. It was Mr. Mullings's horse. Kicked me he did! He kicked me, yer knaw" (louder). "Oi can stand up though" (louder still); "oi can stand up." Then, not quite so loud, but with a slow distinctness of enunciation, meant to give his hearer every chance, "Oi can stand up, but it's walking that bothers me, that bothers me, just here, yer knaw; just here. Oi'm well enough, and comfortable enough, thankee, zur. Now I don't want for nothing, I dawn't, thankee kindly." A shelf half-hidden by a neat curtain held a couple of bottles and a Bible and prayer-book, and a convenient stand at the bed-head served for the veteran's dinner-tray. "I suppose he's very deaf," said his late interlocutor, commiseratingly, as we left him bobbing his head like some huge and bulbous sensitive plant, after his bed-linen and accessories had been examined, and found clean: "I suppose he's very deaf. How old is he?"

"Well, sir, he's eighty-five, and his sight's failing, but his hearing's as good as ever!" This discovery rather weakened the spirit of our cross-examination; but time pressed, and we passed to what was called the old men's day-room. The pseudo deaf man, who, though confined to his bed, looked as hale and strong as any of us, had been a soldier, then a wanderer, then a farm-labourer, but "had never made himself a home," and was locally known as a boisterous Lothario up to the time of his accident "a long time ago, I don't exactly know how long, but he was here when we came in 1855."

A corner cupboard containing an odd volume of a religious work, a soap-dish and shaving-brush, three stale crusts, two small bits of cooked meat, and some odd cups and saucers; a table, a bench, and a Windsor chair with unnaturally long legs, which lifted it from the ground like stilts, and a cottage interior to match the rest, made up the old men's day-room. A pauper, recently deceased, had laboured under a spinal infirmity which compelled him to sit in a certain position, and the chair had been altered by order of the guardians for his benefit. The other inmates, both male and female, are too old and infirm for household work, so a charwoman, and in time of pressure two charwomen, are hired from the village for as many days a week as are necessary to keep the place in order. Everything is on the same cozy scale. The "infectious ward" — it really seems absurd to use these titles when we recall the little place — is the upper room of one of the cottages. It is seldom used. How often? "Oh! perhaps twice or three times a year, perhaps not so much — we had a case of itch here last, but that's five months ago. No, we've never any able-bodied people here, and the others are nearly all of the same class as the old man you've been talking to, who have never made themselves a home. Our guardians relieve out more than in; for if they can help people at their own places, they prefer doing it to breaking up their homes and forcing them into the house. Do I consider it safe to keep two idiots and a young man of suicidal tendencies together, with their medicine bottles within reach to drink from, or ply each other with? Well, it's some months ago since the young man attempted his life last, and he's been a good deal easier in his mind lately. Indeed, sir, if you think the Commissioners of Lunacy ought to know about him, and that he shouldn't be kept here, I'm sure I'll tell the board so, and I dare say they'll have him moved. No, sir, I don't remember that the gentleman from the Poor Law Board ever mentioned this; but you shall see the visiting book directly. May I ask if you're from the *Lancet*, gentlemen? Yes! I thought as much (smiling). Well, I hope you don't find us very bad. I'm sure we try our best, and when there's any one sick I don't think they're badly cared for. I generally nurse myself, and the ladies from the Hall and the clergyman's wife often come to read to the inmates, and lend them books as well; oh yes, the clergyman visits the workhouse regularly. No, sir, there's no service held here, but the ten pounds a year is paid him for coming, don't you see, and he's very good and kind, I'm sure."

Although we had reason to believe that paupers — always excepting the male casuals, who were evidently housed wretchedly on principle — were properly treated in the main, the arrangement under which the workhouse is hired struck us as peculiar. One regulation of the new Poor Law is, that "all contracts to be entered into on behalf of the Union, relating to the maintenance, clothing, *lodging*, employment, or relief of the poor . . . shall be made and entered into by the guardians;" and, in a note to this clause, we find that "heavy penalties are imposed on persons having the management of the poor" — i.e. the guardians — "if concerned in contracts for the supply of goods," — "goods," in this sense, obviously referring to lodging as well as maintenance, "for the use of such poor."

This salutary regulation is, it is well known, frequently evaded. The influential ratepayer, who virtually returns a section of the guardians, is a tradesman whose tenders are not often refused; guardians have nephews, or brothers, or wife's relatives, who sell bread, or groceries, or meat, on such disinterested terms, that it is the bounden duty of the parochial board to deal with them; or guardians sell the raw material out of which the goods for contracts are made, and make their vote contingent upon the tradesman buying of them in return. These things are notorious; and the following anecdote fairly illustrates the system. Not many months ago, a contract for painting a metropolitan workhouse was signed; and, in due course, the painter entered upon his work. On the first day a guardian, who is a wholesale dealer in colours, looked in at the workhouse during the dinner-hour, and while the workmen were away, and in his intense regard for the paupers' comfort, asked to see the wards then being restored, that he might judge for himself how the work was performed. The good man then, without passing a word of censure or comment, wrapped up two minute specimens of the paint, put them in his waistcoat-pocket, and walked quietly away, first telling the workhouse-master to let the contractor know of his visit. The next day this guardian and colour-dealer received in answer to his hint an order for the very paints required to carry out the workhouse contract; so that all unpleasant analyses of the quality, or quibbles as to the work, were promptly avoided. Here was no corruption, no touting, no undue influence. What could be more strictly in accordance with a high-minded guardian's sense of duty than that he should devote his special knowledge to the ensuring fit materials for parish work being used? And how could this end be better attained than by examining them for himself? On the other hand, the contractor was merely anxious to please his customers; and if one of them furnished the paints himself, it was scarcely likely that the board would be dissatisfied; or questions arise as to an inferior description being used, or less work being given; or on the contract generally being performed in a slovenly but inexpensive fashion. The tacit understanding manifested between guardian and contractor was beautifully simple, and in large towns, where parochial boards are mainly composed of small tradesmen, there is no reasonable doubt that similar practices prevail almost universally. But in the agricultural districts, where country gentlemen, magistrates, and their friends serve as guardians, where a patriarchal interest is supposed to be felt in the poor people of the township, or the estate, we expect matters to be managed without taint of jobbery. Yet, in the establishment we are visiting, where we find so much to praise and so comparatively little to blame, the chief guardian lets the workhouse to the rest, and draws his rent from the poor-rates he administers!

It is possible that no very serious wrong ensues. It is possible that the ratepayers are better served than if a workhouse were built, in another portion of the parish; and it is probable that the paupers are more kindly treated, when the squire of the parish serves in the double capacity of landlord and chief guardian. But that the practice is loosely illegal, and open to grave abuse, there cannot be a doubt. Suppose a man to be less high-minded than there is reason to believe this present chairman to be. Suppose other guardians coalesced to purchase, build, and let to each other for the use of the poor. Suppose land to be owned by one guardian, bricks made by another, building undertaken by a third, and so on — what check have we then? The answer is, the Poor Law Board, which, through its representative, the district inspector, undertakes to see that the law is properly observed. Let us turn, then, to the visiting-book, and see how the official visitor, who is already celebrated for his discharge of duty at Farnham, has performed this duty His inspections have been made with great regularity twice a year, and "Wards in good order," "Satisfactory," "Very satisfactory," form the staple of his monotonous remarks. Not a syllable concerning sanitary arrangements, closets, cesspools, classification, or the ownership of the house. Not a grumble, scarcely a suggestion. That some vegetables should be moved from one empty room to another, is positively the most important recommendation made for years. Another entry, in which some minor alterations are suggested, has under it, as the guardians' minute thereupon, "refer to the land-lord, and request him to make the changes advised." That is, refer to our chief, and see whether he will put his hand in his pocket, as owner, to satisfy a request officially made by himself as guardian. Comment is needless upon a system of control which makes this state of things possible, and we left the workhouse honestly wondering that its abuses are so few.

Leek, Staffordshire (1867)

> The second of *All the Year Round*'s workhouse 'probes' took place at what can be identified as Leek, in Staffordshire, where the union had acquired a large new hearse in 1866. As previously, the visitor was probably Joseph Charles Parkinson.[29]

ANOTHER WORKHOUSE PROBE

"Prefer it, sir?" said the Staffordshire workhouse master, energetically; "they're downright fond of it, and proud, too, I can tell you, for there's none of the unions about here has a 'earse to touch it. No difficulty about getting 'em to attend funerals now; all the old men volunteer, and we've six nice suits of black, so that we give most of 'em an out in turn. You see there was a good deal of dissatisfaction before, for a corpse is a heavy thing to carry, our inmates bein' mostly old and infirm, and the ground between this and the cemetery stiff. Consequently, when the old inmates had to git up this hill — you can see it over yonder, sir, between the trees to the right — they grumbled, and said it wasn't fair. To the guardians? Oh, no, sir, they wouldn't go so far as *that* — but to each other; and then some of the board saw 'em struggling on, and almost breaking down with a coffin between 'em in the hot weather; and a motion was brought on and carried, and all was settled, and this beautiful 'earse got in less than three weeks; for our guardians are kind men, sir, and like to bury their paupers well. Can the infirm mourners ride on it? Well, two of 'em can, in front, and the rest follow two and two. I wish you could see 'em, sir; it makes a funeral good enough for anybody; and they're all anxious to go directly we've a death in the house. You see for yourself what the 'earse is" (patting it affectionately, as if it were a favourite snuff-box), "handsome and well proportioned, but yet neat; and I do assure you there aren't one like it in any of the unions in the county. It's curious, downright curious, too, to see how our people have taken to this 'earse. Sometimes, when one of 'em's ill, and it's known he won't get better, they'll talk quite eagerly among themselves as to whose turn it is to follow him as mourners, and what a weight he'd ha' been to carry if the 'earse hadn't been got. You see it's a bit of an out, that's what it is; and now they've something to be proud of; they like funerals, and had rather go to one than stay all day in the house. For there's hardly anything to do in burying an inmate now. Of course they have to carry It from the 'earse to the place where the service is read, and from there to the grave — but that's all; and they're allowed to rest even then. We've a very nice horse that goes out with the bread-van for the out-door relief, and we just put him into the shafts, and he takes the whole affair to the cemetery without bother or trouble to any one. Would you like to look inside? No? Well, it's very roomy and snug, and is as well finished there as you can see it is from here. No, sir; we never refuse 'em permission to follow, if it's their turn, unless they're too old; and it's wonderful — downright wonderful — how eager some of the very oldest of all are to put on one of the black suits and play at mourners, as you may say. There was an old inmate now, eighty-three, and nearly double with rheumatics. He always insisted on his right to go; and when some of the others said it weren't fair, for he was so slow in walking, they always had to wait for him, and no good either at helping to carry It when in the cemetery grounds; so when, on one terribly wet day, we kept him at home out of kindness, blest if he didn't take it so to heart that he kept his bed. I don't say it killed him, because at eighty-three you don't want to look far for reasons for being carried off; but he never fairly looked up after he wasn't allowed to follow the new 'earse. As for the old man you saw peeling potatoes in the back yard, and whose cough you asked after, he's been just a glutton for funerals ever since the carrying by hand was given up, and I've no hesitation in saying, from what I've seen, that this 'earse is a real comfort, as it ought to be, to every inmate in the house. Is there any feeling of sorrow at losing an old companion, or wish to show respect to his memory by following him to the grave? I should say they don't know what it means. It's just the pleasure of walking behind what they know is a handsome thing, and of getting away for a time from here. For there's not much friendship in workhouses. Paupers aren't like other people, paupers aren't; and there's not much caring for one another when they're once in the house.

"Casual wards? Yes, certainly; you shall see them now. But our guardians, I may tell you, are almost unanimous against tramps, and we've fewer of 'em than any workhouse in the neighbourhood. Why? Because" (triumphantly) "*We* give 'em nothing to eat! That's the way, sir, depend on it; and, in my opinion, if tramps weren't fed, there'd be an end of vagrancy. We don't work 'em, mind, or give 'em bedding, or let 'em wash. No, sir. We tried all that sort of new-fangled work, and it didn't answer — not it. They'd eat their suppers or their breakfasts fast enough; but when work-time came, they'd rather run away than do it. System of control — labour-master? Bless you, no. We tried 'em with stone-breaking, we tried 'em with oakum-picking, and we tried 'em with carrying water; but they took to none of 'em, and made off every morning, as regular as the clock came round. Not likely to take to it, unless they're made, your say? Give 'em decent beds and bread and gruel, and take care to make 'em work it out the next morning, as is done successfully elsewhere? Why should we, when our present plan answers as well as it does? Why, we've fewer tramps in our wards than any of the workhouses near, and why? Just because they ain't coddled here, and don't get fed. Why, sir, if my plan was adopted, I'd back myself to clear the whole country of vagrants in three months. What is my plan? Well, let the unions combine — for it's no use trying it, mind you, unless all act alike — and put out a notice saying that, after a certain date, no tramps will be relieved, on any pretence whatever. Now, I've had a good deal of experience — I have; nine-and-twenty years I've been master here, and I say that if a good white board were put outside every workhouse in England, and this notice written on it in large letters, and acted up to, there'd soon be an end of vagrancy. There should be fair notice given 'em — three months, say; and after that, let 'em look out! What are vagrants? That's what I want to know. Nasty good-for-nothing fellows, who leave their parishes, if they ever had parishes — which is doubtful — and come for help to people who've enough to do with their own poor.

Why is it our neighbours get more than we do? Just because they give 'em food, and we don't. However, here we are at the women's tramp-ward; the men's is just like it on the other side, and you can see for yourself how they lie. Straw, sir — good straw, that's all; and I'd like to see the man who'd say it wasn't enough for vagrants. Rugs in cold weather? Clothes to put on, if their own are wet? No, sir, not a scrap; they've got a knack of tearing rags and clothes — tramps have; and we don't choose to put our union to expense; so they just lay down as they are, or naked, if they like it better, and are got rid of in the morning. Washing-place? God bless you, they're not a washing sort — vagrants aren't, and wouldn't care to use it, if we had. Quarrel or behave badly among themselves? Well, then they'd have to make it up again. *We* shouldn't hear them, for this ward, as you may see, is a good way from the house, and they might halloa and screech their hearts out without annoying anybody. But we're never troubled in this way, I assure you; and our vagrants aren't worth speaking of, they're so few since we've treated them properly. Does the Poor Law inspector approve of our sending casuals supperless to bed, and dismissing them breakfastless in the morning? I've no reason to think he doesn't, sir; he's never said so — and he's a very nice gentleman, is our inspector, and much liked by the board. No, sir, not old — about fifty or thereabouts; but enjoying very bad health, as I believe."

The reader will have discovered that this workhouse experience differs from the one recorded last week in every particular but one — the irresponsibility of the discipline and the self-constituted character of the rules. Here, as elsewhere, the management is of the kind in vogue when the New Poor Law wiseacres determined to put down poverty and misfortune thirty years ago, with such modifications and "readings" as perfectly unfettered guardians may devise. The place is beautifully clean, the inmates are tolerably fed, the beds and bedding, day-rooms and sick-wards, are arranged with mathematical precision, and the entire establishment is as sternly repressive and soul-depressing as the most misanthropic could desire. To say the sick are insufficiently cared for, is to repeat that we are in a workhouse; to say that the aged and infirm are left to tend or annoy each other without help or supervision throughout the night, and that the entire establishment does not show a single trace of human interest or fellow-feeling, save the boasted hearse, is to repeat, consistently, that we are in a workhouse. To say that helplessness, misfortune, and infirmity are so many crimes and misdemeanours, is to iterate once more that we are in a workhouse. Yet some of the maladministration within the house seems to arise from sheer wantonness or ignorance, and not from deliberate cruelty, as in the casual wards. Thus, with but ten people ill, and a resident paid nurse to attend to them, we find the door of communication between her room and the male sick ward carefully locked at night, and the medicines administered by a pauper, whose appearance, open-mouthed, hollow-cheeked, and vacant, recalls Smike.[30] He is described as "a very superior young man, who oughtn't to be in here," but he stares idiotically when addressed, and says wonderingly, after promptings by the master and coaxings by the nurse, "Yes, sir, I'm wardsman," in reply to a question as to another pauper's age! "He's hard of hearing: that makes him seem stupid," the master explains; and then, translating a request we have — twice, "Show the gentleman where you sleep, can't you!" precedes us into a room judiciously divided from the nurse's by a stone staircase, three thick doors, a substantial flooring, and a lock and key at night. Some old men, who are too far gone in torpidity and old age to even lift their eyes from the fire they gaze into and sit round, an old man in bed, with eyes closed and sheet tucked under chin, in that terribly suggestive fashion which seems common to bed-ridden paupers, and a much younger man, who rises from his chair near the fire to assures us earnestly that he is as well as he could wish, and would like to be let out that make up the party. "Nothing much the matter with any of them," the nurse explains, nervously plucking at her apron with both fingers, as I have seen witnesses do under cross-examination. "Why does the doctor put them on the sick-list, then?" "Oh, they're too old to be good for anything, for the old man in bed is more than ninety, and one of them sitting by the fire is eighty-five. The younger man is always praying, falling down on his knees in the middle of the day, when nobody expects it" — a compliance with the scriptural injunction concerning prayer without ceasing which has landed him in the infirmary ward. "Not very strong in his head," the master opines; "*though* his father was a mayor, and he has relations well to do, who turned him off because he went speaking of some lawsuit." Old men, helpless from age and infirmity, together with a man "not strong in the head," looked after by a deaf wardsman with an impediment in his brain — this picture suggests such frightful possibilities, that we ask, with some particularity, the nurse's precise duty in regard to them. Indefinite supervision by day, and a generous trustfulness in fate by night, appear to form the code by which that functionary is governed. It is necessary, you see, to lock the door dividing the sick-wards for women from the sick-wards for men; and as the nurse's room is with the latter, it follows that the deaf wardsman has sole charge during the hours when assistance is needed most. "No, sir, there is no bell, and no way of communicating to me from the ward where the old men are; but the young man has only to get up, and come up those stone stairs at the end of the passage, and then along this corridor, and if he kicks at the locked door at the end of it, my room's not far off, and I'm sure to hear if anything's wanted. But it's very seldom, I assure you, that I'm required. Oh, sir! of course I should get up directly, if he came, and he'd be sure to come if anything was the matter." We suggest, diffidently, that locking up aged invalids and incapable paupers together, and leaving it to the conscience and judgment of the latter to decide upon the necessity for leaving a warm bed, and traversing a couple of cold corridors and a stone staircase, to kick at a door until a nurse is roused from her bed some yards off, appears a somewhat elaborate form of How not to do it. But both master and nurse are thoroughly convinced that any departure from the present admirable arrangements — bringing into use, for example, some rooms on the same floor as the nurse's room, in which beds were lying empty, and which have not been used since "the year of the cholera and Irish fever" — would be injudicious and unwise: so we prudently change the subject, and visit the day-room of the old men not on the sick-list. Fireless, comfortless, clean, and cold, and without old men. These are all at work, some in the garden, others about the outhouses; and in one of the latter we come upon a cluster of feeble wretches, some blear-eyed, and either palsied, or shaking with the cold, who are cowering together and coughing against each other this bitter November day in a place flowing with water, without a fire and open to the yard, of which it is a part. The water is not turned on to the brick floor for the sole purpose of giving the dotards cold. Potatoes are being scraped and washed by three or four of the least decrepit, and the others are blinking and winking by their side, because to be sheltered from the biting wind, and to sit down, is less chilling than their other alternative — standing in the open yard. "What is the matter with the old man making the painful noise when he coughs?"

"Well, I didn't notice which one it was; but they're all very old, you see, and liable to coughs." Such a row of helpless, hopeless, withered faces! One of them essays to bow cringingly as we enter; but the rest, like their prototypes round the fire in the sick-ward, eye the potato peeling like worn-out puppets, to whom volition or change of gaze is impossible. The majority seem so torpidly inanimate as to be unconscious of all but cold; and there is not one among them to whom a warm room, kind treatment, and what are called "comforts," are not as necessary as food and clothing are to the healthy and strong. To shut those forlorn people out in a flagged exercise-yard, or to leave them neglected in an open out-house, is simply shortening their lives. Looking at them critically, it was difficult to understand how the line of demarcation is drawn between the sick and the infirm. If to need nursing, medical care, and constant warmth, be "sickness" in a parochial sense, assuredly the men before us were sick. Let the guardians who read this paper make a tour of their spick-and-span model workhouse for themselves, and forgetting for a moment the incomparable virtues of whitewash, and the saving grace of cold water, let them, this winter, talk to the old people who are sent out to work, listen to their ailments, and observe their infirmities; and if their experience does not affect the discipline of the place, our faith in the kindness of Cheshire squires is gone. The house is confessedly occupied by the old and worn out. Out of the *one hundred and twenty-three inmates* it contained at our visit, *there were but two able-bodied men*; yet the whole of the vast gloomy place, which has accommodation for double the number there now, is kept in order, and every domestic function discharged, by people who are admitted to be past work. Either, then, the classification is false, or tasks are improperly thrust upon those unable to discharge them; and as we have seen that the house does not suffer, it is tolerably obvious the paupers do. Those dim-eyed, purposeless old men haunt us. We want to master the details of their daily lives, to know the lying down and getting up of people to whom a funeral of one of their number is a treat, and who take a pride in following the ghastly hearse which they themselves are soon to fill.

We hastily ask the master to conduct us to the old men's sleeping-ward, and this is what we see a long room, light, airy, cold. Beds running down each side, leaving a clear space in the centre and between each. Floor, white and spotless. Walls without so much as a fly-spot to break their uniformity. Windows facing each other at regular intervals, so as to ensure a thorough supply of keen fresh air. Outside the door, and at the stair-head, is a washing-place, with a copious supply of cold water and a couple of towels, which were clean at our visit, and are changed "when necessary." Here the feeble old men in the potato-shed sleep. The door is locked which communicates with the master and the rest of the house, but they are mercifully allowed free access to the staircase, to the cold water, and the closet. There is no bell or other means of communication; no wardsman, no pauper nurses charged with the limited responsibility which it is equally common and wrong to thrust upon them. In this room, which would be excellent for healthy vigorous lads, but is desolately penal for the decrepit wretches sleeping in it, men of seventy, eighty, and ninety spend their nights, unguarded, uncared for, unremembered, until the hour comes for unlocking the door and permitting them to go forth to the yard or potato-shed again. "Is there no one here," we ask, "to act for you in case of accidents? Suppose one of the old men were suddenly taken ill, or had a fit, or were quarrelsome, is there no one in charge?" The workhouse is too well conducted for any possibility of the kind. "Never have any trouble of that sort, I do assure you; and never find it necessary to put any one in charge. Of course the least infirm among them naturally takes the lead; but we've no wardsmen, it ain't necessary. As for a fit, or anything being wanted, one of 'em would get up, of course, and come down-stairs and through the other ward, and then knock at the door nearest my room, and I should be sure to hear directly." "Are paupers always ready to help intractable other? Are there not sometimes bad and intractable characters among them?" "Well, we never meet with any such. All is quiet and orderly when they're once locked up; and as for squabbling or fits, we never have anything of the kind." In short, the arrangements are of the best possible kind; a bell would be a superfluity, and a wards-man or night-nurse rather a nuisance to the people than otherwise. Listening to this, and silenced by the courteous firmness with which the master puts us right, we recall an ugly circumstance which happened at Bethnal-green workhouse a couple of years since. In just such a ward as this, aged and infirm men were locked up at night, without fire or light, as here; but with this apparent advantage over their Staffordshire fellows — a pauper wardsman had strict orders to call the master if anything went wrong. One night an old man suddenly fell out of bed, and lay somewhat unaccountably on the floor. After a time, one of his neighbours called on the pauper in charge, who, finding him "quite cold," refused to rouse any one unnecessarily for a dead pauper, and, after grumbling at being disturbed, retired comfortably to bed again, and the body was removed in the morning. Now, a considerable fuss was made concerning this dead pauper and his fate. Journalists said it was cruel to lock up aged helpless people and leave them to each other's tender mercies. The Poor Law Board, ever watchful, considerate, and kind, instituted an official inquiry, and every one concerned was examined and absolved. The master, since dismissed, was rather complimented than otherwise by the local press; the pauper witnesses contradicted each other and themselves, and made their evidence worthless; and after some fitful indignation on the part of the public, discussion, like the poor wretch who occasioned it, died out and was forgotten.

It had been formally shown that it was a mistake to suppose the ward was isolated; for bells, conveniently hung, and of sonorous ringing powers, were shown to be there only a fortnight after the sad event. It happened, however, to the present writer to feel doubtful concerning this pauper's death, and the circumstances surrounding it, and to inspect the ward and examine witnesses for himself, some days before the official inquiry began. Accompanied by a friendly guardian and the rector of the parish, he obtained admission to the workhouse, and examined the ward and pauper death-bed. *The bells were not then put up*, and the condition of things sworn to at the official inquiry proved not to exist. After the untoward death, and its more untoward publicity, efforts were successfully made to smoothe things over; and by the time the official inquiry was held, all the arrangements and everybody concerned were blamelessly immaculate, except the pauper who obstinately fell out of bed and died for want of help. It was the accident of publicity, and the awkward questions it raised, that made bells necessary. Visiting committees of guardians had examined and reported favourably upon the workhouse arrangements every month, and every other precaution had been taken to show that this was one of the many best possible establishments, produced by the best possible system in the best possible of official worlds. The pauper died, questions were asked, and indignation shown; and lo! bells were affixed, and any such wickedness as locking up the aged and infirm without light or fire earnestly and: successfully repudiated.

How many paupers die thus from neglect, without discovery? Here, for example, the condition of the poor creatures we have just seen coughing

105

in the cold — worn-out agricultural drudges, who seemed to be mutely asking permission to end their days peacefully and without pain — absolutely demanded warmth and care. Their age and infirmities make night-nursing essential, not merely to their comfort, but to their life; and to shut them up together through the long dark hours, without supervision or help, is to bid them die. Who, knowing anything of workhouse pauper-nature, its callousness, its servility, its cruelty, thinks it likely that there would be any disposition to rouse the master in case of the illness of a mere "inmate"? "No use disturbing Mr. Blank when the man's feet were quite cold, and he was as good as dead; for Mr. Blank couldn't bring life back again to a dead man, could he now?" was the reason given to us at Bethnal-green for not knocking up the labour-master. And cases are plentiful in which men and women have died through the neglect and indifference of the fellow-paupers entrusted to look after them.

It was a pauper nurse at the Holborn Union workhouse who, on her own responsibility, plunged the dying Timothy Daly into a warm bath on an inclement day in December; and a pauper nurse who improperly applied fuller's-earth to his sores.[31] It was a pauper nurse who, at last, mercifully killed off Richard Gibson, at the St. Giles's Union, by giving him gin;[32] and a pauper wardsman who left Robert Scolly to die unaided, on finding "he could not, or would not, answer" when asked whether he were ill.[33] The Poor Law Commissioners, in those consolidated orders which have been so carefully framed, and through the non-enforcement of which so much cruelty and misery is caused, insist that in large workhouses a paid porter shall be employed, as they "believe it to be of a rare occurrence that a pauper can be safely trusted to exercise the power and perform the duties of porter;" and this rule should apply a thousand-fold to all positions demanding delicacy and care. If pauper nurses are as thoroughly inefficient as we have seen, what is to be looked for when there is not even a pretence of deputing duties to any one pauper among the rest? The fate of everybody's business is proverbial; and when, as at the sick and old men's wards just seen, there are passages, and stairs, and wards to be traversed before help can be procured, the fate of an old creature, suddenly smitten in the night, can be easily guessed. He would groan, and be told, surlily, to "make less noise." He would struggle, perhaps, and then become still — with the stillness of death — but unless his condition made him actually disagreeable to the rest, it is childish to suppose any one in the house would be roused. On inquiring of the master as to what would happen if a given case occurred, the invariable, "Well, it never does happen, you see — we never have any trouble of the kind," smoothes over all difficulties. We are asked to assume that old men of eighty are never ill until a Union doctor declares infirmary treatment necessary — that a hard-worked master is personally fond of being roused out of bed at night; that Staffordshire and Cheshire paupers are exceptionally full of the milk of human kindness, and without harshness to each other, or sycophancy to those above them — we are asked to assume any or all of these highly probable contingencies, and, in that case, we need have no fear that the paralytic and infirm are at all likely to be killed off. But, with the harsh coughs and death-like looks of the wretches cowering in the potato-shed still before us, the elaborate cleanliness and bare neatness of this long chamber jar upon one as much as if it were a living tomb. Nor is there any more trace of its being the home of people with the same wants and feelings as ourselves, than would be found in a row of trestles upon which corpses were to rest. Not a shelf, not a book, not a tray-stand, not a solitary attempt at cheap decoration, relieved the dreary uniformity. It made one's eyes ache to note the comfortless cleanliness of the chilly chamber and the prison-like regularity of the rows of couches. Not a word can be said against the beds, as beds; though the master was "unable to say" whether at this time they accommodated two inmates each, or one. They are clean and fairly comfortable. It is the absence of all human personal interest, of every trace of individuality, which strikes us as repulsively harsh for any but a criminal class. A prison, cleanly, well ventilated, but still a prison, where the inmates are looked after according to fixed rules, and where any yielding to personal tastes, any attempts at rendering the last earthly resting-place of the unfortunate, the broken-down, and the afflicted, home-like, is against the rules — such was our estimate of this dreary establishment. The axiom enunciated at the tramp-ward, "Starve vagrants, and there'll be an end of vagrancy," is paraphrased within the house into, "Withhold necessaries from paupers, and you'll make pauperism unpopular." This might be defended, if idle, worthless scamps were battening upon the poor-rates. In such a case, by all means make their discipline and regimen harsh. Hem them in by rules and regulations, forbid them comforts, and, while finding them with food and shelter, rigorously exact labour in return. And these admissions may be made with the more confidence, when it is remembered that the present inmates are, almost without an exception, declared by the parish authorities themselves to be unfit for work.

The children are at school, and we enter a large room where an organ and other fittings show that it serves the double duty of chapel and schoolroom. Both boys and girls are being taught here, under a male and female teacher respectively, and lock well fed and happy. There are evidently no undue hardships for them. Their young blood keeps them in a glow in the coldest yard; and as for being locked up in the dark together at night, their only trouble is that the plaguy schoolmaster sleeps in the next room, and has a knack of appearing in his nightgown directly a comfortable pillow fight begins. This is the boys' view, and if field-labour or other out-of-door work could be substituted for this nasty schooling, which never did anybody good yet, and never will, why they would, they think, be tolerably satisfied with their lot. The sacred board-room, with firm-looking chairs, which suggest equal firmness in their users, and a general air of formality judiciously calculated to awe the pauper mind; a board-room, the sole ornament of which is the black harness decorating a corner, and some framed regulations, signed "Courtenay," for the Poor Law Board, is shown next. This harness hasn't been used yet, and is waiting for the guardians to approve it. "You see, what we had was rather worn when we put it along with such a 'earse" — the master, whose talk is not otherwise cocknified, persists in speaking of the gloomy caravan as if it were the dialect of the Gaels — "such a 'earse as ours is: it looked downright shabby; and so our guardians agreed to have new, for, as I said before, they're kind men, and like to bury their paupers well."

Laundries, admirably arranged, are shown, with hot and cold water laid on to each washing tank. In one, an imbecile female dwarf of sixty is rubbing her brown and wizened bust with soapsuds with a slow deliberate motion, as if trying to remodel it a better colour. She responds to the "Now then, Sally, look sharp!" of the master, by making the most grotesquely hideous grimace it has been our fortune to see save in a gurgoyle or a pantomime.

The lavatories, are copiously supplied with water and clean towels. We see a bakery next, in which excellent loaves have just left the oven and their tins, and are being ranged in warm brown rows on racks, by a shrewd baker, whose face and clothes are pervaded, like Mr. Tulliver's,[34] with a general mealiness. We see the old women's day-rooms, with the infirm inmates dotted about like bundles of old clothes, some gibbering affably to the air, and others self-complacent and gossiping, as dowagers at a five o'clock tea. A table, and the means of sitting down to it, comprise the comforts and amusements provided here for old age. The old women have, however, these advantages over their brethren — the windows of their room look out upon the country, instead of a prison-yard, and they are not turned out of it to mope in the damp between meal-times. The tank at the top of the house, immediately under the latticed lanthorn window which is so conspicuous an object from the road, and a loft in which the scent from pauper-grown and pauper-gathered onions strongly asserts its equality with onions differently circumstanced, claim our notice next; and we gradually beat back to the room in which we first found the master. Then came a delicate duty — the duty of making our entry in the visitors' book.

Great people — a living duchess and a dead lord, a duke, and an earl's son; philanthropic people — notably a gentleman from Ireland, whose entry was methodically enthusiastic, and who iterated every item of approval like an inspired appraiser; official people — the guardians and the representative of the Poor Law Board — had all concurred in recording their intense admiration of this workhouse and its arrangements. Her grace's comments are mildly rapturous, with an undercurrent of implied feeling that if a harsh fate had not compelled her to be a duchess, she would choose the Elysian life led by the paupers here. The inspector has not a word to say upon the palpable defiance of the law in the tramp-wards, or about the neglect of the sick and old, but has carefully examined workhouse, infirmaries, and arrangements, a few months since, found everything in capital order, and would report "very favourably" to the Poor Law Board; adding, in a consistent postscript, that the ventilation of one ward is "very defective," and that some air-bricks should be put in.

In the face of these glowing statements, it requires some courage to hint, in writing, that, while the able-bodied and the children are well cared for in this workhouse, the arrangements for the aged and sick are susceptible of improvement, and that the practice of starving casual paupers is not in accordance with the requirements of the day. Yet we make bold to do this, in the name of All the Year Round, on the master asking us "to write something in the visitors' book." Whereupon that worthy, obviously staggered at our audacity, promptly changes the subject to "the new 'earse," which, to his mind, condones all shortcomings, and upon the beauties of which he dilates eloquently until we leave.

Chorlton, Lancashire (1871)

This article was published (with no attribution of authorship) in *The Sphinx* magazine in 1871.[35] It presents a rather sympathetic picture of the Chorlton Union workhouse at Nell Lane, Withington, at the south of Manchester, which at that date could accommodate over 1,500 inmates. Becoming Withington Hospital, the main building survives, now converted to apartments.

A DAY IN THE WITHINGTON WORKHOUSE.

The English ratepayer, receiving at various times slips of paper on which are inscribed definite cash amounts said to be "Due on Demand," has an instinctive knowledge that he must pay the said amounts prior to a given day to certain officers whose names are printed on the papers in question. Being willing to know something of one of the channels down which our coins were said to vanish, and having an idea that workhouse life would present many phases likely to suit our contemplative disposition, we gladly availed ourselves of an invitation to spend a day inside the extensive workhouse of the Chorlton Union at Withington.

It is not generally known that the Withington workhouse stands on its own grounds, or, in other words, is surrounded by a quantity of land, which it farms, raising thereon wheat and oats and bacon for its own use. Crossing these fields and passing by the graveyard, which is the final resting-place of the outcast and helpless who find a temporary shelter in the neighbouring buildings — and which is none the less pretty or tranquil because almost the only memorials of the dead beneath are grass-covered mounds and evergreen bushes — we were ushered through the gates of the workhouse into a fine hall, designed doubtless to suggest to all who enter it, the nobleness of charity. From this place we were escorted along a corridor about four hundred and fifty feet in length, extending from end to end of the house, on each side of which are ranged

The impressive frontage of the Chorlton Union workhouse at Withington.

the various offices, school-rooms, and sitting-rooms; then out again into the open air, and up a flight of steps to an elevated terrace at the back of the house, built on arches, which terrace connects with each other the five pavilions used as hospitals. Standing on this terrace we were enabled fully to enjoy the pleasant rural situation of the buildings. Indeed, so pleasant was the prospect, that it was difficult to realize that poverty lay in front of us, insanity on either hand, and disease and death behind.

After a few preliminaries in the shape of introductions and mutual explanations between ourselves and the gentlemen who had volunteered to be our escort, we were led back into the house in order to witness the ceremony of dining. An immense kitchen, in which potato-hash had apparently been prepared by the cart-load in a series of huge boilers, first attracted our attention. Passing through this apartment we gained the dining-room. This place is fitted up with a series of fixed tables and seats arranged something like the pews in a chapel, the diners being seated side by side and back to back. The women do not sit with the men, but, like Dr. Johnson, at the publisher Cave's, partake of their food behind a screen, which screen runs up the centre of the room. The old people occupy the front seats, the middle-aged and young come next, and the children bring up the rear. Speaking of this system of classification we were glad to learn that in the bed-rooms and day or sitting-rooms a further principle of subdivision is adopted, the moral, orderly, and cleanly people being placed in one series of rooms, and the black sheep in another. To each dining-table there is one saltcellar, which is a fixture. About four hundred people — principally aged — were dining, and the clatter of spoons went on with a mechanical briskness, which seemed to indicate that the company was quite undisturbed by the presence of our party. But though the heads before us were all bowed food, we could not help feeling that our inspection was rather rude, and therefore retreated quickly into a sort of big pantry, in which some hundreds of loaves were being cut into slices for supper. These are served out by weight. When they are too heavy the corners are cut off. We were shown several large baskets filled with these corners which are saved for the use of the children. Every pauper has the right to see his bread weighed if he suspects that it is too light.

Leaving the bread-cutter to his crusty employment, we next visited the interiors of the hospitals. The Withington Workhouse is adapted to accommodate twelve hundred people, but about one-half the inmates are usually stretched on beds of sickness. There are five hospital buildings, connected only by the terrace previously referred to, and containing in all fifteen wards or rooms, and about five hundred beds. The hospital arrangements appeared to us to be perfect. We readily agreed with the doctor that cleanliness and fresh air are no slight helps to the medical man. Anything more clean than the wards we visited, or more orderly and complete than the various appliances and systems of ventilation, it would be difficult to conceive. The beds looked quite inviting, and the floors were spotless. But white as were the sheets, some of the faces were whiter. The patients were of all ages, and suffering from all sorts of complaints, medical and surgical. They were of course classified. Many were people quite able to support themselves respectably when in health, but compelled to come here when overtaken by accident or sickness. We were shown, for instance, the case of a servant maid, who, in slipping down some stairs, had managed to thrust her hand through a window, and thus had severed some of the arteries and tendons at the wrist. Some of the faces wore the glad expression of returning health; others had the listless look which betokened that they were approaching the unknown land which rich and poor must enter alike. The use of one ward was graphically enough indicated to us by the large number of very young

112

infants present. We were told that the adult occupants of the beds were all either servant girls or members of that profession to which it is considered indelicate to allude. If it be true that an increasing population is always a sign of a nation's prosperity, perhaps many of the ratepayers will be satisfied with the necessity of devoting a portion of the rates to this last department of the workhouse.

The doctor having completed his description of the hospitals, we were handed over to the care of the governor, and conducted through the various day, work, and store-rooms. In some of the day-rooms, and in the grounds attached to them, the old men were standing and sitting as if doing nothing but waiting for their clean shirts. Whether our presence caused them to be silent or not we cannot say, but a more listless and aimless company we do not care to look upon. We were much more pleased with the old women. In their clean white caps they looked quite motherly, and many, moreover, were busily engaged with their needles. We have always thought that in this power of being able to work, if they choose, at all times, in the drawing-room as well as in the workhouse, women have a great advantage over men. A woman can take up her tatting when a man is confined to tattling or playing with his fingers. One old lady of about eighty, who was hard at work knitting, had been confirmed, in company with several of her elderly sisters, by the bishop the week before our visit. None of the inmates are compelled to work after they are sixty years of age; and we were informed during our progress through the work rooms that it is difficult to get into the house a sufficiency of able-bodied paupers. We formed a slight idea of the amount of work to be got through when our attention was directed to the immense number of stockings to be kept in repair. The principal work-rooms are the laundries in which the women are employed. These are fitted up with every appliance calculated to expedite the work. Amongst others, huge washing-machines, driven by steam power. There are also shoemakers', joiners', and tailors' shops, in which the lads are taught those various handicrafts.

The store-rooms are very extensive, and they were so suggestive of plenty that it was really pleasant to walk through them. Flour, meal, and tea appeared to be the principal supplies. There was also a quantity of snuff made up into screws to be distributed to the partakers of that luxury, and a supply of tobacco, likewise for distribution. The quantity of the latter given out weekly does not appear to be sufficient for the smokers, and is usually eked out with tea-leaves; but we were informed that the renown of these dainties is sufficient to attract paupers from all the surrounding localities to the Withington Workhouse. We were likewise shown into a cellar well-stocked with barrels of beer and porter for the use of the invalids, and into another containing an extensive supply of mutton-chops, intended for the same persons. In view of the destination of these articles, we do not doubt that many of the inmates are occasionally troubled with mysterious complaints, and we heard a hint that sometimes severe blisters are required in order to convince the sufferers that they are in good health. A very complete system is required to keep so extensive an establishment in order, and one or two of the Workhouse contrivances suggested to us that the ruling genius had discovered the principle of perpetual motion. To take one example: The straw which is got from the crops of wheat on the Workhouse farm is used for stuffing the beds. In order to ensure cleanliness, it is regularly changed; it is then passed on to the pigs, and when the pigs have done with it, it serves as manure for the fields, where, we suppose, it again grows up into wheat.

The inspection of the lunatic wards could not have other than a saddening effect. Mr. Clements, the doctor, again joined our party prior to our entrance to these wards, and considerately accompanied us through them. The first room we entered was occupied by middle aged and old women. Here a poor thing named Nannie sidled up to us in a queer fashion, and, shaking our hand, replied to our enquiry that she was very well, hoped that we were the same, and that we had left all well at home. While talking her body was never still, its movements being compounded of slides and curtsies. The other lunatic women who were standing around looked on with half-pitying, half-apologetic expressions on their faces, as if beseeching us to make allowances for poor Nannie's peculiarities. Another room was appropriated to young creatures, aged from eighteen to twenty-five years, or thereabouts. They were chatting together just as any other assembly of girls would do, and our entrance was the signal for whispered surmises as to who we were. But all the faces wore a strange, unsatisfied look which told us that we were in strange company. One poor girl with bright eyes and glowing cheeks put a thin hand into ours, and, gazing eagerly into our face, strove to recognize us. She told us that she had enjoyed herself very well during her visit, and that it was a very nice place; but she was getting rather tired and would like to see her friends. When we parted from her she gave us her name and address, and begged us with a painful earnestness to call at her home and give her love to all whom we should find there.

In the wards for males we were struck at first with the intelligent cast of features of many of the inmates. One particularly well-made and powerful-looking man advanced to us and, assuring us that he was quite recovered, begged us to bring his overcoat to him and let him go. We half-believed that he was sane, but a glance at the eye, which never rested, soon settled the matter. When we left him he vowed to memorialise Her Majesty the same evening, the result of which action on his part would cost us millions of pounds. To each ward is attached a pleasantly laid-out ground, all grass and shrubs. The majority of the males were reclining on seats in one of these enclosures. Here the spectacle became even sadder. One poor fellow with a bandaged arm was addressing a brick wall in terms of earnest complaint and expostulation. He seemed utterly miserable. From the seats others were watching him with cynical, stony countenances not pleasant to look at. Out in the beautiful sunshine and on the fresh greenness of the hopeful spring, there was an awful weariness about those still figures, which was all the more appalling when we learnt that drink and vice were the chief causes of the ruin they expressed.

The lowest types of humanity shown to us crouched in the ward and on the ground for female idiots. We were led into a snug apartment, resembling a comfortable kitchen. In a corner by the fire sat an object which seemed all head, knees, and feet. It was a girl. On the floor by her side was another. They never looked up or spoke; only jabbered inarticulately. More were squatted over the grass and gravel paths outside. We saw the face of one who was huddled up on a ledge, in a kind of shed, as if on a perch. Call it the face of a monkey or what you will, it was not the face of a human being composed of body, soul, sad spirit. Talking on the subject, our guide told us that the brain of a male idiot, who had died in the workhouse a little while before, had been examined. It was pronounced to be a perfect structure, and, as far as material went, the brain of a highly intelligent man. This statement caused us to be much more impressed by the difference between the faces of the lunatics and those of the idiots. In the former, we fancied we could see an indwelling spirit vainly trying to produce harmony through the chords of a shattered instrument. In the latter we could detect no spirit at all. We wondered whether the first were immortal beings dwelling in ruined tenements? the latter only moving machines pulled about by electric ganglia. The doctor's words "It is a mystery," ended our reflection.

The opening of a door, shrill bursts of joyous laughter, a rushing as of a swarm of bees, and a crowd of little girls have fastened upon the legs and hands and arms of each member of our party. It is like music after despair. For an instant we are so dazed that we stand passively submitting, like Gulliver, to the assaults of the pigmies. Little by little we make out that we are in the girls' playground, and that these are a portion of the workhouse children. Some have rosy cheeks, bright eyes, and dimpled faces; others have faces not so chubby or rosy; but all look merry. There is a shadow of melancholy present, because we can't forget that these are foundlings, picked up in the streets, or born in the workhouse, and dependent for future happiness upon the kindness of strangers. But we fairly enjoy ourselves. Tossing one child into the air, we are deafened by shouts of "me, me." At length, being thoroughly tired, and having had our hands kissed and smoothed and petted all round, we bid our young friends "good-bye," and enter the nursery. Here, seated on the floor, surrounded by an admiring circle of small infants, is a juvenile scarcely large enough to walk, slowly and cautiously blacking its shoes with a brush, which its tiny strength appears just able to move. Outside the circle is a youth of about three summers, apparently the wag of the company, inasmuch as he proceeds to make faces at us, to the intense amusement of a select party of his acquaintances. A promise of cake induces the band to place their diminutive forms on seats provided for them, and to favour us with a song, which we have heard before, beginning, "A little ship was on the sea." Passing through a neighbouring room, we are shown the numerous cradles in which the latest generation of paupers take their rest. One of these cradles, adapted to hold six infants, is declared to be an object which elicits exclamations of delight from all the ladies who visit the workhouse.

In the boy's playground we saw a number of as artful-looking dodgers as we have ever beheld. Upon our entrance, and in obedience to a sign ham the governor the whole of the boys, with one exception, ranged themselves in a crowd before us. The exception alluded to was a little lame fellow who, supported on a leg and a crutch, and whip in hand, was actively pursuing a gyrating top, evidently imagining for the time being that the universe contained nothing but the top and himself. Most of the faces before us had that look of wide-awake intelligence which is the only good gained from a street education, softened somewhat by the discipline of school-life. There was no mistaking the Lancashire extraction of one diminutive personage. The Governor called for six of the biggest boys to run a race for the usual prize to be enjoyed at supper — cake. Six boys stood out from the rest, one of the six being the smallest present. Holding up his head, however, he seemed to think he was decidedly the biggest, and, notwithstanding some objection on the part of his companions, managed to maintain his place. During the enunciation of the "one, two, three," we observed that his stockinged feet were slyly creeping from the encasing clogs, and, when the starting number was given, away he went down the playground and back again, winning the race by about three lengths. On our way to inspect the piggeries we saw several boys gardening, under the superintendence of a paid instructor.

The last department of the Workhouse which we visited was a building appropriately designated "The Test House." It was a narrow apartment, consisting of a passage along the side of a number of wooden cages, to each of which was attached a machine resembling a huge coffee mill. We were informed that able-bodied male applicants for relief, who are supposed to be vagabondish, drunken, or idle, are placed in these cages, there to grind the corn which is raised on the adjoining farm. The men are locked in here at about eight o'clock in the morning, if we remember rightly. The mills are filled three times during the day, and if the grinders have ground the specified quantity they are liberated at about five o'clock. Dinner is served to them in the cages. Behind the grinding-room is the sleeping apartment, and attached to it a barren yard containing a heap of stones. We can assure our fellow ratepayers that no sluggard or drunkard will partake of the workhouse charity until forced by hunger, and that as long as he is an inmate of "The Test House" he earns his living. Indeed it seemed to us that the regulations effectually confine the benefits of the Institution to those sufferers who must ever be the proper objects of charity. Whether in the details of these regulations or in the nature of the benefits there is room for improvement our day did not afford us sufficient opportunity to ascertain. Doubtless there may be. Our courteous guide, the governor, Mr. Brokenshire, told us that the admirable appliances and systems which we saw in thorough working order were the accumulation of the fifteen years which have elapsed since the original building was opened. We believe, however, that very considerable advances in efficiency and towards perfection have been made in the last few years. The institution at present is considered to be one of the most complete and perfect in the kingdom, and improvement is still going on.

Keighley, West Yorkshire (1887)

A Night in the Workhouse was by Carey Craven, a Keighley bookseller. His night in the Keighley casual ward imitated the infamous visit to the Lambeth workhouse by James Greenwood in 1866, whose own account had a similar title.[36] The casual ward no longer exists, but the other buildings on the Oakworth Road site have been converted into Hillworth Village homes for the elderly.

A NIGHT IN THE WORKHOUSE.

Having had a desire for a long time to obtain an insight into the vicissitudes of a vagrant's life, I determined to put a plan into execution which should secure to me at least one night's company amongst the guerrilla element of modern society. How I succeeded will be found in the following narrative, the accuracy of the incidents of which I am prepared to vouch for.

I found no difficulty in obtaining a suitable rig-out in the shape of an old pair of corduroy trousers, a pair of worn-out shoes, together with a dilapidated coat, specially slashed for the occasion, and a greasy nebbed cap. Thus suitably equipped, I perambulated to the police-station, hung about the door hesitatingly for a moment or two, and then screwed up sufficient courage to enter the office. My appearance was greeted, in cheerful tones, by the officer in charge. "Come forward, young man; do you want a ticket?" To this I answered modestly, " Yes, if you please, sir." In reply to his interrogations I gave him the following information concerning my august self:— Name, Charles Burrell, on the road from Bradford to Burnley; trade, mechanic; age, 28; height, 5ft. 5in. This was written upon a ticket, with which I was duly presented, a duplicate being kept in the officer's book. I thanked him kindly, and betook, myself rapidly up Oakworth Road to the Workhouse.

On attempting to enter I was debarred by the stern fixity of the iron gate. After waiting a few moments a window was opened to my right, and a pompous voice exclaimed, "What is it?" I presented my ticket. Again the questions were asked, "Where are you from? Where are you going to? What trade are you?" to all of which I answered as in the first instance. The assistant porter (for I found out afterwards that he wasn't the regular one) then exclaimed in a surly tone, "Pipe and matches!" "What?" replied I. "Pipe and matches!" "Yes, I'll have a pipe and matches." "I want your pipe and matches." "I haven't got any." "Then pass on." I passed on, and after missing my way several times, found myself in the outer room, the dimensions of which were about 4½ yards square, Here a regular pauper was in charge, who at once told me to undress myself. Whilst doing this, a piece of dry bread, about 4oz. in weight, was thrown on a board, with the exclamation, "Thear's yer Tommy." On getting my coat, waistcoat and trousers off, and discovering my underclothing, the attendant exclaimed several times, "*You* don't look as if you hed been on t'road long anyhow." "No!" says I, "this is the first time." He then told me to take my shirt off, and strip myself entirely. "Why take my shirt off?" I asked." Because ther might be sum o' *them thear things abaght*." he replied. "Are there many of those things round about these quarters?" I further interrogated. "Nay, ah doan't think there'll be so monny, we mostly stove 'em when we find onny." With this answer I was somewhat comforted. When I had undressed myself to a state as naked as when I was born, I was told to tie my clothes up, and place them alongside a series of similar bundles laid against the wall. I was then furnished with a couple of rugs and ordered into the inner or sleeping room, and the lock turned on me. All was dark as pitch. My bare feet slipped on what I afterwards found was the vagrants' spattle on the stone floor, and the sensation was cold and slimy. It made me think of snails, and worms, and other loathsome creeping things. I felt glad when my hand clutched the boarding on which my limbs were to rest for the night. The men in the room were conversing freely with one another, and after a time I ventured to inquire if there was any room for me. The one in the partition nearest the door answered that I could sleep alongside him, but must be careful not to upset the tin of water at his feet. I made my way as best I could to the place indicated by the sound of his voice, and got my foot accidently into the tin of water, but soon extricated it. Then covering my naked body as well as I could with the rugs given to me, I laid myself on the hard slanting boards, with bare wood as my pillow, to experience twelve hours' misery.

Do as I would I was unable to make the rugs entirely cover me. There was a cold draught, and I was alternately seized with cramp and neuralgic pains. Now and again I could observe the dim naked forms of the vagrants as they passed to the tub where circumstances of necessity were performed. Needless to say the stench arising from this was anything but pleasant. When the night bad progressed somewhat, the noise arising from snoring and the men talking in their sleep was incessant. One fellow kept calling out "Sixpence." Another said, "You are there, and I am here, and we've another night and day to do," &c. &c.; As the eight o'clock bell rang for the regular inmates to go to rest, there came a sound of sweet music from the outside, as if a batch of church revivalists was indulging just before separating for the night. The vagrants wondered where the singers came from, and one of them exclaimed, "'The Workhouse Door.' Have you ever heard it sung? I heard a young woman sing it the other night, and liked it very well." The conversation turned on various topics. Two of the vagrants had been in Skipton Workhouse the night previous, and one of them related how his bread had been carried away by a ravenous rat as big as a cat. The leading features of the Skipton Workhouse were the severity of the labour in stone breaking, and what a "clever beggar" the porter of the establishment was. Other topics were the new waterworks at Barrowford and Colne, and the probabilities of getting a job there. Also what sort of task-work would be likely to be given to us the day following. The tramp next to me complained that he was suffering from diarrhoea, and that the agony he was undergoing was most excruciating. He had asked three times that day to see the doctor, but every time the attendant pretended not to be able to make out what he had said, and the only effort made to relieve the pain was by giving him a tin of warm water to drink. He stated he had travelled from Wakefield, where he did manage to obtain a bottle of medicine; but at Keighley he had been treated "worse than a dog." From him I also learnt that he had been where he was all Sunday, without putting his clothes on, and that he preferred being inside to outside on that day, because people stared so much, and shunned a tramp, particularly if he was badly dressed. He had passed many a Sunday without even breaking his fast. He intended making his way towards Burnley, where, he stated, there was no vagrants' ward, but that tickets were given for a lodging-house.

I did not sleep a wink all night, and kept fancying "some o' them thear things" were creeping over me. By the time the welcome streaks of morning dawn appeared through the window, my bones felt terribly sore, and I was half starved to death. At about a quarter to seven the key turned in the door, and the order was given for us to "get dressed and bring your rugs in here." Seven naked forms then flitted about in search of their clothes, and commenced to dress. I found the piece of dry bread I had left untouched the night before still remaining. I was asked by one of the vagrants if I wasn't going to take it, and replied in the negative, saying he could have it if he cared to do so. He appeared exceedingly grateful, and at once commenced to devour it. The feet of my fellow-lodgers were of all sizes and shapes, and I had never seen such a collection of corns and bunions before. I found in my pocket a small paper of tobacco, which I shared out as best I could. After getting dressed we carefully folded up the rugs we had slept in, and piled them up in a corner of the room. A few then produced small pieces of soap, which they had secreted about their persons, and endeavoured to wash themselves at the bath, into which at different times I had observed several spit and blow their noses. Whilst waiting for breakfast. I had a good opportunity of noting the appearance of the room we had slept in. I judged it to be about 8 yards long by nearly 5 yards wide, and at one end was a passage, in which was placed a slipper-bath, a long towel on a roller, and the cess-tub. The boarding on which we had laid was divided into three partitions, each of which was supposed to provide accommodation for three vagrants. Two or three windows, strongly barred on the outside, gave a moderate light to the place. The walls were newly whitewashed, and I noticed several inscriptions written thereon in a legible hand, including the following:—

"Dirty days hath September,
April, June, and November;
From January up to May,
The rain it raineth every day;
From May again until July,
There's not a dry cloud in the sky;
All the rest have thirty-one,
Without a blessed ray of sun;
And if any of them had two-and-thirty,
They'd be just as wet and quite as dirty."

Also,

> "If I could stretch from pole to pole,
> And grasp its icy span,
> Although this is but a dirty hole,
> 'Tis better than dry scran."

"Dry scran," I was informed, meant dry bread. Amongst my companions were a tailor, aged 67, decently dressed, a compositor, also respectably attired, and a band-maker, while the remainder could scarcely be classified, except as labourers. Several of them had worked in the town on previous occasions, and on explaining myself as a native of Keighley, I was led into conversations which were remarkably interesting. Breakfast was brought in by a pauper attendant, and consisted of seven pieces of dry bread on a board, each piece weighing 8oz., one for beach vagrant. These wore placed upon the stone floor, while in a surly tone the man who brought them exclaimed, "Thear's yer Tommy." Talk about the haughty pomposity of parish beadles! It was nothing in, comparison with the attitude of the pauper as he deposited Our breakfasts upon the ground. A rusty can was then brought in, containing about two quarts of cold water, which was to serve as a drink for all of us. A strong feeling of indignation rose within me as I observed the Miserable fare, and the contemptuous manner in which it was served out. Although I was told I should need it before the day was finished, I gave my share away, whilst the others seized upon their portions eagerly and devoured them with apparent relish, more than one, though, complaining that in England vagrants were treated worse than criminals were in any other country. After a sufficient time had been allowed for breakfast, we were ordered out to perform our task work. Two were relegated to some lighter labour, whilst five, amongst whom was myself, were set to corn-grinding. We were placed in a room, consisting of but two narrow passages at right angles. Here protruding, from the wall were six wheels with handles attached, and nothing else but the dead wall was discernible. After being ordered to grind away at these, we were locked in. Some of the machines were dreadfully hard to turn, whilst others were not so bad. Fortunately mine was one of the latter, and I was very much envied by the others, when they observed how easily my wheel went round. One of the vagrants, who had been at the game before, had made the calculation that to grind the requisite four bushels of corn, it was necessary to make 8,800 turns at the wheel. He adopted the process of counting the revolutions, and every time he reached 100 he made a note of it on the wall with a pencil, and then rested himself on the wheel handle before commencing the next century. The old tailor performed his work very methodically, if rather slowly; but all were agreed they would not kill themselves with the job. The "comp," who performed next to me, was very weak, and could scarcely work his machine. The most aggravating part of the affair was that none of us could observe how much work had been accomplished. The atmosphere was very warm, and in midsummer must have been nearly stifling. Being in want of something to drink, we thrust a tin through an aperture in the window, with a request to one of the paupers to fill it with water. The tin was taken away, but no water appeared, and nearly an hour elapsed before our wants were supplied in this respect, and then only because of repeated knocks and shoutings. Drearily the hours passed until twelve o'clock, when we were liberated for dinner, consisting of thick soup, which I could not bring myself to taste. From one to five o'clock corn-grinding was again our portion; after which the night was spent much similar to the last one. I was greatly pleased: when my time expired and I was again a free man. I quickly travelled down Oakworth Road, and immediately on reaching home cast off cast off my tramp's garb for ordinary attire.

My impression of the general treatment of vagrants is that the system is much too severe. Making every allowance for the shortcomings of the class constituting them, I am of opinion that the lowest of mankind deserve better treatment than that accorded to pigs, dogs, and other animals of creation. The food furnished was scarcely fit for these last mentioned, whilst about the harsh treatment the less said the better. It is a disgrace to, any civilised country. The only redeeming feature I observed was the general cleanliness of the place. Where, I noticed anything dirty it arose from the habits of the vagrants themselves. I would not again for a substantial sum, be placed in a similar position, if I had any choice in the matter, nor shall I forget for a long time to come, my experience in the Vagrants' Ward of the Keighley Union as an "Amateur Casual."

Macclesfield, Cheshire (1888)

This visit to the Macclesfield union workhouse formed part of *A Walk through the Public Institutions of Macclesfield* published in 1888, author uncredited.[37] Later home to West Park Hospital, the main workhouse building has now been converted into apartments.

A WALK THROUGH THE MACCLESFIELD WORKHOUSE.

Entering at the main gateway, we pass the lodge occupied by the porter and taskmaster, the tramps' wards, stores for clothing, and room and offices, through the garden to the principal entrance to the house, being welcomed by a fresh-looking porter with a cheery "Good afternoon," as he hirples to close the wicket behind his visitors; he is evidently not on hid best behaviour, for as we learn subsequently he can don the politeness of a courtier on the occasion of concerts, and receives the ladies who attend with all the affability of an old-fashioned country swain. The house stands in a nearly quadrangular plot of nine acres, five of which are covered or enclosed with buildings, which comprise porter's and taskmaster's house, tramp wards, stores, clerk's office, board room, stone sheds, piggeries, new hospital, and fever hospital (unoccupied, and used as a tailor's shop, upper storey for spare beds), these being all separate and detached buildings; the main building consists of dining hall with kitchen underneath and stores at back, female wing, imbecile wards, and male wing.

The style of building is of the Tudor architectural character, and there is an appearance of solidity to the jerry builders of to-day. Over the main entrance, a clock tower rears its pinnacle, to the left is the male wing, and beyond the new hospital; to the left rear the stone breaking sheds, and at a convenient distance the piggeries. To the right is the female wing, an exact counterpart of the other, and before entering we note the gardens. With the exception of what is occupied by necessary cartways and walks the vacant ground is placed under cultivation, and there are still imbedded soil crumbling from the effects of a severe but splendid agricultural winter, remains of leeks and onions and garlic, vegetables which brought sad memories to the hearts of the children the hearts of the children of Israel as they tramped, homeless through the deserts of Arabia. Just a thin border has been devoted to flower-plants, along the route to the main entrance. On the lintel of the doorway is the legend, 1843, the year in which Mr. Frost's workmen placed that stone on its bed. A knock on the door brings an aged inmate, quite a curious old man in his way, noted, because he is over 80 years of age, for his active limbs and restless querulousness. Once inside the visitor will be immediately struck with the almost baronial appearance of the interior. A large reception hall, set about with pot shrubs and flowers, tended by inmates in their second childhood. To the left is the master's office, and the call not being expected he is busy at bis duties here. With an affability quite refreshing in a public official Mr. Potts says "certainly, you can see every nook and corner of the house now." Well; we shall see every nook and corner.

Stepping into his retiring room he introduces Mr. Needham, chairman of the House Committee, who turns out to be as intimately acquainted with "every nook and corner," and with the personal history of each inmate as the master is. The chairman of this important committee, the master explains, does not confine his visits to the official routine observed by order of the Guardians, but looks in now and again "to see that all is going right and have a chat with some of the old folks, give a word of encouragement to the youngsters, and assist in keeping an eye on the first beginnings of malpractices." "For you must know, sir," adds Mr. Potts, "we have all shades of characters here, and one cannot be too careful in observing the copybook headline: 'Evil communications corrupt good manners.'" So far, the reception of a visitor: the resident? A person having become infirm and unable to work is considered e fit subject for the Workhouse. Able-bodied men, unless past the prime of life, find no resting-place here. As a rule, the fit subjects for residence within these comfortable walls are people whose friends are also struggling — sometimes successfully — to keep the wolf from the door, and who, even if out-of-door relief were afforded, would be not one whit better off than outcasts.

In answer to the query, "How do people obtain admission?" Mr. Potts explains that a person in destitute circumstances makes his or her wants known to one of the relieving officers, or more frequently to a member of the Board. The officer having visited the applicant and satisfied himself the report is genuine, warns him or her, as the case may be, to attend before the Guardians at their next meeting on Tuesday morning, frequently at the same time granting some temporary assistance. Having considered the facts of the case as reported by the officer, and satisfied themselves from personal inquiry, the Guardians, we will suppose, grant an order for the Workhouse. As a rule, this is the last form of relief a poor person will accept, but it must be submitted to in certain instances. The necessary order having been secured, the holder presents his or herself at the House, and the first ordeal is the bath. In the case of Macclesfield the contents of the bath tub are not "like mutton broth." The capacities of the House boilers and apparatus are such as to afford continuous and ample hot plunge baths during twenty-four hours per day; the town is blessed in having a splendid water supply at all seasons of the year. Next a suit of clothes is provided, and a cot or bed found in a particular department or flat. The new comer's name and age are duly entered in a book kept for that purpose, with date and hour of arrival and admission. Now, he or she is under well-defined *régime*, from which, however, there are many, many gentle digressions; the Master and his underlings, acting under the instructions of the Board — instructions founded on long and well-tried experience as we have already seen — being to their faults a little blind.

It has often been said with an effrontery begotten of ignorance that a Workhouse is little better than a prison. There are even those who aver the food of a prison is superior to that in the Workhouse, and their reason is, the prisoners receive more pounds weight of solid food than Workhouse inmates. But the reason for this is not far to seek. Prisoners are a strong, able-bodied class of men on the average; paupers in a Workhouse are infirm and weak, to whom great quantities of solid food would prove more injurious than nutritious.

Our cicerone first introduces us to the dining-room up a few steps, and at the further side of the entrance hall from the main door. The wood of these steps and the floor of the spacious apartment are of pitch pine, kept in a pretty fair state of polish, and the woodwork of the walls and open roof, where not "the worse for the wear," have a rich and warm tone. The walls immediately inside the door are decorated with frescoes containing the Decalogue, the Apostles' Creed, the Lord's Prayer, encircled in floriate borders, the work of a pauper, a native of Macclesfield. On the walls depend framed full-size woodcuts and oleographs from the illustrated newspapers, and a few which have been presented by warm-hearted friends of the poor. There are mottoes, "No cross, no crown," &c., displayed at convenient spots, and, astounding as it may appear, these are all the work of old men who, past labouring for their daily bread, have been forced to seek a refuge within these kindly walls, and just as they had-a-mind, pottered away at their life-long occupation, and have left, some of them — for there are a few of these workers still alive

— these silent but eloquent memorials of the peace and quiet in which their declining days were spent in the Macclesfield Workhouse. The dining hall, as we shall see in other apartments, is free from that excess of whitewash so prevalent and overpowering in many other institutions of the class. Variety of colour lends a well-intentioned cheerfulness to the surroundings, the windows filled with flowering plants and shrubs, the walls studded with pictures, and the rich graining of the wood combine to produce an apartment much after the style of the servants' hall at some rich man's mansion. Emerging, the first apartment to which our nimble guide directs his steps is on the left of the dining hall.

In this warm room are busy at work a number of infirm women, who do the knitting, darning, and make clothes for the female inmates. Their happy "good afternoon," as the party enter, betokens pleasure in their occupation. Conversation with one elicits that she has not been up stairs of any kind for — she does not remember the number of years; she is only "79 years past now, she is sure," but she is very stiff in her limbs. At work upon a pair of men's stockings, without spectacles, she is by no means the worst-looking in the company. They don't chatter much, she says, and just work when they are not weary. Not being able to walk, some being past feeding themselves chiefly from paralysis or palsy, they are victualled here, and pauper nurses wait on, them with the tenderness of daughters. Between each window bas been hung a neatly-framed picture — the subjects are promiscuous and various — which relieves the monotony of the dead walls.

Next we visit the children's day-room — where bright little cherubs, dressed with faultless cleanliness, are disporting themselves with toys, or playing at games. The day, though dry without, is cold, so nurse thinks it better to keep her twenty-seven little charges indoors. They are bright and healthy-looking — from mewling and puking babes to romping girls of four or five years; even these little tots bid the visitor "Good afternoon," and have learned to reply "Quite well, I thank you, sir." Their cots, are, of course, railed in, and we are shown the very interesting process of preparing their food, according to the most approved maternity hospital rules and data. Then we see the nursing room where the children sleep, the girls' dormitory, and a playroom where they can have games, and amuse themselves when the weather is wet. Girls who have come to such ages as twelve and thirteen are put to useful kinds of employment.

As in the room for infirm women, we see another apartment used as a school in which young maids are taught the "three R's" as well aa knitting, darning, mending women's garments, or making articles of textile natures for use in the House. Other women are washing, the operation being carried on in the old-fashioned style, but the modern wringer turned by a small engine has displaced the severe twisting powers of dames of forty years ago. There are smoothing irons, Italian irons, and other irons in use, and the laundry work keeps some eighteen to twenty women, who cannot be put to other occupations, employed doing a pretty steady turn.

Passing from the main building into the imbecile wards, one not informed of the fact would scarcely guess that these elderly dames, cleanly clad, but evidently doing nothing, more bereft of reason or practically headless so far as will or energy are concerned. This is a part of the House which is practically shut off from all others, having an airing yard, in which a few flowers even at this early day are budding und blooming to delight the eyes and impaired senses of those who may care to wander out. One is pointed out as the "oldest inhabitant." She came from the original workhouse in Waters-green. How long she had been an inmate there no one knows, and she has never left the precincts of the ward or airing yard since her removal hither. The nurse puts her age at 84, as her own nearest guess, but it is evidently inaccurate. There are others of the came class, but this subject is particularly attractive from the fresh colour of her face and the nattiness of her attire.

Close by this ward is a padded room, which though its existence is enjoined by the Lunacy Commissioners, is happily never required for use. In this building is a children's sick ward and a ward for sick imbeciles.

We have now walked through the female side of the House: the male half is its exact counterpart. Following our guide through its various rooms we find less to interest than in the female division. One man in the department for bedridden men is pointed out as wonderful fellow. He is 93 years of age and was a silk weaver. Annually, in summer time, he tramped off to Scotland selling the product of his looms at farmhouses on the way. When his silk wares had been disposed of, he retraced his steps, and for over 60 years this went on with the regularity of the sun in his annual course. But there came a day when our old friend could not undertake the homeward journey; he broke down on the road, and reached Macclesfield only through assistance. He has many racy tales to tell of helps received by the way, of stirring events on which he was an outside onlooker, but his speech is broken and his articulation difficult, and only his nurse and the master can appreciate the full humour of his jokes. Four years ago, after having been several years bedfast, ho resolved to make one last effort to see Scotland again. He applied to be discharged from the House, end his discharge was prepared and handed to him. The spirit was willing but the flesh is weak, and he is still in Macclesfield Workhouse laying plans for bis next summer's journey.

In the old men's day-room, which is next in order, there are several talkative patriarchs of over 88 to 94, moving about like animated mummies Some of them, whose weazened faces betoken their having spent a hard life. Yet they play draughts, backgammon, and other easy games, and have plenty of newspapers to read between the intervals of telling their old world stories. Among them there still moves about old Norbury, once of Sutton, who was "90 four years ago," and he is anxious to buttonhole his visitors because he does not find appreciative listeners "among such old folks as these," little dreaming that he is the oldest, and might easily take the cake for garrulity. The boys are at school, except some few who are sick when we walk through their day-room.

So the school claims next attention. In an airy, clean apartment 41 boys are busy at their lessons. The curriculum begins with divine worship in the morning and then the "three R's." At certain periods of the day those who are old enough are drafted off to the tailors' shop, there to learn the trade which contests with gardening the honour of being the first practised by the hands of man, aye, or of woman either.

The boys' day-room is the last we visit before walking over to the new hospital, which was built in 1879, and in which there were 50 patients, under the charge of a staff at whose head is a very careful and painstaking nurse. For the most part the inmates of these two wards are old people, who, as might be expected, are as easily upset or laid on one side as the merest infant. Above the clean white coverlet some little old faces peep, and but for the motion of the eyelids the visitor would believe he was looking on rows of corpses laid out for burial. Some are in one week and out the next, they come and go as the weather affects their spirits or special ailments, and their little idiosyncrasies must be attended to, for who so querulous as an ailing old man or woman. Our attention is drawn to one patient from Poynton, 83 years of age, whose wife, the companion of his joys and sorrows for nearly sixty years, died four years ago, and in mercy — it may be mistaken tenderness — the event has never been communicated to him. She had for a number of years been in receipt of outdoor relief, and could not come to see him ere she passed away. He lives on happy in the thought he shall meet his first love hereafter; he has no hope of ever leaving the Hospital to embrace her on this side the grave. It gives rise to curious reflections on the changes which time and circumstances effect, to be told as we emerge from the hospital, that seven years ago this comfortable building was only a shed, and that since its completion as an hospital it has never been either empty or completely filled.

As we leave the hospital a gang of strong-looking men of ages apparently ranging from forty-five years to fifty-five or sixty pass. They are engaged in occupations connected with the internal economy of the house. Many of them have been silk weavers, and temporary distress has driven them to this haven. Stone-breaking is the employment usually allocated to the ordinary inmate who is under 60 years, and those who cannot be set to this are told off for oakum picking. Our weaver has no such manual labour awarded him. Some Guardians, whose hearts are as tender as their judgment is inaccurate, believe if a silk weaver is put to stone-breaking, he is for ever after rendered incompetent for his own trade. Carrying out this belief, other kinds of works are found for such as have been silk hands, such as potato peeling, washing up, and other necessary occupations in and around the house.

Having completed a full tour of the main building, the party step over to the stone shed where the able-bodied are at work. Many of these do not sojourn in the house; work is found them by the Guardians, and what they earn they are paid, some making as much as 9s and 10s a week. In consequence of their being unskilled, — even stone-breaking requires a certain amount of technical education — their wages do not reach more. Stone-breakers in the employment of the Highway Board, Mr. Needham says, make from 18s to 22s a week, at a price very little above that paid by the Guardians. The cause of this striking difference is that the labour is new to them, and the toil, if not hard, is painful. Half a ton of stone is not, ordinarily, a good day's work, some of the men say; one breaks easily 15 to 16 cwt., and is paid proportionately high. Stone-breaking is in no sense a "test," for a man out of his usual occupation is simply set to this work — the only remunerative employment they can give him — by the authorities. What he earns he is paid, and he may dispose of his wages as pleases himself best. Usually, only men with families are set on to this work, the single-minded tramp has his supper of gruel, is housed for the night, gets a "hunk" of bread and gruel in the morning, and having broken as many stones as pay for the eatables, he is passed on his way, generally murmuring.

When these matters have been noted and explained by Mr. Potts, six o'clock arrives, and an adjournment is made to the parlour whence we started. A cup of refreshing tea invigorates after this panoramic walk, and while indulging the innocent liquor, the Master imparts the information that the routine of the House for those who are well and able to be about is 6 45a.m., out of bed; 7 30 to 8 o'clock breakfast; dinner, 12 to 1, noon; and six o'clock, when all labour ceases, supper. After which repose, and at 9 p.m. bed. Reckoning up the people seen on our walk, it will be found there are 79 old women and 90 old men; 21 washers, 22 sewers and knitters, 12 scrubbers, 12 assisting women, 4 in the kitchen, 4 in the nursery, 4 stocking darners. The girls are taught sewing, knitting, plain cooking, washing and ordinary laundry work; so that they may, if they choose, and opportunity offers, accept situations es domestic servants, or take themselves off to other occupations where their abilities in these branches of domestic economy are valuable. There is necessarily a greater diversity of occupation among the males. Two are joiners, 1 slater, 1 upholsterer, 1 blacksmith, 3 assist the porter with the tramps, 6 men attend the boilers, 3 attend the stoneshed men, 4 whitewashers, I attend the pigs, 2 look after sanitary matters, 1 regulates the coal supply, 13 are potato peelers, 1 messenger, 26 ward men and 2 doorkeepers, and 12 boys are at work in the tailor's shop.

Setting out with an old domicile capable of sleeping 230, the Board has now a House in which there is room for 500, and the average number of inmates now is about 360. On the night of our visit, 346, exclusive of officers and tramps, went to bed under the Workhouse roofs.

It is now half-past six o'clock, and the tramps are beginning to arrive. On our way out to see these gentry, we deviate to inspect the pigs. Several well-fed porkers are busy guzzling messes prepared from the food unused in the House. Each inmate has a certain allowance for a meal, and with rare exceptions this is ample; in many cases it is occasionally too profuse. With the fragments, which are carefully collected that nothing be lost, the pigs are for the most part fed, and like the inmates of the House they thrive on their supplies. When ready for the butcher, these animals are sold and the cash received placed to the credit of the ratepayers.

Opportunity, it should be mentioned, is given every Tuesday for all who have anything to com-plain of, to lay their grievances before the House Committee. In ninety-nine cases out of the hundred, the old people are the most frequent grumblers, and as may well be imagined the lazy make up the percentage. The majority of the presentments are of a really frivolous nature, and in default of satisfaction being obtained at the hands of the committee there is always the Local Government Board to fall back upon. As matter of fact, only one case has come up during the past year, and that complaint was by a man who had a glass of medicine given to him to cure slothful and dirty habits.

The tramps as a rule begin to turn up at dusk — from six to eight o'clock is the hour for admission. There are no "qualifications" required of the wayfarer farther than to be homeless, penniless, and without other shelter. He is asked his name, age, nationality, trade (if he has any), where he slept last night, and his destination on the morrow. In a book kept by the lodgekeeper for that purpose, his answers are recorded. Your tramp is next walked off to the bathroom, where he is well soused in tepid water with plenty of soap in solution, a liquid which, within a very few minutes, assumes the "mutton-broth" hue attributed to it by the "amateur casual."[38] The tramp's clothes are returned to him, and he is next supplied with a pint of gruel and a piece of bread. The gruel is a savoury drink, made not merely from meal and water, but partaking largely of the qualities of soup-stock and oatmeal, a mixture at once strengthening and warming. Next he is handed a rug and conducted to his cell for the night. These "cells" are boxes partitioned off from one another in the tramp ward. Women and children are not thus secluded from one another, but enjoy the luxury of an open apartment, in the fireplace of which a huge fire blazes. Both wards are heated with hot water besides.

When the reveille bell sounds next day, the men, having been supplied with a repetition of the bill-of-fare for supper, are marched off to the stone shed, where each must break 5 cwt. of stone. This occupies till about 11 a.m., when each is at liberty to go. Ninety per cent. of these wanderers are professionals who live by the way daring the day, sleeping in strawyards and barns when they have money to buy food, and driven only from stress of weather and want to the tramp ward. In a matter of police the tramp record is most valuable, as it enables the authorities readily to hunt down those who, when opportunity offers, pick up "unconsidered trifles" about country houses, farms, and cottages, and leaves traces of others who "bully" unprotected children and women in order to obtain alms.

About 10 per cent. of the tramps are novices, men who, out of work, are moving from place to place "looking for a job." To such indulgence is shown; they are really in distress, and are allowed to depart as soon as breakfast is over and without the stone-breaking task. Mr. Potts assures us the professional is easy distinguishable, and on comparing notes of four who have passed in, it certainly is true; three have come from Stockport and are making for Stoke, the fourth is on his way from Yarmouth to Liverpool. Women are employed in cleaning up and other domestic duties; if they are too numerous a selection is made. Those who have been longest on the road are put to house work, cleaning up, &c; the "old 'uns" pick oakum. We are at the gates as the affable manager imparts this last information, and bidding him good afternoon, we too pass away grounded in the belief, that on people overtaken by misfortune and helplessness the money of the ratepayers is well spent, and with a due regard for the present and future interests of the poor and needy.

St Pancras, London (1889)

Although published in 1889, Mary de Morgan's 'Recollections of a London Workhouse Forty Years Ago' could be said to be out of sequence in this chronologically ordered collection as it records the author's memories of a visit paid to London's St Pancras workhouse in around 1850.[39]

Seeing the building from the road no one would have guessed what was its internal condition. Only the high walls and bolted doors recalled the idea of a prison. There was a flower garden before it which was cultivated by able-bodied paupers for the use of the Master and Matron. The Infirmary wards were approached by a door on the right, which opened into a paved yard surrounded by high walls. This had to be crossed to enter the Infirmary, the visitor passing through a number of idiotic, epileptic and lunatic women and girls, all harmless, but distressing objects, especially some of the girls, who caught hold of the visitor's dress and clamoured either for sweets, or to be let out. Among these one often met with poor women afflicted with different forms of disease and distortion. The gibbering and loud quarrelling of these poor creatures, who had no chance of recovery or release, made it a real *Inferno* — "Whoso entered there, left all hope behind."

As I now write of what I saw nearly forty years ago, I cannot profess to describe with any accuracy the form of the workhouse, or the position of the wards relatively to each other. I can only tell of those sad scenes by which my memory was most strongly impressed, and which I hope are now even more modified than they were soon after the work of the new Guardians and their friends began.

The men, as I remember the place, occupied wards on the left side, the women on the right of the building, but this arrangement was not carried throughout. We used to meet the poor, aged, and infirm people, generally the women, wandering about the dreary stone passages and corridors, and in answer to a word of greeting we were always met by a sad history of hardships and privations, generally not without foundation, especially in the matter of food. This was a real trouble to the old and infirm, who could not eat the very hard boiled beef, of the coarsest fibre, which was given to them three or four times a week. On the alternate days they had the liquor in which these "stickings of beef" had been boiled, though with the addition of a few peas. It was indescribably bad. These troubles, and many more, might have been remedied at no expense except a little good feeling and practical thought.

The patients in the sick wards seemed to me to be in a less pitiable case than the aged and infirm, especially after the overhauling of the whole establishment, for then the sick people were more carefully nursed. And the doctor was appointed with a view to his real merits and fitness for the task. Moreover, a large number of the nurses in the Infirmary were *paid*, while in the old people's wards the attendants were inmates of the House — aged people, often partly blind or deaf, and glad to get gin or brandy whenever they could. No one who has seen much of the monotonous wards and dreary stone corridors of a workhouse can wonder at the craving for drink which prevails throughout the whole place. If I am wrong in saying this *is* the case, I trust my readers will correct me. That it *was* the case in my time I am certain. I hope that the beneficent work of the ladies' committee and the efforts of many excellent chaplains may have done much to remedy it, but where a rigid classification prevails, and all the old men are put together, and the old women, too, shut in their own wards, and no intermixing such as takes place in happier grades of society, allowed, the want of variety and of interest, and the exceeding dreariness of life which falls to the lot of the aged poor in a workhouse form a very sufficient excuse for the longing for any kind of stimulus. I do not see how the exceeding monotony, which is the fruit of the rigid classification insisted on, can be prevented, except by the constant attention and care of the educated and benevolent, who can read and talk to these unhappy people, for they cannot generally read, and their surroundings are not productive of new or cheerful thoughts. It is difficult to imagine what system can take the place of the strict classification now generally supposed to be the best arrangement. But it is very different from what we see around us in nature or social lift, in which the division into families is the work of the highest wisdom, and in which, as education and culture prevail, the distinct lines of separation between classes fade away.

With reference to separation and classification, I thought the old lying-in ward one of the most objectionable. It was extensive, but low pitched, and packed full of beds far too near each other. I knew of outbreaks of fever in this ward, which would have been far less likely to take place if the patients had occupied four or five smaller rooms instead of one large one Here, too, there was no attempt at discrimination of the characters of the women, the most worthless being placed in near proximity to the decent married ones, who were often, I found, distressed and harassed by the language of their neighbours.

In the children's ward we found a melancholy instance of the want of thought which was more or less apparent everywhere. This ward contained between twenty and thirty children, the youngest unable to run alone. The older ones four of five years of age. These poor little things presented a melancholy appearance, every one without exception having ophthalmia. "They catch it as soon as they are brought in," we were told; but when I asked why the healthy were placed among those already affected, I got a very unsatisfactory reply.

The ward in which the boys slept was in a terrible state. The atmosphere of the whole house was bad, except where opened windows of doors admitted the air, which came in sometimes too strongly for the old and rheumatic. But the boys' ward is difficult to describe in plain language. It contained no furniture of any kind except the forty small beds, which were placed very near together and filled one side of the room. They were scantily covered and far from clean; moreover, there was not a bed for each boy. The total absence of all accommodation, such as is usually found in bedrooms, was supplied by an open gutter running along the side of the room opposite to the beds, and terminating at one end in a drain connected with a large pipe outside the building. It was the sewer gas arising from this arrangement which made the air of the ward unfit to breathe. There was no convenience for washing, nor any bath or basin whatever.

The lunatic wards were crowded to a degree which was quite needless, and which would not have taken place if the order for removal of the patients to the County Lunatic Asylum at the earliest period possible after their reception in the House had been attended to. The head physician of the Colney Hatch Asylum told me that nearly half of the cases sent from the workhouses might be cured if taken in time, before the insanity was quite confirmed. The old lunatic wards in St. Pancras did not afford a chance of recovery, from the crowding together of large numbers of these afflicted creatures, and the certainty of increasing their malady by the constant irritation produced by being together in a condition of nervous excitement. This evil was in some degree amended when the new Infirmary was completed. The worst patients were removed at once to the County Asylum, and there was more space for those who remained. Still there was and is room for great improvement, as there must always be when many insane patients are kept in too close proximity. Perhaps nothing can convey a better idea of the dirty, neglected, and miserable state of the aged poor and sick at St. Pancras Workhouse, as I first saw it, than the following fact. When the new Infirmary was completed, the beds and bedding had to be removed into die new wards. It was intended to wash such of the sheets and blankets as were not worn out. But this was found to be impossible; so a large fire was made in a yard behind the house, and the blankets, sheets, and much of the bedding were burnt at midnight. On questioning the pauper nurses who had been the only attendants on the infirm and sick, we found, by comparing their evidence, that these sheets and blankets had not been changed for sixteen weeks, and some of the blankets for even a longer time.

Almost all the associations about the workhouse were sorrowful or gloomy. This need not be so in the case of those poor old people who enter there by no fault of their own, or in that of the destitute children. Ail

136

these last have been better cared for since the formation of the District Schools, on leaving which for service the girls are well looked alter by the Association for Befriending Young Servants, first projected by Mrs, Nassau Senior, the first and, I believe, the only woman Inspector of Workhouses. But many of these girls, who are too old or otherwise ineligible for the schools, still alternate between the streets and the workhouse, and seemingly hopeless as is the task of trying to improve their condition, it has more chance of being well executed by a mixed body of men and women than if treated by men alone.

I may add one little recollection to those already given. There is a good-sized hall containing an organ, and used as a chapel when wanted; at other times for a workroom. It was held to be a privilege to get into this room and do needlework. I was told "it was so beautiful and light. There were plants there, and you could see the trees in the garden from the windows." So one day I went in. There was cutting out and tacking going on by some, and sewing by others. The material was a coarse, stiff calico, and I asked an old woman what they were all making. "Shrouds," was the answer; "we've been at them all this week. There's a many wanted now. We shall want them ourselves soon." This was true enough, but not cheerful; neither was the work of the carpenter, who was sawing and planing in a shed, while two or three lads, supposed to be helping him, were looking on while he made a rough shell or coffin. I found that this "joiner's" work comprised nearly all the carpentering taught in the House.

The condition of things of which the foregoing is the slightest possible sketch, given chiefly from memory, prevailed in a large London workhouse many years ago, and, as far as I could learn, many workhouses and unions were then not much better. But they are certainly improving, possibly owing to the share taken by ladies in visiting them. And, whether in the way of procuring comforts for the sick and aged, showing kindness and care for girls, little children, and babies, or that quick detection of growing abuses which women are so much more ready than men to perceive and correct, it cannot be questioned that the work and thought of some women on a Board of Guardians will add greatly to the efficiency of the body.

It often struck me, when trying to suggest improvements at St. Pancras, that such suggestions would be better understood and carried out if the Master of the House were, like the governors of our prisons and lunatic asylums, a man of some education and culture. We have physicians at the head of our lunatic asylums, and officers of the army over our large prisons. The whole control and management of a workhouse, containing many hundred people of different ages, characters, and conditions, surely demand as much intellectual and moral power as is required for the management of a prison or an asylum, and not less urgent is the need of an educated woman as matron over these mixed populations, which, whether large or small, call everywhere for skilful management, and kindly yet firm and sympathetic control.

St Pancras (Streatham), London (1889)

'Workhouse Worries', by Rev. Frederick Hastings, describes St Anne's Home, the St Pancras branch workhouse at Streatham Hill.[40] The elegant building was erected in 1829 by the Royal Asylum of St Anne's Society to house and educate poor children. Pullman Court flats now occupy the site.

In rough brown cloth with brass buttons, and lightish corduroy trousers, kerchief of whitely-spotted blue around the neck, and with low felt hat in hand, an old man stood in the passage-way. I did not recognise him at first under his altered aspect, but soon remembered where I had first seen him as a tradesman in a busy thoroughfare.

When, after his failure, I first saw him under the brown and brass, he was walking out of the workhouse chapel, at the close of a service, and put out his hand to clasp mine. I had not known of his ruin, as he had not been one of my flock. A half-crown I then slipped into his palm brought tears to his eyes. He told me afterwards he had for months been without money, and he could hardly believe that he was so rich in possessing that bit of silver. Poor old gentleman! When he gets his card of leave, he comes ever and anon to get me to repeat the dose. He had been removed from St. Pancras workhouse over to the costly new branch of that institution at Streatham. He walked this morning all the way from that place to Camden Town in order to see me. As I looked at the bulky form and short limbs, and thought of the long walk, I could not but feel still deeper pity for the Old man. I was glad to be at home, that he might not be disappointed in his hope.

138

The story of his life may be briefly told. The lease of his business place had run out. He had been promised renewal of it, but when he thought it was all settled, he found that a publican had offered twice as much as it was agreed he should pay for the place. The publican wished to increase the accommodation and attractiveness of his place of temptation. The old tradesman could not raise the extra amount. He had to clear out, and to take another small place at a great disadvantage. Here, alas! he did not succeed. He then obtained for a time a situation, but soon found a younger man was required. Thus he drifted to the workhouse. As he sits in my study he makes me realise something of what life in the workhouse must be to a man who wears the uniform of the brown and brass.

It is one thing to go and address a congregation half of men in this brown uniform, and the other half of women in the white cap, small reddish plaid shawl, and blue cotton gown, and quite another thing to live among them, or to have to be one of them. As the old man tells me of his daily life. I get a clearer conception of the worries under the workhouse garb.

"We get up at half-past six; breakfast at seven," says the old man. "Half-past seven we come out of the dining-hall. Our breakfast consists of tea and five ounces of bread and butter. We have dinner at twelve. About eleven I generally feel very hungry, so I eat a bit of bread and butter which I save from my breakfast allowance. You are not supposed to take away anything you can't eat, but the officials kindly wink at the action of us old men. Dinner is a pint of soup and bread. Of course we get tired of having the same regulation diet. I very rarely take all my soup. We get a bit of meat on Tuesday. It is steamed. We often get a great deal of bone, for it weighs in. The potatoes are nice. On Wednesday we have soup again. On Thursday Irish stew, which is still soup, with a little potatoes and meat added. On Friday we have meat again, and on Saturday one pound of suet pudding, with treacle, but no soup or meat. On Sunday we have bacon and greens and potatoes." The old man's eyes glistened as he spoke of the added delicacy of the cabbage.

"We have tea at five, with bread and butter. The men who are in for a short time get skilly instead of tea, which is only for the regulars. The short-timers have their skilly with salt in another hall. We have to pick oakum, and if we don't do our right amount we are put on bread and water. Between breakfast and dinner some go into the oakum shed, others go to tailoring or boot repairing. The place in which we dwell is really a beautiful mansion, but I cannot be happy there. One not only thinks of his past losses, but has to be too jealous about one's comrades. Some are very greedy, and we have to 'come the old soldier' and hide things. I used to go to church, but some would sneer and say, 'Here comes one of the chaplain's pupils!' The regular chaplain comes round and speaks kindly to us all, but some don't seem to appreciate his kindness as they should.

"I sleep in a ward with about forty men. Some of them snore terribly. When they do so, the next-door neighbour will catch hold of their clothes and pull them off, and at this there will be some hard words muttered. You can go to bed directly after tea. Those wake up the earliest who go soonest to bed, but they are not allowed to leave the ward. At five they will be seated on the edge of their beds, ready for a leap, and will rush like a lot of wild racehorses down-stairs directly the signal is given. Officers try to stop us from being aroused. If any attempt to go down before time, they have their cards taken away for a month, or perhaps three. If it is taken away, it takes three months to get another.

"We go to bed at eight o'clock, and some get tired of bed. The officers come round at half-past eight, and turn the gas low: they keep it burning all night. . . . Very few persons have been ill since we have been at the new place. Most of them are aged men. They are not too affable. If in the grounds you take the seat of one of them, he takes you by the collar of your coat, and out you come in no time. Places to which they have been accustomed they regard as their own. Why, I have had that seat nineteen years, and you have only just come into the house: how dare you take it' said one of my fellows to a new-comer to old St. Pancras one day in my hearing. The persons who complain of the workhouse authorities are persons who are the most undeserving. The master over the wall said to me one day, 'Here's some plums: some of my own growing.' I took them, but it soon went over the whole building. I gave one each to the men as far as they would go, and then the mean grumblers only said, 'Can't you get any more?' Jealousy is our great bother.

"When you come out you have to ask the master for leave. You hand him your card, and he puts his initials on it. Directly some get out, they will go among their friends. They get asked to drink, and so eager are they, that they will almost 'bite the beer.' They know the public-houses where their friends go, and some find them out to get treated.

"I have to pick oakum all the afternoon; I cannot do much. After tea we walk, or lounge, or go to the service. We have no prayers regular, only on

140

Wednesday and once on Sunday. Sometimes ladies come on Sunday evening and sing, and bring tracts, and give us a little talk before the regular service. One lady has more and more people to listen to her each time she comes. I saw one man crying like a child — and not crocodile tears, sir. They don't know the good that a little human sympathy does to us poor cast-off hulks. We used to have an entertainment in St. Pancras, but we get none now. Sometimes we hear the music of the Salvation Army, and that is a pleasure to us for a time, as it passes; and even they don't know the cheer they give us poor fellows inside.

"When we are out some of the people look at us as if we were carrion. Some of the residents think our place lets down the value of their property.

"I got new clothes when I left the old workhouse. I thought I should get a better fit in the old workhouse than in the new. You see, sir, there's pride in the cobbler's dog yet." The old man tipped his hat, and lifted his eye, and looked somewhat like his old self.

"A parcel of young fellows are there who are strong, but won't work. They will go out and get a drop of beer, and back they come again. They have always lived in the workhouse, were born there, and have grown up there, and some of them will say, 'We would not go out of the workhouse for a pension.' They don't care so long as they can eat and drink and sleep; they are happy at other people's expense. When asleep, they won't be disturbed if possible. If you wake me up again I'll punch your head,' said one to me when I nudged him to tell him a friend wanted him. It pains me to see how greedy some are. One man often has three men's dinners, for some are too old to eat much. That man keeps back generally, and peeps into every vessel to see if anything is left. He will drink up that which is left by the others. Another will always finish early, and be on the lookout for that which another can't eat. This is not because he doesn't get enough, but it is only gluttony. But there, sir, one has to live among such and make the best of it. It do seem hard after my life as a tradesman to find I have to be shut up with some of them. Still. I am thankful I have such a place to rest in instead of wandering — dirty, hungry, shelterless — through the streets of this great city."

I knew the old man was a teetotaller, and so I could trust him not to go and get intoxicated with that which was given him. Lunch was just on the table, and I asked him to come in and have some. He looked at me unbelievingly, and then said, "No, sir, I can't come in to eat with you in this coat. No, sir, I am too full to eat more. The cakes were as much as I could manage." Away he went. I watched him down the square with pitying eye, mingled with some amusement at the alacrity with which stumpy legs carried a heavy body.

I have often been in the wards of various workhouses: have visited the lunatic wards, and those set apart for the aged and infirm. I have seen painful sights of men lying in cribs, because too infirm or childish to be trusted in a bed without sides up to keep them from falling out. I have talked with many, and have done my best to cheer them when taking my turn in the religious service, but I never met with any who gave me such a clear glimpse of the worries of a workhouse from the pauper's standpoint as the poor old decayed tradesman to whom I have just said "Good-bye."

The worries are not confined to the men's wards. Those old ladies who move in blue cotton dresses, with little red plaid shawls over their shoulders, white caps on when indoors, and plain straw bonnets with single ribbon when out — have their worries too. "Don't let the others see you give me anything," said one to whom I always gave a trifle; "they will be so jealous. I have to keep to myself, or I could not live. You don't know how they can talk." I could hear them, and could imagine how — , in a large ward, with little variety of things to engage their thoughts, trifles would be magnified, and every word and movement bitterly criticised. The attendants have to be very firm sometimes in suppressing the bitterness of the inmates towards one another. Ah! as you go by a great building like that in St. Pancras Road — a building with its two hundred windows beautifully arranged in bays — and as you see the placid faces of the old dames who dwell there at the public expense, you little know how much of sorrow and bitterness can be hidden beneath those cleanly white caps. And you can little imagine, also, how much of deep piety some of them possess. Here is one. She is feeble, beyond threescore and ten. She staggers almost from one place to another. A little assistance to her place brings warm blessings. "Ah, sir! I have no one to care for me now. I have buried my husband two years ago. He died in the men's ward. I have also lost nine children. Haven't a relative to wish me well, or when I die to close my eyes. It is hard to bear, but God helps me. He, too, will bring me to that world where I shall see my dear ones again."

One is thankful to know that never were the poor stranded mortals better treated in our workhouses than at present. The attendants really are very kind. Considering the trying nature of their work, in bearing with all the unattractiveness, pettiness, fretfulness, and selfishness of many who are placed under their care, they discharge their duties with an alacrity and thoughtfulness that are really delightful to witness. Those who have spare periodicals, magazines, books, and chess-boards might help to greatly lessen the worries and weariness of many of the unfortunate inmates of our workhouses by sending them. They will not know how thankful many will feel, but they may rest assured that they have done a good work.

St Marylebone, London (1889)

In 1889-90, the magazine *The Sunday at Home* published a sequence of articles under the heading 'Workhouse Life in Town and Country', all written by Mrs Emma Brewer. This description of the St Marylebone workhouse was originally printed as two separate articles.[41] The institution stood on the Marylebone Road, opposite Madame Tussaud's.

A VISIT TO ST MARYLEBONE WORKHOUSE.

Before starting on our tour of inspection, we were given many interesting facts by Mrs. Douglas, the matron, who subsequently conducted us over the whole building.

We learned that utter destitution is the only recommendation required for admittance into the workhouse, that no one is too old, too young, too wicked, or too depraved to be admitted; and once in, they cannot be turned out, nor can they be refused, however often they come back, if they present the overseer's order.

All cases are received: the old and infirm, children, lying-in cases, sick and insane. The two last, however, are passed on, one to the infirmary, the other to the asylum, except when the disease is not serious, and yields to treatment. The workhouse is certified to take in eighteen hundred inmates. Among them are representatives of many classes. Here, for example, occasionally may be seen a prince, a count, a barrister, a doctor of music. Here, too, we saw a skilful dressmaker from one of our best London houses, who had found her way to this workhouse several times — the cause, Drink. People of many nations have drifted here: French,

143

Germans, Russians, Egyptians, and Chinese, the three last speaking no word of English.

We further learned that the able-bodied women are by far the most troublesome of the inmates. As a rule they object to going out to service, but now and then will yield for the sake of the outfit. They soon get tired of a respectable way of living, behave badly, are sent away, and drift back to the house.

There are twelve female paid officers, among whom are two for the lying-in ward, one for the insane, one for the old and infirm women, including the Temporary Sick Ward (which is kept for cases of sickness occurring in the house, or for persons brought in sick by the police without notice), a laundry superintendent, a labour mistress, and a receiving officer.

Owing to the lack of a common dining-room, the work is greatly increased, for the food has to be carried to twenty-one halls and wards. One consequence of this arrangement is that it is almost an impossibility to give proper supervision to the inmates at meal times. Of course a room must be large indeed to accommodate all the inmates at one time, for this workhouse is one of the largest in London.

We commenced our inspection with the chapel, which has been fitted up in one of the wards. The Roman Catholic service is held here at eight o'clock on Sundays and on special days. The priest also attends on Fridays, and he gives his services gratuitously.

The Church of England service is held every Sunday at eleven and three o'clock, and in the evening of every day but Monday; and the wards are regularly visited by the chaplain.

The few Nonconformists are permitted to attend their places of worship on Sunday.

The chaplain has charge of a library, and supplies books to about a hundred of the inmates every week.

Fifteen ladies and gentlemen visit the aged and infirm twice in each week.

All the Roman Catholic women have been placed on the chapel floor in order to facilitate matters; but they do not like it, and would far rather be mixed up with the Protestants in the old style.

We found the beds in this ward were very clean, and arranged down the three aisles. The walls were covered with bright pictures and texts. A pleasant temperature was kept up by means of hot pipes round the rooms; and there was excellent cross-ventilation through the ceiling.

The women, who were mostly very old, were collected round the tables in the three large bow windows. They were occupied, some in reading the papers and books provided, but the majority of them were working busily at shirt-making. The shirts were beautifully made, and the matron astonished me by saying that the work done by the women for firms outside the house amounts on an average to £35 a quarter.

Two were sitting apart, making shrouds, which is the work they prefer; and one woman, an exceptionally good worker, was making an elaborate music-case.

In one ward we noticed a bright-looking old woman reading a newspaper. On asking her age, she answered —

"Only ninety-two, my dear!"

Clean sheets and pillow-cases are supplied to each bed every week, and once a year each piece of bedding is thoroughly cleansed. Nothing is forgotten for the comfort of the old people; a bag containing a brush and comb hangs at the head of every bed, together with a towel which the woman takes with her to the bath-room.

We were allowed to take a look into the sewing mistress's room at the end of the ward, which she has made pretty with her own little treasures. The dark curtains drawn in front of the bed give her a little sitting-room at the same time. She is with the women from half-past seven in the morning till twelve, all the afternoon till half-past four, and then again until eight in the evening. The receiving-officer takes charge of them at meal-times.

We noticed that the passages outside this ward were artistically painted, and heard that they had been done by an old inmate over seventy.

We went through many such wards, and were struck throughout with the cheerful content expressed in the faces of the old women, their cleanliness and neatness, the quick way in which their fingers moved, and the bright ready smile with which they greeted the matron's entrance. On every floor, and at the end of each ward, there are bath-rooms heated with stoves, lavatories, all sweet, clean, and fresh, and amply supplied with water.

We next went to the kitchen, a huge place, with quite an army of cooks busy in preparing the immense number of dinners.

Being Friday, it proved to be fish they were cooking, good fresh haddocks, and very appetising they all looked. When cooked, they were laid in rows on trays and covered with large sheets of clean white muslin to keep the steam in and preserve the heat.

Large good potatoes, cooked to perfection, were also waiting to be served, and the place was as busy, orderly, and cheerful as could be.

Parted off from the kitchen is a sort of larder where the bread is kept, all of which is made and baked in this department. It is made in rations like so many French rolls, so that, as the matron laughingly remarked, "Betsey Brown cannot say she has all the crust while Sally Smith has all the crumb, since each little loaf is exactly alike." And very good white and sweet bread it was.

We next came to the laundry, a comparatively new building, and of which the matron is very proud.

The superintendent of this department, together with all the paid officers in the house, wears a dark brown dress, white cap and apron. She has forty workers under her, selected from the more respectable of the able-bodied women who like the laundry work better than any other in the house.

All is done here by machinery, which is of the best kind. Eighty shirts, for example, can be washed in a quarter of an hour. The wringing-machine has a basket underneath to receive the clothes, which are almost dry when they fall out.

The drying-room is provided with sliding cupboards, such as we have seen in our visits to the hospitals. Every bit of linen is marked — for example, K Ward,25 — so that there is no possibility of the inmates wearing each other's clothes. We were glad to hear that every person over fifty years of age wears flannel underclothing. The delivery-room was stacked up to the ceiling with clean linen. Two thousand five hundred sheets are washed every week. From beginning to end the laundry work is excellent.

From this beautiful modern laundry, where such a vast amount of work is done daily, we stepped out into the cold air, and made our way to the old married couples' quarters.

They are on two floors — four rooms downstairs, six up. They open on to a long balcony. Each room is furnished with a double bed, a toilet table and glass, and an iron washstand furnished with a plugged basin, and hot and cold water. The matron has with her own hands made for each a scarlet night-dress bag which keeps the room neat, and looks pretty. The toilet cover is of scarlet American cloth, another of the matron's ideas, which she says can be wiped free of all dust and looks cheerful.

Bright pictures and comforting texts cover the walls, and in some cases, little ornaments stand on the mantelpiece.

All the ten rooms were alike, and the sanitary accommodation is of the best.

Attached to these rooms is a day room, where the old people may read or work, and take their meals. It possesses arm-chairs and tables, and is very comfortable.

Imagine the comfort it is to these old couples that they may make their own five o'clock tea — a privilege which they alone in the workhouse are permitted. There is a cupboard under the stairs where they keep all things for this purpose, and it is like everything in this house, clean and orderly.

The matron told us that the selection for the privilege of occupying these married couples' quarters is made with the utmost care — generally from the new-comers, as those who have been long in the house have become accustomed to the old way and like it best.

The old Paddington burial ground, on which these rooms open, has been given them for a recreation garden by the vestry, and seats are placed about so that the old folk can sit and rest.

On our way to the men's wards, we passed through the cutting-out room where the assistant matron was busy cutting and giving out work.

All the clothes used and made in the house, except the men's outer garments, are cut out by the matron and her assistant-a giant work even if it stood alone.

A bale of three hundred shirts ready cut out was standing in the room.

We came into the men's wards just as they were sitting down to the dinner we had seen in the course of preparation, and so were able to witness the cleanliness and dispatch with which it was being served.

Large trays of the smoking fish, and huge pails of potatoes stood on the tables, and two haddocks and three large potatoes were served to each person.

We were amused at the sight of a pail of melted butter being carried round and ladled out.

One blind old man made his way up to the table with his three potatoes in his hand, and complained that they were small and therefore not sufficient, and on being served with a large one extra, went back to his place satisfied. One could not help thinking of poor Oliver Twist asking for" more," and how differently his appeal was met — the two cases forming a very good illustration of the difference between old times and the present.

We come next to the dormitories. There were seventy-five beds in the first, a comb and brush bag hanging on each; and everything thoroughly clean and sweet, the beds and their coverings being also exposed to our view.

The matron said that all the paint and whitewash was house labour, and exceedingly well done it was.

On the men's side, the day room is apart from the dormitories, but wherever we went, we found the same air of cheerful comfort reigning.

We were admiring the bright pictures and engravings on the walls, which caused the matron to remark that when she and her husband (the master) came there thirty years ago, there was nothing on the bare whitewashed walls, and she well remembered the joy they both felt when Lady Radstock sent them some printed texts to hang up in the wards.

We next visited what had been the children's ward, but in which fifty able-bodied women slept now. Rather close quarters, but when the new building which is in course of erection is finished, these premises will be vacated.

We passed through what was formerly the children's garden railed off, one side for girls, and the other for boys, and into the day room where the able-bodied women were having their dinner. These are the people who give the most trouble.

Entering the men's imbecile ward, while they were at dinner, I was surprised to see them using knives and forks; they were, however, what are termed lunatic instruments. The paid officer in charge had his little room at the end of the ward, which he had made bright, and there he uses his spare moments in mechanical contrivances.

The next ward visited was that of the bedridden old women — both they and their surroundings were as clean as possible. One old woman was a great politician, and knew all about the questions of the day. She had formerly been a Scripture reader.

Another, who was as fragile as she could be, and extremely old, announced her intention of getting up and going out into the world again soon; while yet a third who had evidently enjoyed her meal, and was busily engaged folding up the little cloth which had been spread on the bed, on being spoken to by the matron repeated unceasingly: "Yer very kind to me; I'm very grateful ter ye, my dear."

Another old woman, ninety-eight years old, has been in her bed twelve years, and she has not even a scratch on her skin.

We left this ward with its pathetic sights and sounds behind us, and found ourselves in the oldest part of the whole building, and after mounting the narrow stairs, arrived at the lying-in-wards. A little babe had been born that morning. There was the weighing machine for the baby, and the wheeled chair in which when well enough the patient is taken into a second room well provided with carbonised bed and bedding. A midwife and nurse are in attendance on these patients, and the doctor visits them morning and evening.

I could not help thinking how cruel an heritage it is for a woman to bestow on her child, that of birth in a workhouse — but I comforted myself by the thought that at least a few so born had made their mark in the world.

A notice hangs up in this ward, giving the address of a lady from whom the women can seek advice and help on leaving the house. We peeped into the superintendent's quaint low ceilinged room, with a door opening on to a long stretch of leads, which made one believe oneself in a foreign southern city.

Our next visit was to the female imbecile ward — where the officer in charge was a bright, pleasant, trusty-looking girl. One could not help feeling surprised that she should have chosen such a branch of nursing, but she evidently understood it, and performed her duty well, for her patients were well cared for and quite comfortable. The day room of these patients opens on to a garden where they can sit in warm weather, and there are two padded rooms in case of violence or fits.

The superintendent has her room at the end of the ward from which she can see every one. It was in this ward we saw the superior dressmaker I mentioned before; and here too was a poor blind child eaten up with disease who had lately been brought in, and was even now, I heard, much better.

The workshops are interesting, where the able-bodied men are occupied in tailoring, carpentering, book-binding, wood-chopping, etc., each trade working under supervision.

We came next to a small room occupied by what are known as *remand boys*; that is boys accused of begging in the streets or such like, and who are to appear before a magistrate in a week or ten days.

It is far better for them to be taken care of here than to be in prison herding with bad men. There were only three on this day, and a man had charge of them.

From this I begged the matron to be so kind as to use her latch-key and take us into the casual wards, which are quite apart from the workhouse and have a separate entrance.

There is a covered shed with seats in the yard where those wanting shelter can come in at four o'clock if they please and rest until the time for opening the wards, which is at six o'clock.

If a casual has not been seen in any other casual ward in the metropolis, he or she .is kept two nights and a day and allowed to leave early in the morning.

The cells, for one person only, are clean and neat, provided with an electric bell, iron bedstead and bedding. There is a rather larger cell at the end of the passage, in case a mother and child should come in together.

For supper each casual receives a pint of gruel and six ounces of bread, after which a compulsory bath and then to bed. The water is changed for each person, the days of pea-soup baths for the poor creatures, such as the "Amateur Casual" had at Lambeth, are things of the past.

The clothes they arrive in, if wet, are dried and disinfected during the night. In the morning they are called at a quarter to seven, and receive for breakfast the same as they had for supper, gruel and bread. We saw for ourselves that both were good. Those who have to pass the day there are set to work, the women to house-cleaning or to shirt-making for the workhouse, but the superintendent said the latter was doubtful help. If incapable of either of these tasks, a woman is set to pick oakum, two pounds being the allowance for the women and four pounds for the men.

It is easy to see if the arrivals are used to this work, the untried hands are hours over their tasks, while the others get it done before the morning is over.

The dinner for the casuals is eight ounces of bread and rather less of cheese. Of course many grumble at the food, but the matron said they would most likely do that if they were fed every day on ham and chicken. We thought the store room much too small for the needs of this part of the house.

Of course everything has to be under lock and key, for among the casuals are often those of the lowest class who would not scruple to appropriate anything they saw about.

We felt very thankful that those of a better class, whom misfortune or accident had driven in, need not associate with the vicious ones as formerly. At all events each has a room to himself or herself, and can rest in peace. The superintendent of the casuals seemed very pleased that she had been allowed to add some tins of condensed milk to the stores for the babies, who are often brought in late at night when it is impossible to get fresh milk. The last thing we saw was the ambulance waggon standing in the yard ready for every emergency.

Two things impressed me greatly in going over this workhouse: the first was the large-hearted, tender sympathy shown — especially for the old and infirm — and the unceasing energy and supervision that must be exercised in order to keep everything as we found it. There was not a dirty corner in the place, and every face brightened as the matron appeared. I was extremely tired after the inspection, and yet she had been through every part of the house previous to our visit, and would do the same again in the evening!

The second thing which impressed us is the great care the master has taken for the proper classification of the inmates. To use his own words, "a well classified workhouse is a necessity to enable the guardians to deal effectually with pauperism. It affords protection to the deserving, and is a deterrent to the undeserving."

Speaking of the workhouse for a whole year the master said that not a single ounce of ale, porter, gin, whisky, or brandy had been ordered by t he medical officer, and except on Christmas Day no fermented or spirituous liquors had been consumed by the inmates.

One of the great advantages of removing the sick from the workhouse besides the direct benefit to the sick themselves, is the space secured for other purposes. It is now set apart for occupation; suitable to old men inmates. Two hundred old men, for example, whose ages vary from sixty to sixty-six, work in the wood-shed. The amount of wood leaving the house is about thirty tons a week, and the revenue realised from this department during one year is £2,764.

Thus the Marylebone institution may be taken to represent workhouse life under the most favourable conditions.

St Marylebone Infirmary, London (1889)

St Marylebone's workhouse infirmary was opened in 1881 at Rackham Street, North Kensington, one of several separate-site infirmaries established by London poor law authorities from the 1870s onwards. This account by Mrs Emma Brewer followed her articles on the St Marylebone workhouse.[42] The site is now home to the St Charles Centre for Health and Well-being.

MARYLEBONE INFIRMARY AND NURSES' HOME.

The Marylebone Infirmary is situated in the parish of North Kensington, near to Wormwood Scrubs, about half an hour's drive from the workhouse proper. It is an imposing collection of red-brick pavilions guarded by iron gates, and a porter's lodge.

The main building is on the right of the entrance and the Nurses' Home on, the left. This last was built later than the infirmary, and was opened in 1884 by Princess Christian, who, for a long time past, has thrown her whole energy and interest into the subject of nurses and nurses' homes. This special home, which is a training school for nurses, was the first of its kind attached to a poor-law infirmary, and it is carried on under the combined direction of the Nightingale and Infirmary Committees.

It is hardly a digression to state that this home affords a grand opportunity to Protestant ladies who are desirous of becoming nurses. The training obtained here is quite as extensive and varied as in any of our London hospitals; and it will probably be considered a privilege that the nurses attached to this infirmary are not required to do any housework, their duties being confined strictly to nursing. Ladies offering themselves to the infirmary are of the same class, if not of a higher, than those in the hospitals. The matron told me that, roughly speaking, she has three hundred applications in a year.

There are sixty-six nurses and probationers, whose salaries are paid by the Nightingale Fund, and twenty-four staff-nurses and five sisters in the infirmary, all of whom were trained here.

The probationers start with a salary of £10 and the gift of a uniform. After being trained for a year they, in due course, become nurses and ward-nurses in the infirmary, which means a transfer of themselves to the Local Government Board, which henceforth pays the salaries. Each one so passed on to the infirmary leaves a vacancy in the home.

About fifteen probationers are trained here yearly, and are much sought after. One is now at the Paddington Infirmary, a second at Southampton, and others in various places. It is very desirable that all corning for training should remain three years. Efficiency cannot be obtained without it.

This home is three stories high, and contains forty rooms, one of which is a large and airy sitting-room, and well fitted-up as a lecture-room.

Its chief attraction lies in its cupboard well-stocked with specimens, and containing a large lay-figure for experiments and demonstration. The table-drawers again are filled with numbered divisions, occupied by bones, for the clearer and better understanding of the lectures which are given frequently by the medical superintendent, and twice a week by the assistant matron. Here too the nurses are taught bandaging, and the position of the main arteries, and how to apply pressure for the preservation of life, which, the matron said, had been done successfully by several of them.

Whether probationer or nurse, each has a simply-furnished, clean, and airy bedroom. The only difference between one and another is in the personal belongings scattered about.

The fourteen night nurses are separated from the day nurses and probationers by a red baize door, and great care is taken not to disturb their rest which is taken between half-past eleven and seven.

There is a small sitting and bedroom, set apart for the use of any nurse or probationer who may break down in her work and require special care. Both doctor and matron said that so much depended upon the nurses, it was needful to take great care of them, for many broke down in hospitals, not because they had been reared in luxurious homes, but because they worked beyond their strength.

The dress of both nurses and probationers is a bluish grey gingham, a quaint white cap, something like the Sister Dora cap, and a brown holland apron for the nurses, and a cheque cotton for the probationers.

The home is warmed by hot-water pipes and is well ventilated; and the fire-hose in the passages simply arranged and quite easy to set in motion.

By those who have not gone into the matter thoroughly, it has been thought that trained nurses are an extra expense and mean a heavier burden on the ratepayers, but it has been proved to be quite the opposite, owing to the quicker and more thorough cure of the sick in the unions.

We now crossed the road and entered the main building through an archway. It is considered a very perfect specimen of what an infirmary should be. The cost of building, fittings, etc., was £143,000, that is to say, about £192 per bed (seven hundred and forty-four beds).

On either side of the archway is a receiving-room, one for men and the other for women, with a bath attached, where the patients, if not too ill, are bathed before inspection. These rooms are under the care of a man and his wife and are kept scrupulously clean.

We come next to the medical superintendent's office or library, an interesting room full of books and papers, among others a register of all the acute cases within the last six months, the nurses' reports, notes, and temperature charts, for to take these correctly is part of their training. These charts, taken every four hours, look so pretty with their small squares, dots, and fine lines, that they might be termed the fancy work of a nurse's occupation. On one side of this room there are several pigeon-holes for giving out papers, books, and notices for the various wards, for no nurse, under any pretence whatever, is allowed to enter either this or the dispensing room.

We next go into the steward's room, with its lining of lockers and huge tins. This officer controls all the stores, whether of food, furniture, or material.

Everything is found in the house, and everything must be accounted for: thus so many yards of calico, given from this room, must make so many garments, which, when made, must be brought here, entered, and stored till wanted.

The matron withdraws all worn out clothes two or three times a year; tells the steward how many new ones she requires, and receives them from him direct.

No nurse can obtain any article for the patients, not even food, without a written order, defining size, amount, quantity; this card, being first checked off in the library, is brought to the steward and entered on a large sheet neatly divided and subdivided, showing the material used, the quantity and value. This is signed by the doctor, the steward, the nurse, and the clerk. These sheets are bound up into a book and are so clearly and beautifully kept that even an unpractised eye can see the amount and cost of any special article used in a year. I never saw such clearness and neatness, except in the papers kept by the sisters of St. Vincent de Paul in the Milan hospital.

We cross the passage and pass into the kitchen — an immense place worked by a female cook and four assistants. There is only one gas-stove, all the rest being ordinary coal grates. They send out from here every day seven hundred dinners of meat, potatoes, and rice pudding, seventy fish diets — eight ounces making one diet — and hash for one block, beside a large quantity of broth and beef-tea. Breakfast and tea are prepared in the wards. The first meal is taken at seven o'clock, lunch at ten, and dinner from twelve to one, tea and bread and butter at half-past four, and supper at seven. The food is carried to the various wards on large hot-water tins, having many divisions, so that the patients get it hot and appetising.

The meat comes in fresh every morning from the market, and the bread is made and baked in the house. The oven is immense, and well it may be, for eleven sacks of flour are made up every week.

The amount of milk which comes in twice a day is sixty-nine bar gallons,[43] and it is kept in a cool pleasant dairy lined with white tiles and provided with slate shelves.

We now go to the engine-room in the basement to see the three twenty-four horse-power engines, which supply all the water used in the infirmary. The amount used daily is fifty-five thousand gallons, and it is supplied by an artesian well, five hundred and two feet deep.

From here we pass through one passage where the oil stores are kept, into another devoted to mustard, salt and such-like articles, on to a room used for the storage of household goods in the shape of brooms, brushes, pans, pails, crockery and glass. Nothing is given out but in exchange, that is to say, the old broom or brush must be brought back before a new one goes out, and if the bristles are gone, the handle must be given in, and the same with all articles required. The last room in the basement was occupied by soap, huge columns of which were stacked from floor to ceiling. It struck me as good management so to utilise all the space underground.

We next come to the laundry, a very important department, and managed with the same care and efficiency as marked the rest of the infirmary. It is worked by a head laundress, two laundry-maids and eighteen women helpers from outside. Thirty-five scrubbers are also employed in the Infirmary from seven till eleven o'clock daily.

Fourteen to fifteen thousand pieces of linen are washed here every week. The dirty linen is washed in an upper room, just under the water tower; it is then sent down a shaft to the open-air drying-ground, which occupies three sides of a square, also high up in the building, from whence one obtains a splendid and extensive view. From here it is sent down a shaft again to the mangling, ironing, and sorting rooms. When sorted it is packed into large square baskets and run on trollies to the various wards. The drying presses are on the same principles as those we are accustomed to, but they are deficient in number.

Having seen with what care and good management the necessities of the sick are considered, we proceed to the apartments of those who devote their young lives to them.

The nurses' lavatories, provided with swing basins, and hot and cold water, are excellent. Their dining-room, and that for the sisters, which is separate, are large, airy, and cheerful.

The recreation-room is a bright and pleasant apartment, looking out on a garden, and it is supplied with pictures, piano, and American organ.

Next let us look into the dispensary, which is supplied by contract. The stock mixtures, or those most generally needed, are kept in a row of neat shining barrels, each with a little white cup underneath to catch the drops. There is a small glass aquarium containing leeches; and a huge tub of linseed meal. There is one dispenser; and as no nurse is allowed inside the dispensary, a window with a sliding glass shutter is provided where medicines can be asked for and obtained.

In an inner room the laughing-gas is kept, and, here, also, in a cupboard lined with green baize, are rows upon rows of terrible looking shining surgical instruments. Beside it hangs a card, whereon can be seen at a glance, if and where any instrument has been taken for operations. Here, as elsewhere, the most perfect order prevails.

And now through the well-warmed passages we pass into one of the wards with twenty-eight beds. Noticing the quantity of flowers and plants we heard that a small sum is allowed for them, but this is supplemented out of the sisters' and nurses' own pockets, who take a pride in their wards. Last Christmas some gentleman gave ten pounds' worth to the infirmary. Pictures and engravings adorn the walls, and are the gifts of friends who take an interest in the poor.

The committee allow the daily papers and books in the wards, so we found many of the patients sitting up in bed reading, particularly on the men's side. The women were occupied for the most part with various kinds of needlework; and we were told by the matron that every garment, sheet, and pillow-case used in the infirmary is cut out and made up by the nurses and patients.

One old woman has the privilege of darning all the stockings, which she does beautifully.

Some of the men also were doing needlework, putting in gathers in a wonderful way.

It is easy to see, in passing from bed to bed, that the diseases of the people admitted here are, as a rule, of a chronic character.

In the centre of each ward is a stove with fire back and front, and a vase on the top containing water, which being warmed a slight vapour arises and moistens the air. The flues from each stove descend and pass right and left under the floors to the outer walls, in which they are continued to the chimney-shafts above the roof. It seems an exceedingly clever arrangement.

We found in each ward several pretty bright screens made by the nurses, and covered with Christmas pictures and cards.

Wheel-chairs are provided for those who cannot otherwise get about. Patients, who feel sufficiently well, are allowed to clear away the meals and help wash up in the little scullery attached to the ward. It both amuses and occupies them.

The pottery used in the infirmary is white; that for the patients has a blue badge, and that for the nurses a red one.

On each floor is a bandage-cupboard, full of the neat little rolls with which, by this time, we are familiar, and each ward has its own inventory. It has, too, its own medicine-cupboard with the POISON shelf clearly marked to prevent mistakes.

There are smaller wards for the more serious cases, containing only two or three beds, where the patients can have special attention. The male patients, who are well enough to get up, have a recreation-room, in which they can sit and read, and a garden also, where they are allowed to smoke.

The male and female wards are in all respects the same; the latter, perhaps, looked brighter, because of the red shawls wrapped round those who were sitting up. There is no special ward for the children who are scattered about among the adults. One poor little girl of twelve or thirteen, we saw, who is paralysed, and who will never be able to sit up or walk all her life.

The eye-ward was darkened with green curtains.

Lady visitors are permitted in the wards, and are a comfort to the patients. Many were looking for scripture references, and trying to find answers to questions put by the ladies in their last visit.

The women convalescents have a garden, which looked gay with the children in red hoods and the women in red shawls. They have also a dayroom, where they sit and work or read.

There is a corridor, which connects two portions of the building, over which is an open balcony, making a pleasant promenade for the old people in summer.

The chapel is a beautiful building, in which services are held both on Sunday and week days; but why it has been placed so high I cannot imagine. It is reached only by a high flight of stone steps, which to the sick and weary must indeed be a penance; it seats two hundred. The handsome lectern was given by Mr. Debenham, and the nurses subscribed for the stand to match. The chaplain attends daily, holding Bible-classes and services in the wards beside those in the chapel.

The Roman Catholics have their service in the wards.

We asked the matron as we came away if there was any special thing she needed for the inmates. Her answer was that she would be thankful for story-books in Moon's type for the blind patients.

The amount of valuable knowledge to be gained in an infirmary like this, and of a character not to be found even in hospitals, makes one sorry that medical students are not admitted as in hospitals, but perhaps this will come later.

The order, control, and discipline, which pervades every corner of this large infirmary should be a matter of deep thankfulness to the rate-payers in the metropolis. The old and the sick are cared for, neither pampered nor neglected.

Islington, London (1889)

This instalment in the 'Workhouse Life in Town and Country' series by Mrs Emma Brewer records her visit to the Islington workhouse in north London.[44] The site later became Hillside Public Assistance Institution. Only a small portion of the workhouse buildings still exist.

A VISIT TO ISLINGTON WORKHOUSE.

The Islington workhouse is an immense pile of buildings, raised from the level of the road by grass terraces and stone steps, and made pleasant to the eye by a row of young budding trees behind the handsome railing which divides the grounds from the road.

It is situate in St. John's road, Upper Holloway, in the north of London, and furnishes an example of workhouse and infirmary under the same roof.

This house contains mostly old people, the younger ones being sent on to Shadwell House, a sort of workhouse of ease to this one, which accommodates six hundred and ten inmates.

The thought repeats itself with every new workhouse we visit, that the aged and infirm inmates, more than any other people, stand in need of gentleness and tenderness, for to many of them this is their last earthly home, and one in which they must wait patiently for the Master's call to begin life once again.

I never so saw many old people together, and although it made one unhappy to see such numbers bereft of home and all that makes home lovely, yet certainly they were not miserable, nor did they give one the idea of being cast aside as useless.

All were busily engaged in work of some kind suitable to their age and capabilities.

In the large, airy day-room, many of the women were reading; some were at needlework or at the knitting-machines, for all the stockings are made here with a soft kind of fingering; while in the work-room, presided over by a paid needle-mistress, an immense amount of work was going on to the tune of sewing-machines and chatter, which gave a tone of cheerful activity to the room. The whole of the making and mending of clothes for the men and women is done here. The bedding for 1,400 inmates is made, together with several hundred articles for the school belonging to this workhouse; last year as many as seven hundred were

159

The Islington workhouse on St John's Road, Upper Holloway.

made in this room. Still further, they make clothes and bedding for the vestry to disburse to those whose property has been destroyed through infectious diseases. Last year £60 8s. 7d. was earned, in addition to all this, for needlework done for warehouses. When we think of so much being done by the old people, we are struck by the results. It is plain that age is not "useless" here.

Noticing that each person went about her work in a very capable manner, we heard that, as far as possible, they were given the same occupation as they had been accustomed to outside.

As we made our way through the spotless corridors, we enquired what provision was made for old married couples, and were very grieved to hear that while formerly they were accommodated with separate and comfortable quarters, now, owing to want of space, these have been taken back and turned into wards.

We now came to the babies' part of the house — first a small neat kitchen, then an ante-room, and next a bright sunny large day-room, liberally supplied with toys, rocking-horses, swings suspended from the ceiling, and bright pictures on the walls, presided over by a motherly paid nurse, who was occupied when we entered, sewing up an unfortunate and decrepit doll, to the great satisfaction of a little baby-girl.

All the children here were under three years old. One, a bright laughing baby-girl, was found some eighteen months ago in a corner of a locked-up deserted room, life almost extinct, and with no sign to tell who her parents are or what her name is.

At mid-day the mothers are allowed to come in and feed the babies. The food of those a little older is prepared in the matron's kitchen, and consists of mutton broth, beef tea, rice pudding and such like food.

At the age of three they are sent to the schools belonging to the workhouse, where there are four hundred children.

We next went to the ward where lunatics are kept until passed on to an asylum. The paid nurse was trained at Caterham. She told us a sad story of a woman here who had been a gentleman's nurse. He died and left her a legacy which seems to have unsettled her mind; for the first thing she did was to marry a man old enough to be her father, who wanted her money more than herself. After discovering this, she gradually grew worse till she had come down to this — a lunatic in a workhouse ward. She is most uncertain in her humours, sometimes quite quiet, and at others quite unmanageable. We found her in bed in a strait waistcoat, and she told us a long rigmarole about her early life and her future plans. Beside this woman there was quite a young girl suffering from "delirium tremens." This lunatic division of the house consists of the nurse's room, a small bright day-room, and a night ward containing seven beds. The nurse has a woman-pauper to clean the place, and to assist in managing the refractory patients. An able-bodied pauper sits up at night, beside the regular night attendant who goes round the house to see that all is right.

We now made our way upstairs to the women's dormitories, or night wards — they are large and airy but a little crowded.

The bedsteads are iron, the beds flock, and the rest of the bedding good and sufficient with warm-looking red quilts.

The night nursery is a splendid room, with a good open view from the windows, and looking so pretty with the many tiny cots covered with blue and white quilts, and the pictures on the walls. A nurse sits up here all night

A large ward is set apart for nursing mothers and babies.

The large store-room with shelves reaching to the ceiling, was amply supplied with neatly covered and folded articles. Bales of stuffs ready to be cut up lay on the long tables; and on the mantelpiece were dozens of neatly rolled bandages made here. A smaller room running out of this was stocked with men's clothes, made under the supervision of the paid tailor on the premises, and boots and shoes made by the paupers under the resident shoemaker.

We next came to the beautiful chapel, with its polished wood seats and its organ, presented by Sir James Tyler. The lectern, which is wonderfully carved, is said to have been done by a lunatic. The chaplain attends the infirmary daily, and conducts Divine service in the chapel twice on Sundays and on Wednesday afternoons.

The Roman Catholic priest also visits the infirmary daily, but the Roman Catholic inmates go out every Sunday to their service — so also do the Nonconformists.

All inmates of whatever creed, over sixty years of age can, if they will, go out on Sundays, and one week day in the month.

We passed on to the spacious dining-hall, well furnished with tables and seats, leaving an alley down the centre: one side being for men, the other for women.

Breakfast commences at half-past six in the morning: cocoa or tea, and bread and butter. Dinner is at twelve. On Sundays, Australian meat and potatoes; Monday, pea soup; Tuesday, stew; Wednesday, bacon and rice; Thursday, pea-soup; Friday, fish, and Saturday, suet pudding. Tea is at four o'clock, but the inmates provide their own tea, each putting a pinch into one of the large urns we saw in the day-room. They also provide for themselves condensed milk, and jam if they like it. Supper is at six.

As it was Tuesday, we watched the cook weighing out the stew, four or five ounces to each person. Think of the number to be provided for, viz.: 866 in the house, and 540 in the infirmary; of course it is done with the utmost rapidity. The stew was very good, and the contrivance for carrying the food about was excellent: a tin fits into another filled with hot water, and the two are placed in a square box, with lid lined with green baize, and handles and straps outside by which it can be easily carried.

The kitchen was a large busy place with huge coppers and other cooking apparatus. On the walls hung diet tables, with the names of the various wards attached, and others with the days and hours when boilers and flues were to be attended to. Joining the kitchen was the bakery. The baker and his assistant work fifteen and sixteen hours a day. The hours need not be so long if another oven were added and a little extra help given. Forty-three to forty-eight sacks of flour are made up every week.

The laundry consists of a set of rooms, high, light and airy. There are twenty-three women washers and men assistants, besides engineer, stoker, and handy-man. The machines and hot presses are all good; and we found quiet and order throughout.

From this we went to the infirmary, leaving the men's side of the house till later. Each floor is divided by a partition running down the centre of the principal corridor, the men's wards being on one side, the women's on the other. There is, as a rule, a trained nurse to each ward, under whom paupers are employed "with safety and efficiency," the master says.

The names of the wards are peculiar, viz:—

MEN'S WARDS: Abraham, Isaac, Jacob, Luke, John, Matthew, Mark, Stephen, Daniel, Samuel.

WOMEN'S WARDS: Charlotte, Rachel, Ruth, Leah, Hannah, Martha, Mary, Esther, Elizabeth, Eve (Lying-in), Sarah.

ISOLATED BLOCK — INFECTIOUS, SKIN DISEASES, ETC.
MEN'S WARD: Lazarus.
WOMEN'S WARD: Magdalen.

LUNATIC.
MEN'S WARD: Ishmael.
WOMEN'S WARD: Hagar.

I asked if there was any special reason for the names, and the master said No — he had chosen Scriptural names with one exception for they were easy to remember and pronounce.

In the Isaac ward there were thirty cases, nineteen of which wore advanced consumption.

Accidents happening outside are brought into the infirmary, though not so often as formerly, the Great Northern Hospital relieving them in this direction.

There is a very curious case of dementia here: a man who will persist that he is older than his mother, and when one tries to convince him of the contrary he is extremely angry. They not infrequently have doctors, lawyers, and clergymen in these wards, many of whom have been thus reduced by drink.

On our way to the upper floors, we looked in at what may be termed the kitchen-of-ease, where mutton broth, beef-tea and extras are prepared and served for the infirmary.

We next visited the women's wards which were made bright and pleasant with flowers, birds and plants. Tile lavatories and baths are at one and of each ward, and the nurse's sitting- and bedroom at the other.

The most depressing sight I ever saw was the lying-in ward. Most of the patients occupying the beds were domestic servants.

The old women's ward, which we next went into, was cheerful in comparison, with its red quilts and bright flowers, and spotless cleanliness. The head nurse in this ward had been trained at Guy's.

Leaving the infirmary, we made our way to the men's quarters, passing on the outside an iron staircase to be used in case of fire.

In the oakum room were about two hundred and thirty men sitting in rows, wearily picking away at the bundles of rope, reducing it to the fluffy condition in which it is used for caulking ships. Many of the faces were good and refined; and one old white-haired spectacled man was pointed out to us as having formerly been a man of property, and as having kept hunters.

We asked if it were not very hopeless work, and were told the men much preferred it to sitting and doing nothing, which is given as a punishment. When a man has behaved badly, his punishment is to sit in the master's office with him all day, to have his meals there, and be content to sit silent and idle. The master says he rarely has the same man a second time.

We now went down to the basement, every corner of which is utilised. In one part men were chopping up the preserved meat boxes for firewood, which has not been bought for a very long time. Then came the carpenter's shop, where some very beautiful work was being done under a skilful artisan.

The tailor's shop came next, pervaded by an unpleasant smell of corduroy, but the scene of cheerful industry was quite different from one's idea of workhouse life.

Another room contained a storage of rags, and men were sorting the white from the coloured, ready for sale.

Again we saw heaps of lead paper, such as is used for wrapping up tea, and asked what good they were. We learned that, as a rule, these were sold, but that lately when some of the pipes wanted repairing lead papers had been melted down by a pauper who understood the work, and had been used for the pipes.

Then came a room where the women's own clothes are kept for two years, and at the end of that time are sold.

Last, not least, was a large airy bath-room, where the women bathe, well provided with baths and towels.

Asking how much water was daily used in the house and infirmary, we learned that about 26,000 gallons was the amount.

Gas is used throughout the building.

The basement, like other parts of the house, was clean, light, and airy.

A paid bricklayer and carpenter reside on the premises.

The arrangements for casuals are exceedingly good. They are open wards with twenty-four single beds, and six double for women with babies. These beds are all provided with mattresses stuffed with cocoanut fibre, and having red woollen coverings. The allowance of food is one pint of gruel and six ounces of bread for supper, the same for breakfast, and bread and cheese for dinner.

Passing through the hall we saw a locked letter box, where the inmates put their letters for post and which is cleared five times a day. Out into a large yard we went next and saw the imbecile men walking about; and so on to the carpenter's shop, where a large amount of work is done, seeing that no outside labour is used for anything in the house and infirmary.

These buildings consist of three pavilions, and cover an area of seven and a half acres. The average expense of each pauper is 5s. a week. Paid labour consists of:— 1 superintendent nurse; 12 day nurses; 3 night nurses in infirmary; 1 night nurse in workhouse; 2 lunatic nurses; 1 nursery nurse; carpenter, bricklayer, labour-master, needle woman, assistant matron; all the rest being pauper labour. This last is undoubtedly good and efficacious, under the excellent master and matron who are now in authority, but how would it be if they were removed? Pauper labour reduces expenses, but it is only good when under close supervision.

The social questions of the great city are repeated in the workhouses. Dark and depressing as some of them are, there is yet reason to hope that the energy and charity which have effected so many improvements in these great establishments, may be enabled to answer them. The only sufficient cure for the worst evils is to be sought in individual reformation.

Shoreditch, London (1889)

> This instalment in the 'Workhouse Life in Town and Country' series by Mrs Emma Brewer records her visit to the Shoreditch workhouse.[45] The site later became St Leonard's Hospital. It is now a centre for supporting community services and health centres. Some of the old workhouse buildings survive.

ST. LEONARD'S, SHOREDITCH.

We have already seen Marylebone Workhouse in the north-west, and St. Mary's, Islington, in the north, and we proceed now to visit St. Leonard's, Shoreditch, in the east of London.

It may be remembered that this workhouse, together with its sick wards, was one of those condemned by the *Lancet* Commission; it was, therefore, with a special kind of interest we made our way thither.

It is a huge building in the Kingsland Road, in a populous parish (pop. 127,000), and is an example of workhouse and infirmary joining each other, but being under entirely different management, and having entrances in separate streets.

It is capable of holding eight hundred inmates. The day we were there, the number within its walls was seven hundred and twenty-seven; and the highest number last winter was seven hundred and ninety — the proportion of men and women being about equal.

Among them are the very old, the infirm, and the able-bodied. Those over the age of sixty, compared with those under, are as four to one, and many of those under sixty, perhaps one-half, so it seemed to us, were afflicted with physical deformity, paralysis, defective eyesight, imbecility and infirmity of some kind or other. Among the able-bodied are some who have been here for years.

The arrangements for the infirm are extremely good. Their day-rooms, dining-halls, night ward and lavatories are all on the same floors, to prevent their having fatigue in mounting steps. I speak of both sides of the house.

The women's day-room is bright with a clock, pictures, and flowers; and a number of them, some thirty or forty, were sitting there in blue gowns, white caps, and red shawls, which is the uniform of the house. On our asking how it was they had no work to do, the matron said they were mostly too infirm for any exertion, and that they liked chatting and reading books and newspapers, and that visitors came often to talk with and read to them. These are not allowed to go out, the matron remarking very justly that if they are too infirm to work they must needs be too infirm to go out into the streets alone.

Their night-ward is opposite their day-room, with a row of large windows on one side and sky-lights into the passage affording both light and ventilation. Here, again, pictures and texts brighten up the room; and everything is scrupulously clean. We looked through the beds, and found them covered with white quilts, a contrast, indeed, to a quarter of a century ago. The beds are flock. Sheets and pillow-cases are changed weekly.

The lavatory for the infirm is next door to the night-ward, and is supplied with round towels which are changed every day. When a special case occurs, such as of skin disease, or a fastidious pauper desires it, an extra and separate towel is allowed. Formerly these old people were farmed out to the infirmary; this certainly is an improvement.

On this same corridor is the officers' mess-room, neat and airy, where the assistant matron, the porter, the labour-master, the female attendant, the laundress take their meals. These, by the way, are all paid, otherwise the house is served by pauper labour.

Such of the old people as are not too infirm go out every fortnight; but, unfortunately, they often abuse their freedom by returning home drunk in the evening, in which case they are reported to the visiting committee and their liberty stopped for three months.

That which struck us as the most pleasant and noteworthy feature of this workhouse was the married couples' quarters, each couple having a room to themselves, six in the front of the house and two on the men's side. They are quite large high rooms, with a table, chairs, nice bed, a convenient little grate, and a washstand. Pictures adorn the walls, and on the mantelpiece remnants of decorations add to the brightness. These old couples are allowed tea and sugar, and have their dinner sent to them. It is considered a great privilege to inhabit one of these rooms, which struck me as some of the pleasantest I had seen.

There is here a blind-ward, fitted with green Venetian blinds, though all using it are not quite blind. As we left the ward we met a blind man going in, led by a little girl-guide. He was a frequent visitor, the matron said, and his special object was to read and talk with the sightless inmates.

The women have earned the same character here as elsewhere, that of being much more troublesome and difficult to manage than the men. The pauper children are at present farmed out; but the guardians are building new schools at Hornchurch, near Romsey, in the guise of little villas, each in its own garden, and with a chapel in the midst.

'In the nursery, well-lighted and ventilated, a fire burning in the grate, and pictures on the walls, we found eleven tiny babies, two of whose mothers only were married. On the floor were little basket-cots, which the matron considers safer than any other kind. The lying-in ward is not in the workhouse, but in the infirmary. Opposite the nursery was the lavatory, provided well with tiny baths, which, the matron said, frightened the children less than being put into large ones.

On the same floor was a night-ward, where the mothers are allowed to sleep with their children until they are two years old. They are sent to school at the age of three, unless they are very backward, in which case they are kept here until the matron considers them capable of learning.

On our way to the basement, the first room we looked into was stored with the rations of bread and butter upon the same plan as that adopted at Marylebone, viz., the half-ounce pat of butter and a roll. There was also a pail of clean, sweet dripping, an ounce of which is given out on Tuesdays and Fridays instead of butter. The paupers much prefer the butter, as they shrewdly suspect the dripping is given for the sake of economy and that they are being defrauded. The mode of making the pat of butter is ingenious. The little wooden mould having the print at the bottom, is struck into the butter and brings up exactly half an ounce and no more, with the pattern stamped on it. It looks much more appetising, and is less wasteful than a rough-hewn piece dabbed on the plate. A similar process is gone through to get the ounce of dripping, only instead of the wooden mould a piece of metal is used with a groove down the centre equal to one ounce, which it measures off accurately.

The bakery is managed by a paid superintendent and pauper-labour. Next came the room for storing flour, potatoes, rice, and oatmeal — the latter is given every morning for breakfast; and when the paupers complain of it they are easily silenced by hearing that the master takes it himself.

All the food is contracted for, and seemed to us of excellent quality. The grocery-room was well stocked.

Next came the shoe-store, well stocked with boots and shoes of all sizes; they are all handmade by men over sixty years of age, under a superintendent. Those who work in this department are allowed tea and bread and butter at three o'clock. Their work is both good and abundant; they make and mend for the house; they make the surgical boots for the infirmary, and supply the Harold Court School (100 children) with boots and shoes. Ten men were working in this room the day we saw it; as a rule there are many more shoemakers than tailors in the house, Shoreditch being essentially a shoe-making district.

We next looked into the tailors' shop, where all the clothes are made and repaired by house labour, under a paid tailor, who receives thirty shillings a week. Eight men were working here when we visited it.

Next came the painters' shop. In the carpenters' shop a good deal was going on, for the paupers execute all repairs, make furniture, cupboards, sideboards and even wardrobes.

In the blacksmiths' shop the paupers alone repair the iron and tin wares, and make cans, trays, saucepans and other articles.

From here we went to the wood-cutting, in which work above sixty men are employed. A ready sale is found for the bundles of wood, although the price charged is higher than in the outside market. During the half-year ending March, the men chopped 250,000 bundles, which were sold at 3s. 3d. a hundred to shops, and 3s. 7d. to private customers.

Some of the very old men pick a little oakum to pass the time away, but are not tasked. The oldest and most infirm of the men have no work to do, but are allowed to read or play games, and, as has been already stated, they have ward and yard separate from the others. The able-bodied men have to scrub and clean windows on the men's side of the house.

It will be seen that the work of the inmates is very varied: a great advantage where so many have to be employed. While speaking of their occupations, it must be stated that the women perform all the ordinary domestic work — including eighteen young women who are told off daily to go to the infirmary laundry. The older ones do most of the making and mending for the house and the infirmary.

Our next visit was to the laundry, which was well fitted up with all things necessary, with a good washhouse and ironing-room attached, and plenty of drying-closets. The labour employed is that of the able-bodied women paupers under a paid laundress. We remarked what a good colour the linen had, and were told that as far as possible it was dried outdoors.

And now for the kitchen. It has a glass roof and good ventilation, and capital scullery and larder attached. The head man-cook is a pauper who has never once been behind with his meals for seven years, and as his cooking is very good he is quite looked up to.

It was close upon the dinner hour. The stew, hot and savoury, was standing ready in huge pails to be taken into the large dining-hall which runs the height of the house and is really a beautiful room.

This hall is fitted up at one end with pulpit and reading-desk, and there is an organ in the gallery, for it is used also by the chaplain to hold service in.

As we entered, one side was filled with men, the other by women, all waiting to be served. These masses of paupers affect one with a sadness impossible to describe. It would be depressing enough if one of these huge buildings and its living freight represented the unsuccessful life of the whole of London; but when one remembers that it is only a gathering up of one district it is appalling.

And, now wishing the master and matron goodbye, and thanking them for their courtesy, we left the workhouse proper, and, through a long glass corridor, made our way to the door of the infirmary. We were shown into the doctor's room to await his return from the wards: it was a dreary apartment looking on to blank walls.

Dr. Forbes, the chief medical officer of this infirmary, is identified with many of the improvements which have taken place in the metropolitan infirmaries.

At the time of his appointment, the infirmary was regarded as part and parcel of the workhouse, and those who ministered to the sick wore paupers; any Sairey Gamp[46] indeed who happened to be in the workhouse was put to the task. This close intimacy between the workhouse proper and its sick-wards gave rise to grave scandals, the paupers placed in authority abusing the trust by trafficking in the food and stimulants, and levying blackmail on the patients and their friends.

On the opening of this building, in 1872, the sick-wards were entirely separated from the workhouse proper, and, in spite of opposition, the doctor succeeded in obtaining permission to replace pauper with paid trained labour.

The opposition was of course based on the ground that paid labour would add to the rates, and so increase the local burdens, while paupers were on the spot having nothing to do. Whereas, the doctor contended, it

170

would be a great saving all round to do away with pauper labour altogether, and the result proved him in the right. So beneficial was the result that the Local Government Board ordered the facts to be printed and sent round to the London Guardians.

There are now trained nurses throughout the infirmary, and permission has just been obtained to take probationers, who are to have £10 for the first year, and if then they pass the examination successfully to become assistant nurses at £17 a year. After remaining three years their salaries are to be raised one pound each year till they reach £20, when they are to become head-nurses, with an increasing salary till it reaches £26.

This infirmary is really the hospital of the district. It is certified for 472 patients, but has just now only 430; but during the year 2248 cases were treated here, and 2738 in the workhouse which were not sufficiently serious to need being brought into the infirmary.

Three hundred and twenty-four deaths occurred during the year. The cost of each patient per head for fifty-three weeks is £34 18s. 3d.

Dr. Forbes contends that a man coming into the infirmary ought not for that reason to be stigmatised thenceforth as a pauper. He thinks it positively cruel that a patient must needs pass through the workhouse when he is sufficiently well to return home; it is an atmosphere of pauperism, and therefore to be avoided.

The doctor considers that it would be true benevolence, and a saving to the parish, if the guardians would afford help to the wife and family to keep up the home for the bread-winner to return to when he leaves the infirmary. Disease and sickness should be no stain on a man's character.

An admirable plan is adopted here in case of fire which is that of outside light iron balconies running from one ward to another, the indoor stairs, of course, being used on all other occasions. It was by this extraordinary means we made our way to some of the night wards.

There were bright, pleasant pictures on the walls, plants on the tables, and screens standing about. The bedsteads were excellent, being wire, chain, or wire springs. The nurses' faces too were bright and sympathetic, as they should be in the midst of sick people.

We were very pleased with the order and classification of the drug cupboard at the end of each ward. The poisons were in bottles of distinct colour and shape, and those containing stimulants were divided into doses and clearly marked with the patients' names. Under each cupboard was a drawer filled with neatly made bandages. Beside this there is a stock cupboard to each ward, so that the nurse has everything to hand. Each patient had a locker by his bed, made after a model shown to the guardians by Dr. Forbes; it contains a cupboard and drawers, and is of the greatest convenience and comfort to the sick man or woman.

We noticed with pleasure the bright copper baths on castors which can be moved to the bedside of any patient too ill to be moved out of the ward and yet requiring the comfort of a bath.

There is an apparatus in use here for lifting helpless patients out of bed, but it is much more clumsy than that we saw in the Carola House in Dresden.[47]

Again we heard the same opinion expressed that the men are so much more grateful for what is done for them than the women. How strange this seems.

We next visited the dispensing departments. Out-patients are received in a large, airy room with red washing tiles on the walls. On a blackboard facing them as they enter, the hours and names of the various doctors are written. They can get medicines and consult the doctors from eleven to one o'clock, and from four to six.

The consulting room joins this.

The officer in charge calls out the names of the patients in order, and in this way they see the doctor, who gives them a prescription. They pass on to the dispensary, where they stand at the window, give in their paper and receive the medicine. The dispenser can dispense thirty in an hour.

The chemist's room for the in-patients is quite separate and much larger, but the two adjoin, to enable the dispenser to attend to all without loss of time.

The water for both workhouse and infirmary is obtained from an artesian well nearly three hundred feet deep, but they have communication with the water companies, lest at any time the well should fail. The infirmary tanks are always filled first.

We noticed the hose and pails in the passage in case of fire, and were glad to hear that the porters were trained once a week in the fire brigade.

The doctor has in his bedroom a tell-tale clock under glass, by which he can tell at what part of his duty the night superintendent has arrived.

The casual wards here are on the cell system. The superintendent of these is an ex-lifeguardsman, a very giant of a man, whose presence alone suffices to subdue the casuals if they are at all inclined to be troublesome.

Dr. Forbes has his own ideas upon the casual wards, as he has upon most things. He says that the whole casual system is a relic of barbarism, for in the present day, when there are so many societies which give their members the means of going and looking for work, the casual wards are not necessary, and that it is only the lazy ones who take advantage of them. He conceives that there should be a place where the lazy should be made to work, and not come into the casual wards at all.

Lambeth, London (1890)

This instalment in the 'Workhouse Life in Town and Country' series by Mrs Emma Brewer records her visit to the Lambeth workhouse on Princes (now Black Prince) Road.[48]

LAMBETH.

To have visited Lambeth Workhouse twenty-five years ago would have been an insane act on the part of any one not obliged to do so. It was too filthy and disorganised for decent people to put their heads into.

This became known through the length and breadth of the land by the revelations of "A Night in a London Workhouse."

To-day, thank God, things are different. Nowhere can be found a better example of the beneficent work of order and cleanliness which has taken the place of misrule and neglect.

The Lambeth New Workhouse, situate in the Renfrew Road, Kennington Lane, and built some eighteen or twenty years ago, is a large and imposing collection of buildings. It is next door to the police court, and close to a fire-station, so that the whole block is a type of law and order.

It is certified for 1235 inmates, but on the day we were there only 1100 were present — yet this number is large indeed for one parish, taking into consideration that the children and insane and sick are not included.

One of the peculiarities of this house is that no stimulants whatever are used. The master is a blue-ribbon man, and carries out strictly what he himself believes in; and it speaks well for his influence and judicious management that the inmates, eighty per cent. of whom are there through drink, seem content and cheerful under the restriction.

Both paid and pauper labour are employed here, and the making and mending for the house, the infirmary, and the schools are done by the old women under a paid labour mistress.

The room where the needlework was being done is large. Windows on both sides let in plenty of light and air, and pictures and flowers give it a look of homeliness, to which a sort of picturesqueness was added by the dress of the old women, consisting of blue cotton dresses, red shawls, and clean white caps.

The laundry is good, and its walls of white tiles give it a clean and cheerful aspect. Forty women were working away here with a good will. Running out of this are passages, with drying closets on either side, leading to two rooms for folding, ironing, and sorting.

The store-room was full of bins, each of which contained a complete outfit of cap, apron, dress, shawl, and linen. To those who have been in the habit of wearing flannel and night-dress those articles are allowed, not otherwise. Among the women who drift in here, there is a great love of secreting. On their return from a day out it is necessary to search them, otherwise spirits and food, equally injurious, would find their way to the lockers. Men give less trouble in this respect and are more to be trusted.

The infirm wards, whose pink walls and chocolate-coloured dado were further adorned with red banners and shields with texts in bold letters on them, looked quite cheerful with the clean beds, and pictures hanging at intervals.

At the head of each bed was a card with the name, age, religion, date of admission, and address of the nearest friend of the occupant, in case of sudden or serious illness, written clearly on it.

The children's ward is large and had a low division down the centre, as most of the adult wards had. They are kept here eighteen months, and a paid attendant looks after them. Little cots, wee tables and forms made up the furniture, while bright pictures on the walls, and the little inmates themselves in red frocks and clean pinafores, made no unpleasing picture.

The kitchen, with its white and red tiles, was very clean and airy, and every one in it was busy as we passed through, for the dinner-hour was close at hand. From this the food is passed through a trap door into the dining-halls, so that there is no time for it to get cold. The diet is varied, viz., boiled legs of mutton, and potatoes in their skins; stew, bacon and cabbage, and plain baked pudding. The master would like to give stewed fruit now and then if those people who have large gardens would send him some of their windfalls.

No tablecloths are used in the dining-halls, but the tables are scrubbed so white that their absence is not noticed.

As we made our way to the men's side we learned that five years ago some abled-bodied young men inmates banded together and gave great trouble; but by good and judicious management the clique was broken up, and some of the men induced to go to Canada. Only a few weeks ago one of these very rebels wrote a capital letter to the master, enclosing five pounds to help some other man over.

There is no oakum-picking in this workhouse; but a large sum is made annually by the chopping of wood.

The old men's quarters are quite as comfortable as the women's, and there are green plots in the yards for them to look out on. As we passed through one of these yards we were attracted by the sight of an old man and woman who were holding an earnest conversation together. Seeing the master with us, the man came up and pleaded earnestly that he might not be separated from his wife, adding pathetically, that he was quite well and strong now, and needed not to go into the Infirmary. He and his wife came from Yorkshire, and were reduced to their present condition by speculation. Our conductor listened calmly and sympathetically to all the man said, and finally told him that they should not be separated. The old man's joy scarcely allowed him to express his thanks, as ho hurried off to impart the news to his wife.

We visited the infirm men's ward while they were at dinner; some were quite unable to help themselves to food, but were assisted with great gentleness by those less infirm. This was a very large room, divided in half by a low skirting of wood, the second half forming a day room, well supplied with books and papers, and made bright by a scarlet cloth on the table and pictures on the walls. The journals are supplied by a box at the railway station, into which people are asked to put the papers they have done with.

Among the infirm inmates we saw a solicitor reduced by drink, a head city clerk by embezzlement, and a chief clerk to guardians also by drink.

The married people's quarters pleased us greatly, eight couples are accommodated; their bedrooms were cosy and snug, with looking-glass, carpet, and every necessary for their use; outside was a little kitchen for making tea, etc.

The married couples dine together, in a room set apart for them in their own quarters.

As a rule, however, the married couples do not consider it a privilege to dwell together in separate rooms; the old man having had enough of the old woman, or vice versa. On being asked to give a reason, they have often no better excuse than "that his cough keeps her awake," or "her tongue, it do nag that dreadful."

The women are, as a rule, braver and more enduring than the men, and will often remain out working long after the men have given up and taken refuge in the "House."

The day we were there the authorities had ninety *remand* boys in charge; but as the large oakum shed has been turned into a dormitory for them there is no difficulty in accommodating them in large numbers, and it is surely more merciful to the boys than sending them to prison.

The casual hall is large, high, bare, and clean. There are more casuals in winter than in summer, and there is an officer always there to receive and certify them.

In the board-room is a portrait of the present chairman by a pauper named Hughes. In the yard outside, grass, flowers, and pigeons give grace to the place.

The chaplain holds service in the chapel on Sunday mornings and Thursday evenings. On other evenings lady-singers and soloists come from outside, and give the inmates beautiful music, or join with them in singing hymns, chiefly those of Moody and Sankey, which are very popular. This is a break in the monotony of workhouse life, and one that is greatly appreciated. One woman, a noted bad character, who has been before the magistrate forty times, has been greatly improved by her residence here, and she declares it is the music!

And now for the Infirmary, which adjoins the workhouse, but is under different management.

The entrance to the Lambeth Infirmary is in Brook Street, Kennington Lane, and not through the workhouse; still the admissions are by means of the relieving officer, and consequently the stigma of pauperism attaches itself to the inmates.

It was built eleven years ago, upon the pavilion principle, the administrative block being in the centre. The superintendent and responsible head is the chief Medical Officer, Dr. Lloyd.

There are one or two features in this Infirmary which single it out for special notice; one is, that ever since it was first opened, it has trained its own nurses; another, that throughout the building pauper labour is remarkable for its absence. Other features will be apparent as we go on.

There is a day and a night staff of nurses, and assistant nurses, the former ranking highest. The dress, which is given them, is pretty; for head nurses, dark-blue stuff dress, large white bibbed apron and lace cap with lace lappets; for assistant nurses, light blue cotton, white apron, and cap without lappets. The medical superintendent finds that he gets the best nurses from the upper set of the better servant class, who are prepared for, and not afraid of work, and are besides steady and reliable.

Lady nurses he considers as generally too hot and enthusiastic at first, and it is his experience that when the enthusiasm has died out the deep interest in their work is lost. He prefers them young, not older certainly than twenty-three or four, and if only nineteen, so much the better.

On first being admitted, the nurses get £17 a year, rising to £20, with board, lodging, uniform, and washing. At the end of twelve months they may become night nurses, with a salary of £20, rising to £25, and at the end of another year they may, if capable, become head day nurses, with a salary of £25, rising to £32. As a reward for good service they are allowed to serve in the Lying-in Ward.

The hours of the day nurses are from half-past six in the morning to half-past seven at night, from which time until ten o'clock they are free to go out. The night nurses come on at half-past seven and remain until half-past six next morning. This plan has answered well. Many of the nurses have been here for years, and are decorated with medals, and as to diplomas, they will be able to cover the walls of their sitting-room with them when they get homes of their own.

No one can pass through the wards of this Infirmary without perceiving that the nursing is excellent; and we quite agreed with the doctor, that a barrister in receipt of a good income ill of pneumonia in his chambers in the Temple is nothing like so well off as the patient here.

The nurses are well accommodated, both in their mess-room, sitting-room, and bedrooms. There are altogether six hundred and twenty-two beds, and the admissions are from three to four thousand a year. There are but few accidents brought here, St. Thomas's being so close.

The wards are large, some of them containing sixty-eight beds, the space being divided in the centre by a low skirting. But the doctor does not approve of this system, as he maintains that in consequence of it there is a certain amount of air which never moves at all. No ward, he thinks, should be over 24 feet wide, and these are 44 feet across.

A ward is in charge of one head nurse, and two assistants. Attached to each ward is a linen closet and tiny kitchen for hot water, beef tea, or any little thing required. Bibles and hymn books were on the tables, placed there by the chaplain, who visits the wards daily.

We asked if the women able to get up did any work, or read much, and were told that they preferred sitting round the fire, doing nothing; that they were not very intelligent, many of them having rarely gone beyond their own street or neighbourhood.

All medicines are kept in cupboards with glass doors, so that the doctor in passing through the wards can see at a glance anything out of order; it is an excellent plan.

The men's wards differed from the women's in that most of the inmates were reading, or amusing themselves in some way. Many of them were very intelligent and educated men; several soldiers and sailors, who had seen the world, talked well.

There were one or two sad cases amongst them, one of a book-maker, who took cold at Newmarket a few years ago, and in some curious way has since lost the use of his joints, so that he cannot raise a finger, even to brush off a fly. He is a great favourite, being very intelligent and grateful. The doctor has had a light frame-work made, covered with book-muslin, to put over his bed to keep the flies from worrying him.

The beds are excellent. First comes a wire spring mattress, called the "Dominion of Canada wire wove mattress," seen by the doctor at the Healtheries[49] — they are good for all cases except broken thighs or legs, and for these they bend too easily. Then on this is an air mattress; over which is a waterproof sheet; and the usual amount of sheets and blankets, all spotlessly clean.

Connecting the pavilion is a roofed but open-sided corridor. Into this, on a clear bright day, the patients who can bear it are often brought bodily, beds and all, to enjoy the fresh air and change of scene.

The want of daily papers and illustrated journals is greatly felt; it would be a real kindness If people would sow and then send a packet to Dr. Lloyd for the use of the patients. It would wonderfully relieve the monotony of their life. While on the subject of wants, let me add that tickets for convalescent homes would be a great boon to the Infirmary.

The expense per week of each patient for food and clothing is, roughly speaking, about six shillings. I wish all interested in the poor could see this Infirmary, and the care and skill bestowed upon the sick. The number of admissions in a year varies from 3800 to 4100, and the number of deaths from 450 to 540. The stimulants, which formerly amounted to some hundreds of pounds, do not now exceed ten pounds in the year.

Chorlton, Lancashire (1890)

This instalment in Emma Brewer's 'Workhouse Life in Town and Country' series records a visit to the Chorlton union workhouse in south Manchester.[50] It provides an interesting comparison with the 1871 visit included earlier in this collection. For example, the institution now had a telephone.

MANCHESTER.

The drive from Manchester to Chorlton[51] Union is through an extremely pretty suburb of Manchester, and seeing it from a distance it looks like a town, so large are the buildings which go to make up this pauper abode.

It differs from any we have seen hitherto in that it has all its family in the one set of buildings, viz., children, old people, imbeciles, idiots, and sick—in fact, schools, infirmary, asylum and refuge all together; and it was for this reason we selected it in preference to the other large Manchester Workhouse.[52]

The master was absent getting a few days' rest, but we could not have had a better guide through its intricacies than the matron, who knew every face and the history of each individual.

The schools, which have been built nine years, stand on one side of the road, and the Infirmary, House and asylum on the other. Our first visit was to the schools, consisting of various sets of buildings called *homes*, an administrative block and two large schoolrooms. The homes are six in number, three for girls and three for boys, each containing sixty children, and each being in charge of a woman, who, from the nature of her responsibilities, is called a *mother*.

Both inside and out attempts have been made, by flowers and by coloured walls and tiled dados, to make these homes as little like a workhouse as possible. Each home has a bright day-room, and three dormitories, containing twenty beds each. The mattresses are of straw; a clean pillow-case is given to every child weekly, but only one clean sheet fortnightly. It would be little enough to have one each week, and there ought to be no difficulty in supplying this, as there are plenty of hands in the laundry.

Should a child fall ill, he or she is at once sent off to the infirmary across the road, and if on examination the doctor discovers that the child is suffering from anything infectious he sends word to the mother to have the bedding and clothing at once disinfected and removed.

The mother of the home has a little sitting-room on the ground floor, and a bedroom on the first, and the two pauper-helps sleep at the top in a room to themselves.

The six mothers have a small neat messroom next the kitchen where they take their meals.

From the homes, which are all alike, we went into the girls' schoolroom filled with rows of bright happy-looking children, who were busy at lessons, and whose faces smiled all over as the matron entered. They had short hair, blue-striped cotton dresses, and white pinafores; this is their dress winter and summer, but they have good cloth jackets to wear in cold weather. Some of the girls were pointed out to us as among those going to Canada the following week. We were pleased with the writing, spelling, and arithmetic, which were all we could spare time for.

Bidding the children good-bye, we made our way to the administrative department, passing on our way the sewing-room where classes are held in the afternoons under a mistress for learning sewing and knitting.

We next came to a large dining-hall for both girls and boys, and here they dine daily at half-past twelve. Bread and milk is their fare for breakfast, and for dinner the day we were there it was peasoup and bread. The kitchen was bright, clean, and busy. One little girl was scrubbing the table to a state of immaculate whiteness, others were busy stirring the soup, and two hard at work in the scullery adjoining.

We next went into the laundry, where the little girls were in full force, folding, packing and ironing. The paid laundress assured us that some of them were beautiful ironers. They are so well trained that there is no difficulty in obtaining good situations for them; but it is at this point that the relations turn up to their hurt, hampering them in their struggles to be good and independent.

We were pleased with a large shallow white-tiled swimming bath, with a dressing-room attached, where the girls bathe on Wednesday nights and the boys twice a week. We could well understand the children's pleasure in this, and also that for an offence requiring punishment it is quite sufficient to deprive them of their bath.

On the boys' side, which is in most respects like the girls, we went into the tailor's shop and that of the shoemakers, where six boys at a time are taught by a paid man, those who are at school in the morning attending here in the afternoon, and *vice versa*.

Many of the boys were out in the grounds at work, for many of them are sent to Canada, and this sort of training is admirable for them.

The boys wear clogs, and, as they came running out of school to exercise on the parallel bars in the recreation ground, we thought of the song, "Oh, the clang o' the wooden shoon!"

Twenty-six of these boys were about starting for Canada.

The head master has a charming little house to himself, bright with flowers; the chief mistress also has a house to herself; while the under masters and mistresses have apartments in the blocks close by, consisting of a sitting-room and bedroom each. The engineer and his wife have a home; so also have the bandmaster and his wife, for the boys have a brass band and play very well.

We now crossed the road and began our inspection of the mass of buildings there, by looking into the probationary ward for children, where they remain until admitted to the homes, and then into the bathroom where people are bathed before entering the buildings. We could not help laughing at the story of an old woman who went down on her knees to the person in charge begging and entreating not to be bathed, for she said, "I've never washed all over since I was a baby, and it'ull kill me!" Here close by was a small receiving ward and tiny bedroom for women, who are, when they first come, inexpressibly dirty.

The chapel is in the centre of the whole block facing the road. Church of England service is held here twice on Sunday, and the Wesleyan service once a fortnight. The Roman Catholics have their service in the dining-hall.

On passing the lodge we noticed that the gatekeeper was an old Crimean soldier, having on his breast two medals, and on enquiry found he had been in the Balaclava charge.

We looked into the sewing-room, well supplied with sewing machines, and then inspected two day-rooms, clean, airy, and bright, where several old women were sitting who did not like pea. soup, and, as that was the day's dinner, had elected to remain here during the hour in which it was being eaten. Is it not possible to get a substitute for peasoup? I asked them why they did not go in to dinner, and one answered, "Not becos it's not good, mum, but 'cos it don't agree with us." They are well fed with nourishing food, as a rule, for they have boiled meat and potatoes on Sundays, and Australian meat and potatoes on Mondays.

From here we went into the nursery, where were forty-two little creatures. In the middle of the room stood a rocking-horse and rocking-chair, a present from some friend of little children; a small room adjoining had a large bed with six compartments, where the little ones take their mid-day rest. When we saw them they were lively enough, and stroked our gloves, examined our dress, and entreated to hear the "tick." No sooner was this granted than they came toddling from all parts of the room crying, "and me too" "and me too" till we had much to do to get away at all.

As we crossed their large recreation ground and stepped through a door in the wall, their merry shrill voices pursued us, and formed a contrast to the sad scene awaiting us.

This part of the house was devoted to the imbeciles and epileptics, all of whom were dressed in brown. There is a large grass plot set apart for their use, surrounded by paths and trees, provided with seats, and here we found them sitting in the sun or wandering aimlessly up and down, some of them talking and gesticulating wildly, others with a vacant smile or mirthless laugh. The block devoted to their service is necessarily large, for there are a hundred and twenty women and girls thus afflicted. We looked at their day-room, padded rooms, and night-wards, all made as comfortable and cheerful as possible for them.

Divided from this block by a door is a sort of home for old women, who were found sitting in a day-room with a fire carefully wired in, and a sleek cat in whom they evidently took much pride, one old lady declaring "She can do everything but speak." The night-wards were clean and comfortable, and the pink and blue quilts and pictures on the walls and screens added cheerfulness also. A sick-ward for the lunatics was the next we passed through; it was nursed by two trained day-nurses and one night-nurse. For the whole house there are three resident doctors.

Our next visit was to the nurses' home, which has accommodation for thirty-five nurses, each of whom has a bedroom to herself, furnished by the guardians, and made pretty by their own private possessions. In this home there is a dining-hall, a drawing-room and a kitchen. The superintendent's room was pretty and bright.

The fever cases are nursed by special nurses kept quite apart from the others, while employed in it. The Infirmary is on the pavilion system, and the seven pavilions are` joined together by a roofed open-sided passage running from end to end. Rules hung on the doors and walls of the wards, for the guidance of patients and visitors. All the cooking for the Infirmary is done in the house, but there are small sculleries at the end of each ward for making beef-tea, and for washing up as in ordinary hospitals. One small room on each landing is set aside for any special case requiring extra. care and quiet, but the large wards are the more cheerful with their grey and white-tiled dado, easy wheel-chairs, tables with plants, and drawers full of deftly rolled bandages, pictures on the walls, and neat-handed pleasant-looking nurses flitting about, ministering to the patients.

At the end of each ward was a convalescent room, where those capable of doing so were sitting up. The bathroom and lavatory for each ward were all that could be desired.

The old wards (for part of the Infirmary is older than the rest) are not quite so nice in their arrangements, not having all the modern im-provements possessed by the others, but they are kept sweet and clean and made the best of. The infectious cases are kept quite separate at the top of one of the pavilions. The day we were there, there were nine cases of scarlet fever.

Leaving the Infirmary we went to the kitchen, which is necessarily very large, as on an average between eighteen and nineteen hundred dinners are sent out daily. It is pauper labour here under a paid cook. The bakehouse was full of sweet-smelling bread; whole loaves are cut up at a time by means of a long, sharp two-handled knife. Different-sized loaves are made for the men and women—the former being five ounces, and those for the latter four ounces.

The dining-hall is divided down the centre by a wooden partition, on one side of which the men sit, and on the other the women. Pictures and a large clock were the only ornaments.

We next visited the store of clothing, every article of which passes through the matron's hands. All articles worn out are condemned by her.

183

This ceremony goes on in an adjoining room called the condemned room. A third room is devoted to giving out the clothes, which are neatly rolled up in bundles and stacked away in bins round the walls. Every bundle as it is given out is written down in a book with the name of the recipient so that no mistake is possible. Each person has two suits. A list book is also kept here with the names of the inmates, and dates of entering and leaving.

The laundry came next under our notice. We thought it too low. It was, however, large, and had a good wash-house, and a small room for the dirty linen, which is thrown into a tank as it arrives. There were good drying closets, and the goffering was done by steam.

The women are largely employed in the laundry work, while the men are occupied in picking oakum, wool and cotton waste, and in wood chopping, but the young men grind corn. All this is done under the superintendence of two labour-masters.

We glanced in at the smithy, and at the bakery, where eight sacks of flour a day are worked up in the summer, and in the winter as many as ten and eleven are used, as outdoor and indoor poor are supplied from this bakery.

The furnaces are very large and good, and reminded us of china factory furnaces.

We next saw the building in which the corn is ground. Idle dangerous characters among the men who will not submit to discipline are employed here.

Each man is locked into a sort of cell, quite dark, and separated by partitions from his neighbours, whom he cannot see, but with whom he can speak. On the other sides are receptacles for the Indian corn fixed into the wall, and bins are put underneath to receive it as it falls through, ground ready for the pigs and horses. One hundred weight a day is the task allotted to each.

We looked into the carpenters' shops and yards, and passed a large water tank, kept ready in case of a break down. We then walked through the large farm attached to the house. They have a hundred and fifty pigs, whose stys occupy a large portion of ground; a kitchen opposite is devoted to preparing food for them. Bones, and such garden produce as is not needed, are sold; but they lack fruit very much, and presents, even of windfalls, would be most acceptable to the inmates of the house and schools.

The farm bailiff has a house on the premises, and a very pretty one it is.

Last Christmas there were two thousand two hundred people in the house!

A telephone connects the buildings with the offices in Grosvenor Square, Manchester, and with the Fire Brigade.

No stimulants are allowed anywhere in the house.

The matron gave us some curious glimpses into the inner life of the workhouse. She told us that people in Manchester having relatives or friends in the Workhouse invariably address their letters to Withington Hospital, in order to avoid the appearance of pauperism. Another fact was, that the married couples generally prefer to live apart. Only one couple to her knowledge begged not to be separated, and their desire being granted, they requested at the end of a fortnight to be parted She also stated, that as no stimulants are allowed, a very little drink affects the inmates, or, as the matron euphemistically put it, " makes them happy," and when the old women have been out for the day they frequently return in this sadly " happy state of mind," but if they go to bed quietly, without a fuss, no notice is taken of it by the authorities.

We thought this Institution very well managed, and that the superintendents showed much kindness and forbearance to the inmates both old and young, sick and well, and were evidently regarded as friends.

Liverpool, Lancashire (1890)

Emma Brewer's 'Workhouse Life in Town and Country' series visits Liverpool workhouse, the largest in England.[53] Its Brownlow Hill site is now occupied by the city's Metropolitan Cathedral.

LIVERPOOL WORKHOUSE AND INFIRMARY.

This is another huge barrack-like collection of buildings, a city within a city, and a very depressing one indeed, though managed as well as it is possible, considering the numbers within its walls, and the peculiar class of its inmates.

It was the most bewildering place I had ever been through, and I did not keep the same opinion of it ten minutes together. At one time I thought the inmates the roughest and coarsest I had ever seen, and then

In 1905, Liverpool's workhouse at Brownlow Hill could house 3,000 inmates.

bending my steps to the old people's portion of the building, I thought them superior to others that had come under my notice. Again, the maternity ward filled one with intense sadness that the women and girls resting there should feel no shame at the thought of the inheritance with which they had endowed their little ones. Then the walk through the nursery, which contained the babies brought back by these mothers after having had them a few weeks in their degraded homes, was a sight never to be forgotten; and lastly the cells containing young girls with delirium tremens made one for a moment despair before the appalling evils that have to be overcome in attempting to improve the condition of the poor.

It was a relief to find no children over the baby age here, they are kept at the schools two or three miles distant, and when we were there the number was 794.[54]

The able-bodied class of pauper is gradually disappearing, while, on the other hand, the infirm and sick are rapidly increasing, as may be seen by the numbers. In 1869 the out-relief amounted to £39,673. In 1888, £11,678. The number of recipients in 1868, was 11,986. In 1888, 2272.

Pauper labour is used throughout for scrubbing and cleaning, and a rougher class of women I never saw.

It was strange to us to be called sharply to account two or three times on our way from the gate to the master's office, and our name and business at each point demanded. t length we gained the large entrance hall, round which were the enquiry office, the master's room, the receiving wards and the dispensary.

The master set out with us on our tour through this pauper town, and as it was the dinner hour he took us first to the dining hall, where such as were able to move about had their meals, the men in one block, the women in another. It is a large room with a pulpit in it, which opens out into an ornate altar for the use of the Roman Catholics. From here we went into the kitchen, manned by a small army of cooks, and with a huge cooking range fixed against the wall, but which would be more convenient if situated so as to allow the cooks to get round it. Only boiling can be done here; the day's dinner was pea-soup, seasoned with mint as a sort of relish.

From this to the general stores was but a step. It is an immense place, under the superintendence of a store-keeper, whose notice nothing escapes. On the table lay a tabulated paper containing the amounts and quality of the ordinary and extra diets and their various ingredients. The food throughout the building is both good and abundant.

At the time of our visit they were using weekly a hundred dozen of mineral waters, a hundred and twelve chickens, four thousand five hundred eggs, and one thousand six hundred and forty-five gallons of milk. This will give a little idea of the requirements of this place.

From the store-room down a flight of stops we came to the bakery, a very large place with huge ovens. All the bread for the house, infirmary, and outside poor is made here, and mostly by paid labour.

On asking what became of the refuse of the whole establishment, we learned that it was sold and tenders invited for it.

We next came to the dairies, dark and cool. In the one used for sweet milk is a cupboard provided with shelves on which rest test glasses. The exact quantity of cream agreed upon is rigorously exacted, and when deficient a penny a gallon is deducted.

We were now made over to the care of the assistant matron, whom the master begged to be our guide through the infirmary, in the absence of the matron, who was taking a much-needed holiday. This sister had been trained in the Marylebone Infirmary, and in every particular showed how good and thorough her training had been.

The infirmary is one of the largest in England, and interesting as being the first to adopt trained, in the place of pauper, nurses. This it did in 1865, and at once raised the salaries and rations from £15,482 to £19,550.

There are altogether a hundred wards in this infirmary, each of which belongs to a certain district or division. For example, each division has its two landings, consisting of four or five large wards and some smaller ones, a medicine store, a small kitchen, and a large bath-room.

The allowance of attendance to each landing is one nurse, one probationer, and on the men's side, one wardsman or wardswoman in addition. A nightwoman is appointed to every two wards during the night, but she has nothing whatever to do but watch, her orders being to call the nurse if she find it needful, or if the patients require anything. It struck me that this service was insufficient.

The medicine is under the care of a special nurse, and is kept supplied by the dispensary. Every medicine required is noted in a book by the store sister, and this is sent daily to the dispensers. It is to these landing stores that the nurses come to fill the bottles for their patients, the medicines being all mixed and ready for use. The poison-cupboard is kept locked, so is the store of spirits, every ounce of which must be accounted for by the sister in charge.

The small landing-kitchen is for the preparation of special dinners, of which, on an average, there are sixteen daily for each landing. From the large kitchen, which supplies all the ordinary dinners, there is a lift — a great advantage where so many patients are to be served with hot food.

The wards are immense, but they are made pleasant by ornaments, pictures, and flowers; touches of brightness are imparted to those on the men's side by the red jackets they wear, and by the blue quilts on the beds.

The men's wards would look, and be more comfortable, if blinds to the windows wore supplied; they have them on the women's side, and it seems odd that they should have been omitted for the men. The men's surgical wards are made as pretty as possible, but we thought them rather crowded.

A low-ceilinged room is set apart for the helpless sick, and called the Crib, as the beds are provided with side-pieces to prevent the patients from falling out. The male operating-room is light, airy, and large.

The women's part of the infirmary is some distance from the men's, for this building is neither on the pavilion nor on the corridor system, the wards running out of each other in an irregular sort of way. The women's medical and surgical wards are exactly like those on the men's side, with like kitchens, medicine-stores, and bath-rooms. The inmates of the maternity wards have already been alluded to.

The babies' ward, with fire, bright pictures, and gay red quilts, looked pretty, but the sights there were heart-rending. The head-nurse, tender and gentle (as a mother I was going to say), was holding in her arms a wee mite of a baby, literally a living skeleton; it wailed piteously and unceasingly, as did many others. Nurse said the babe might probably live for a week in that condition. The sight of that suffering little creature will never pass from my memory, and yet that was one of many in that room.

Nurse said that the babies, when born, are plump healthy little things, but the mothers take them out, and, in the course of a few weeks, bring them back in the condition we saw.

A little apart from the infirmary stands the nurses' perfectly-appointed home. It was built ten years ago, and contains, at the present time, eighty-five nurses — three for fever, twelve for night-work, and the remainder for ordinary nursing.

The probationers wear pink cotton dresses, and the nurses blue. Each nurse has a separate bedroom, furnished simply, but made pretty by her own possessions. Lectures are given every week by the doctors, of whom there are three resident and three consulting. Classes also are held in the large class-room by the assistant matron, with the help of skeletons, and other appliances.

From the home and infirmary, in which last there were nine hundred and thirty-three patients the day we were there, we went to the church — a large, handsome building, containing a marble monument of great interest to the memory of Agnes Elizabeth Jones, who first introduced trained nursing here. On one side of the pedestal, which supports the angel-figure, is an inscription by Miss Nightingale, and on the other side a poem, two lines of which run—

Death came to thee
Not in the cool breath of the silver sea,
But in the city hospital's hot ward.

There are two Roman Catholics to every Protestant in this workhouse and infirmary, so that comparatively only a small number worship here, the majority having their service in the large dining-hall.

Coming out we passed through a yard crowded with helpless and infirm old women, sitting and sunning themselves. Their day-room was large and airy, and the old folk seemed content and cheerful. Visitors come twice a week to real and talk with them. Several were occupied in reading books and newspapers to themselves. One nice-looking old grannie appeared very comfortable, seated in an easy chair, and holding in her hands a book in which she seemed completely absorbed. She attracted and interested me, and, going up to her, I said —

"Have you a very interesting book?"

"Oh, very, ma'am!"

"May I see it?" I asked.

"Oh, yes! Isn't it beautiful?" and she added proudly, "I'm nearly through it."

Perhaps a story-book, some one suggests. Not at all, it was a dry, difficult geography.

"How old are you?"

"Eighty-six, ma'am, and I'm nearly through it." Evidently proud of getting through the book.

Others were knitting a little, or darning, and were very pleased when we took it, and after examining it, gave a word of praise.

They are extremely well-cared for — a certain number being placed under a superintendent, who is at once kind, gentle, and vigorous — and the old people evidently like these superintendents. Large lavatories, bath-rooms and plenty of towels are provided, and their cleanliness and comfort well looked after.

The bedrooms lead out of each other, and are brightened by pictures and bits of colour. The beds are of straw; but sheets and blankets were all clean.

One old woman, whose mind was very weak, began to cry piteously as we were about to leave, begging to be allowed to see her mother, who, of course, had been dead many years, for this old woman was over eighty — but the master neither laughed nor showed impatience or hurry — he listened gravely and comforted her, by saying he would see about it.

The sewing-room which we passed through was a large cheerful chamber, busy with the hum of sewing machines, and the sound of many voices. A staircase leads up out of it, at the top of which the sewing mistress sits, cuts out and superintends. She has to account for every yard of stuff given out to her.

We next descended to the basement, where small cells and a neat kitchen are provided for the inebriates. The cells lock up, and have a small window in the door through which the woman in charge can survey her patient without opening the door. One of these poor creatures was quite a girl. I spoke to an older woman who lay there — she seemed sorry and ashamed, I thought.

There are no applications here for married couples' quarters, for by the time they reach this place, one or other of the old people is ill, and the man or woman is usually glad to be relieved of the burden and anxiety of nursing. The struggle for existence seems to have crushed the love out of their hearts if it had ever shelter there.

When we came to what would be the married couples' quarters, we found that since there was no application for them, they had been used to put decent respectable old women in, who have come to the workhouse through no wrong-doing, but from life being, as they say, dead against them. These quarters form the bright side of the workhouse, and gave us a pleasant surprise. There are seventy-one nice old women here, three having a room together, except in two cases — the messenger who runs errands for them all has only one old woman in her room; and another room, being very large, holds four.

They themselves keep the rooms tidy and dusted, but an able-bodied woman does the rough work — and very bright and clean they are. Although August, there was a little fire in each of the rooms, and on the walls hung portraits of the occupiers' favourite statesmen, and pictures from the illustrated papers. I think Lord Salisbury and Gladstone alike would have felt a choking sensation at the pathetic sight, and a little amusement, too, that both one and other were adding brightness to the rooms of workhouse women.

Almost every old woman was working at something — either knitting or sewing. Each room had its shelf of books, and those who were not at the moment working were reading the daily papers.

To this portion of the workhouse there is a paved yard with seats, where on warm days they can sit and sun themselves. There was an air of content and happiness about these old people which showed that they valued the privilege of ending their days in peace and without want. They are all on a special diet, which includes tea, sugar, and butter. I noticed that the master while in this part of the building lost his look of care. I should like every one interested in workhouses to see these old people's quarters.

From here we went to the insane wards for men, which are under the charge of a young man who thoroughly understands his work. Here were sailors of all nationalities — Negroes, Spaniards, German, and French. One handsome young sailor was suffering from melancholia, brought on by having been ill when his own ship had left on its return journey and his inability to get into another after his recovery. One in this ward was amusing himself by copying and colouring popular advertisements. There were several padded rooms, and a large airy dormitory provided with low beds for those subject to fits.

We now passed on to where the old men were picking hair, which, as the master said, was untidier and more disagreeable than oakum picking, but easier and softer for the fingers.

We next made our way through a long array of so-called able-bodied men's dormitories, all painfully alike, and noticeable only for their extreme neatness and cleanliness. There are two officers on each landing, and one sleeps at each end.

We looked through the little kitchens and carpenters', cobblers', and tailors' shops, and then found ourselves in the dispensary where the same method and order reigned as in other parts of this great building. Three dispensers are fully engaged up to twelve o'clock, and two after that hour. Certain stock medicines are always ready, and the drugs are contracted for in Liverpool. The cost of the medicine last year was £3,373, and for the first half of this year, £1,810 was spent for drugs alone. Men appointed carry baskets all day long between the infirmary and the dispensary. The requirements of the nurses are sent down clearly written on sheets of paper, on which are inscribed also the name, diet, disease, and time of arrival of every patient. These papers are collected by one of the nurses, and sent to the dispensary in tin boxes. The books here are splendidly kept, and at a glance one can follow out the amount and cost of a drug and the treatment of a patient. This dispensary supplies not only the workhouse and infirmary but the parish as well, consequently the whole of the indoor and outdoor poor.

In going over such a place as this it is possible only to give the merest outline. We went there without giving notice, and saw the usual daily routine which we have tried to put on paper.

Cirencester, Gloucestershire (1890)

> This instalment in Emma Brewer's 'Workhouse Life in Town and Country' series records her visit to the Cirencester union workhouse.[55] In more recent times, the buildings, on Trinity Road, have housed District Council offices.

AGRICULTURAL. —CIRENCESTER.

The Cirencester Union occupies seven acres of land on the outskirts of the town, half a mile from the railway station, and stands in the midst of gardens.

We found ourselves at the gate at half-past ten in the morning, and while waiting for admission noticed the printed order that the inmates are allowed to see their friends on Mondays and Fridays, from one o'clock till four, and on no other occasions, except under special circumstances.

The gate being opened, our eyes rested with pleasure on a garden bright with wallflowers and other plants, and our ears were greeted with the singing of birds and the cawing of rooks, and we were almost inclined to think that we had made a mistake, and entered the grounds of a country house.

This workhouse was built in 1836, on the site of a very ancient "poor house," and consists of three blocks, with schools, workshops, and infirmary, all under the same administration.

The master and matron have been here ten years, and evidently take a pride and pleasure in their work.

As the district is purely agricultural, the inmates are chiefly of that class. The average wage of the day labourer is nine shillings a week; and as it is a matter of impossibility that the man and wife can bring up a family and save out of this for old age, even if they do get a nice little cottage and bit of garden for five pounds a year, it is but natural that they should end their days here, when work fails them through old age or sickness.

There were many more old men than women in the house the day we were there; and we heard from the matron that the old women can postpone their coming in for weeks or even months by the variety of work they can put their hands to — whereas the men can do but one kind of work, and when that fails all is over with them. Those, not agricultural labourers, who find themselves paupers, have as a rule arrived at this condition through drink.

The children here, as at other workhouses, are almost all illegitimate. The orphans, twelve at present, are boarded out in the villages round about. A lady visitor is supposed to pay constant visits to the several homes, and keep a supervision over them in order that the little ones may be well treated. However vigilantly this plan is carried out, a better plan, I think, is that adopted by the "Enfants Assistés" in Paris, which compels the foster-mother to bring the child at stated intervals to the council, who bestow a reward if they find the child altogether prosperous.

One of the great obstacles to a child's well-being in a workhouse is that just as the matron and teacher are beginning to see a decided improvement in a girl or boy, the mother may come and take them away, and, after exposing them to every kind of foul living, bring them back again. It makes the reclaiming and teaching them well-nigh hopeless.

We found everything spotlessly clean but very bare. Take the boys' day-room for example, which had stone floor, bare walls and two forms for furniture, their play-yard outside being equally bare; there was an absence of pictures and games, or of anything that would afford the slightest amusement.

We were exceedingly pleased with the schoolroom, its thirty scholars and gentle little schoolmistress, the daughter of the master and matron. The children looked happy and industrious; their sewing, writing, and spelling were good. The chaplain who lives in the town comes once a month to give religious instruction.

As a rule, the children are docile and easily managed.

For the infirmary there is a trained nurse under the authority of the matron; she has a sitting-room and bedroom, and a bell communicating with her apartments hangs in each sick ward.

Infectious diseases are not admitted, but are taken to a building a mile off, provided and governed by the sanitary authorities.

The chronic sick ward was the brightest we had seen, with its yellow quilts, gay pictures, books and flowers.

There should be, I think, a comb and brush for each bed; as it is, there are four or five brushes, and but one comb for each ward!

The children's tick ward was happily quite unoccupied.

In the nursery were four babies. One pretty little mite of two years old was fast pining away, and her mother, who was only twenty-one and of course single, had two other children in the house! We saw her helping in the kitchen with apparently no shame at her position.

One dormitory is devoted to mothers with babies, who are allowed to keep them at night until they are two years old.

There is a nice little laundry supplied with drying closets, and a separate washhouse with hot and cold water laid on.

The old people breakfast on porridge and bread, while the infirm, the laundry women and the wardswomen have bread, butter, tea, milk and sugar and at night, all except the children, have tea.

In the kitchen the inevitable pea-soup was being prepared for dinner for all the inmates, except the children, who were going to have rice and milk. A pound and a half of meat goes to the gallon of water; but it so happens that now and then they boil a large quantity of beef, and then the liquor is used instead of water, and with the addition of vegetables an exceedingly good soup is made.

The dining hall is of fair size, and here all take food together in the presence of a superintendent; and here on Sundays the chaplain holds service.

I think the food is very good and varied and well cooked. Two days in the week they have boiled bacon and two vegetables, two days meat and two vegetables, two days pea-soup, and another day beef and potatoes. The average cost per head for maintenance and clothing is 3s. 8½d. a week.

They deal with the casuals on the Berkshire system, which is that the tramp obtains from the police a pass with his name and age written on it together with his destination. This he takes to the union, and on his leaving the master fills in the name of the next union on the direct route to his destination, and also the places on the road where he may get bread. So, if a man comes with a brand-new ticket, or one showing he is out of his proper route, he is deprived of his liberty for a day and made to work, as be is considered a loafer. Of course the men do what they can to circumvent this, tearing up their tickets whenever they get a chance, and sometimes the lane outside is strewn with torn-up tickets.

The employment given is stone-breaking, oakum-picking, and gardening.

Gloucester, Gloucestershire (1890)

This instalment in the 'Workhouse Life in Town and Country' series by Mrs Emma Brewer records her visit to the Gloucester workhouse.[56] The site, on Great Western Road, is now a car park.

AGRICULTURAL. —GLOUCESTER.

The Gloucester Workhouse stands practically on the railway, just outside the station.

It is an imposing-looking building of red brick, built in 1836, and the day we were there contained two hundred and thirty inmates, and thirty children.

An infirmary was added in 1860, which appears to us unsatisfactory. For example, the stairs are too steep and twisty, and the passages so narrow that it is impossible to carry a stretcher with a bad case on it up to the wards.

Ten years ago this workhouse was so filthy and neglected that, we are assured, it would have been impossible for us to have gone through it, and now, notwithstanding its proximity to the railway, everything in it and about it is scrupulously clean and orderly. In fact, it is as good a specimen of what ten years have effected in workhouse management as could be seen.

Among the inmates there are many old agricultural labourers, and a large number of factory women, dock labourers and waggon hands, beside many deserted women and women with families — drink being in a great measure the cause of the latter classes finding themselves here.

Beside the master and matron, the paid officers consist of the schoolmaster and mistress, an industrial trainer, a nurse, porter, cook, tramp master and mistress, a tailor and shoemaker. The two last teach their trades to the boys, who not infrequently develop into very good shoemakers, tailors, and gardeners, trades which serve them in good stead both here and in the Colonies, whither many of the boys go after leaving the house.

The children are kept until they are twelve or fourteen, and have passed the fourth standard, which, being the minimum necessary for the wage-earning community, means reading with intelligence, writing clearly and correctly from dictation, and working sums rapidly in the compound rules of arithmetic.

One of the great wants in the workhouse for the girls who have to go out to service has been the industrial training necessary for a small household. Everything is on so large a scale that when they first go out to service they are confused at finding themselves in a small kitchen; for example, they cannot light an ordinary fire, they know nothing of the use of the saucepan or gridiron, they are unable from sheer ignorance of their surroundings to perform the duties of their new position, and they lose heart and often head too, and turn out a failure.

Dr. Clutterbuck, the Poor Law Inspector, has long tried to remedy this, and it must be a pleasure to him, as it was to us, to note that Gloucester has recognised that a workhouse school should be a real practical school of cookery and household training, from whence little kitchen maids, parlour-maids, housemaids, and nurses could go out into the world to better themselves.

It has provided a tiny bright kitchen and scullery outside the girls' day-room, where all this is taught by the industrial trainer. Here, a few weeks ago, one of the girls aged thirteen cooked and served up a nice little dinner, quite unaided, on the occasion of the inspector's visit. He was very pleased, fur this special training has been one of his hobbies.

Another departure from ordinary rules struck us pleasantly, and this was giving the children twice a week bread cake, instead of bread and cheese. It is ordinary bread with currants and a little sugar; it delights the little ones, and is much more wholesome for them than bread and cheese.

We were very pleased with the women's sitting-room, which was exceptionally pretty and cheerful, with its crimson curtains and table covers, its bright pictures and flowers; the women themselves seemed happy, and were occupied with needlework for the house.

Another part of the house which we would gladly have spent some time in was the day-room and little kitchen for the girls. In the former, the girls wore very busy at needlework and knitting, both of which were good and did credit to the industrial trainer, a kind sensible woman. The room was adorned with pictures, and on one side hung a neat row of brush and comb bags, each child having its own. Everything in the little kitchen adjoining was bright as the girls could make it.

The food is good and varied; instead of porridge, the adults have tea and bread and butter, while the children have bread and milk.

The wardswomen and washers are allowed half a pint of beer a day, and the old men over sixty an ounce of tobacco a week. There is accommodation for a married couple, but it is not in demand.

The infirmary is exceedingly well cared for, the wards are bright, and there is a nice little hospital kitchen, where beef tea or any little extra is prepared. There is also a well-supplied surgery. A paid dispenser comes in twice a day for half an hour, and dispenses for three doctors.

The chapel is small but pretty, and well cared for. Service is held twice on Sundays.

The casual wards are on the cell system.

The death rate is very low.

Altogether this workhouse is a credit to the master and matron as well as to the guardians.

Swindon, Wiltshire (1890)

This instalment in the 'Workhouse Life in Town and Country' series by Mrs Emma Brewer records her visit to the Swindon workhouse.[57] Its Highworth Road site, later St Margaret's Hospital, is now covered by modern housing.

AGRICULTURAL. —SWINDON.

Swindon workhouse is an agreeable surprise. A three-mile drive across pretty country brings you to a grey and white stone building, approached by an avenue of trees, and standing in the midst of a garden gay with flowers, and well stocked with fruit trees and vegetables. Violets and primroses perfumed the air. Three railed-off portions of grass, with paths and seats, were devoted to the men, women, and children. The house and gardens occupy eight acres of land.

It was built forty years ago to accommodate four hundred and sixty inmates, but at the time of our visit there were but one hundred and sixty there. Here, as at Cirencester and Gloucester, the old, the young, and the sick are all under the same roof. At Swindon they take in infectious cases also, but nurse them in an isolated building on the further side of the garden.

The orphans are boarded out in various villages, and a lady on the spot is asked to keep watch over the one child near to her. This is better than in other districts, but still not so effective as the plan adopted in Paris.

Whole families of paupers have taken up their abode here: one man whom we saw came in quite young; went out, and came back married; he is old now, but still here, and so are his children.

The inmates go out when they please by giving seventy-two hours' notice.

The people who find their way here, as a rule, belong to the agricultural and manufacturing class; those of the latter more often than not through want of thrift and indulgence in drink.

There were thirty old women and twenty-one young ones in the house the day we were there, and the knowledge that these last can come in when they please has a very demoralising effect.

The master, matron, porter, trained nurse, and industrial trainer are the only paid officers. The work of the house is done by paupers.

The board-room and passages are abundantly supplied with beautifully made mats — the work of the inmates.

The old women, of whom the majority are widows, were sitting in a very cheerful room, busily employed in making corduroy trousers and coats, for one of the features of this house is that every single article of clothing for men, women, and children is made by the inmates. One old woman, a beautiful worker, volunteered that they were all quite happy.

On my asking how such an industrious and good worker happened to be here, the answer came — which I feared — Drink.

The day nursery was the brightest and most home-like of all that had come under our notice. There were plenty of toys, the gifts principally of the Great Western Railway workpeople; and in the boys' dayroom we were delighted to see cricket bats.

The workpeople on the Great Western take a deep interest in this workhouse. They collect among themselves a penny a week from each person for some weeks in the year, and with the produce take the old people into Swindon Park for a day's outing, and give them besides sixpence each. At Christmas they give young and old a treat — the foreman of the works and a certain number of the men being appointed to be present to see that their wishes are carried out.

The older children attend the Board Schools in the village, and being dressed neatly in dark blue serge (a kind thought of the matron) instead of the usual dingy brown derry, they are not distinguishable from the children they mix with.

The clothes' store room might with truth be labelled Industry and Ingenuity. Coats, trousers, dresses — in fact, everything made in the house — were here neatly folded in compartments, ready for use: there were tiny stays made out of bits torn from the flannel or ends of cloth neatly joined together, kettle holders made out of bits of corduroy left from making the trousers, and boys' caps made of bits of serge left from the girls' dresses; every strip of material was most ingeniously worked up.

Entering the old men's ward we were greeted by the sight of the first clock we had seen in a workhouse ward, and we found a second before we had finished our round.

The beds are stuffed with cocoa-nut fibre, which is, I think, hard and uncomfortable. The tick is laced up so as to allow the hand to pass in and pick it.

The food is good; no stimulants are allowed, milk and sugar being given instead.

In the summer the children have plenty of fruit: a basket of strawberries being a frequent treat. The value of the garden produce consumed by the inmates during the last half year was £46 16s. 6d.

The trained nurse evidently has a good deal of influence over the sick people, whom she keeps absolutely clean and comfortable.

The matron was greeted with smiles of welcome everywhere, and her influence, especially over the young mothers, is of the utmost service. She spends every gift she possesses, even her voice, which is sweet, upon the inmates. When she has five minutes to spare she goes into a ward and sings a hymn or a ballad to the old and the sick, whom it cheers and comforts.

Three-fourths of the old men are over eighty, and one old woman of eighty-nine years does an immense amount of needlework and without the use of spectacles.

But for one or two things, for example the children sleeping two in a bed, I should say this was one of the best workhouses and least depressing of any we had seen.

For work for the casuals old railway sleepers are bought at fourteen shillings a ton, which being chopped up yield a good profit.

Newhaven, Sussex (1890)

This instalment in the 'Workhouse Life in Town and Country' series by Mrs Emma Brewer records her visit to the Newhaven workhouse.[58] Later home to Newhave Downs Hospital, the building is currently occupied by Newhaven Polyclinic and Rehabilitation Centre.

NEWHAVEN.

The Newhaven workhouse specially deals with the South Downs district. It is a well-built square house situate on a steep hill and with a good and well-kept garden, and two fields in front of it.

The breezes from the downs and the sea blow straight on to it, and so in point of situation it is well off.

The master is an energetic, sensible man, and well suited to his work. He said that of course a good many found their way here from the vessels in the harbour, but not in sufficient numbers to deprive it of its character as an Agricultural Workhouse.

Fifty or sixty is the number of the inmates. The children over six are sent to the Hurstpierpoint Orphanage, which is under Government inspection, and to that in Willington, which is under the care of the Hon. Mrs. Campion.

Poverty brought on by drink is found to be the cause of pauperism here as elsewhere, and two-thirds of the children are deserted. As a rule, the fathers are sailors, who having been away on long voyages return home to find that the wives have behaved badly. In their anger they break up the homes and go off never to return, and the wives and children end by coming in here.

Strange people are every now and then admitted here: one a tailor who had owned a large establishment in a good part of London. One day a tall handsome young man, describing himself as a decorator, applied for admittance through the relieving officer. His manner and speech proclaimed him a gentleman, and there was reason to believe he had not given his right name; but there was no time to prove this, for one morning he died suddenly, leaving no clue behind him, and the authorities were never able to discover his friends.

Nearly all the present inmates are chronic invalids, helpless from age, or imbeciles. Very rarely do they get an able-bodied man, which is an improvement upon eight years ago, when a large number of strong fellows were inmates, and might be seen loafing about Newhaven with pipes in their mouths.

The amount of out-door relief, I am sorry to say, has gone up. In the house, the expense per head is three shillings and tenpence halfpenny. Beer used to be freely given to all, but this has been stopped. This leads to many complaints, and it would be well if good beef tea or something like it could be substituted.

The food is good, and the master does his best to vary it; but the guardians here as elsewhere are slow to agree to any innovations which mean extra expense.

A little needlework is done after a fashion by the women, but is of no real use.

The walls and passages are kept whitewashed and painted by tramps.

The night wards contained eight iron bedsteads each, provided with chaff beds much too short. These bedsteads are a mistake, being very clumsy and heavy indeed; much too heavy for one strong man to move.

Seeing how narrow the passages were, and how small the wards, we inquired if the house had been originally built for a workhouse, and were told "certainly"; and, further, that it was built by Lord Chichester, who paid the workmen in pence.

The men's infirmary is at the top of the house, and possesses a lovely view over downs and sea. Five or six old people occupied it; there were pictures, arm-chairs, and a good fire.

The nurse, a good woman, but not certificated, looks after the old men; and as there is no paid cook, she and both master and matron have constantly to turn their hand to the cooking, or there would be nothing to eat.

In the women's sick ward we saw a ship's stewardess aged eighty-five who had just cut two teeth, a poor girl subject to fits, and a woman with a paralysed hand.

The store-rooms were neat and well stocked, and here we found the tired, overworked matron performing the tasks which in other workhouses are done by the able-bodied women; but here there was no one sufficiently capable even to put on a patch decently.

We found the kitchen in the care of a half-witted girl, the daughter of one of the inmates. Outside the kitchen is a deep well which supplies all the water, and to our surprise this again was under the care of an idiot assisted by a tramp. We asked if it were not dangerous to permit this man to have the care of the well, the answer was Yes, but that there was no help for it, and that he was accustomed to it.

In the disused bakehouse the guardians have had a fixed bath built, which is of great benefit.

The last to be visited was the women's day room. There were nine occupants, all more or less imbecile, sitting round the fire and amusing themselves each after her own fashion. One of them had formerly been in the royal service. A second, a tall powerful old woman, took an interest in us and became so demonstrative that the master had to interfere; she has a violent temper, and bites or stabs any one who crosses her. She has many children somewhere in the world, besides two grown-up idiots here, one sitting by her side and the other the woman whom we noticed in the kitchen. The greatest solace and amusement of this woman at present is a large doll, which she exhibited with much pride.

On our way to the casual wards we came upon the only little bit of poetry in the building. We heard a great cooing and rustling, and on the master calling "Charlie," a beautiful blue rock pigeon came flying to him. The manner in which it became an inmate of the workhouse is peculiar. One cold day, two years ago, the master was writing in his office, and a good fire was burning in the grate, when suddenly down the chimney into the fire fell a pigeon, burning its wings and feet badly. One of the old men, who is still in the house, took charge of it and nursed it with tenderness back to health; and now that it is quite well it singles him out for special attention, visiting him in the sick ward and resting on his neck. Evidently the pigeon has no thought of leaving the house; it is quite content, and resists all attempts to give it companions of its own kind.

The casual wards have fixed wooden bunks and rugs, nothing more; they are warmed in cold weather by fires from without. The employment given to tramps is gardening and oakum picking.

There is an isolated block for contagious diseases, should any break out in the house; it was unoccupied and unfurnished when we were there. We thought it a convenient and compact little block, with its two wards and little kitchen and scullery.

The back garden is devoted to vegetables, and looks flourishing. One year it yielded £40 profit, another year £25, but if nothing were made of it, it would yet be a blessing to the master, whose sole recreation it is.

The house is square and well built, but it wants money spent upon it inside, and more paid labour. It is a very depressing place, from the fact that youth, health, and brightness are all absent from it, and that the work falling upon so few drags down their spirit and energy.

The only thing of beauty about it is the pigeon, and the only hopeful work the garden.

Haverfordwest, Pembrokeshire (1894)

In 1894-5, as part of its campaign to improve the nursing and medical facilities in provincial workhouse infirmaries, the *British Medical Journal* published a series of reports detailing its visits to around fifty such institutions in England and Wales. Below are extracts from its report on the Haverfordwest union workhouse.[59] The premises, on Union Hill, later operated as St Thomas's Hospital but have now been converted into flats.

HAVERFORDWEST, SOUTH WALES.

It has rarely been our lot to visit a workhouse infirmary more unsuited for its purpose, or more ill-provided with all that is necessary for the comfort of the sick. The master readily acceded to the request of Dr. Williams, the medical officer, to show us the infirmary; but we must confess to a feeling of surprise that the matron, whom we only saw for a brief moment, did not respond to the master's suggestion that she should accompany us through the female department.

This union embraces a large extent of country, and takes paupers from sixty-six parishes; the town is the centre of a wide district.

The workhouse is well situated on a hill, and has extensive grounds around it; it is an old house, and in every part is quite behind the times. It is built round four courts, which form the airing courts of the various departments.

There is accommodation for thirty-two sick, and there is besides a fever ward placed at the top of the house, at the present time empty. The wards are of variable size, and are distributed on the ground and first floors; the largest is for eleven beds, and the smaller wards hold two or three beds; the arrangement on the male and female side is the same. The wards are dreary places, the walls dirty, washed over with dingy yellow colouring, windows on one side, only one fireplace at one end, looking bare of furniture for the sick.

The iron bedsteads are low and on them are three planks held by a crosspiece, not always laid close, and on this a chaff mattress about three inches thick. We saw the helpless bedridden old people lying on these beds, and they must have found them a sorry rest for their weary bones. There are about four spring beds distributed in the wards, but they have only the chaff mattress over the springs. There is no means of ventilation but by the windows, and, as the fireplace in some of the wards is small it is hardly probable that the atmosphere is changed in the night.

The system of warming is peculiar to this part of the country. "Culm," which is clay and anthracitic slack kneaded into balls, is used in the grates; when quite alight it is red hot and must throw out a good heat, but it is slow in kindling and can hardly be of service for obtaining a fire quickly.

The classes of patients are of the usual description found in the workhouses. On one of the spring beds there was an old woman with hemiplegia, helpless all but one hand and unable to turn herself; in the male ward was a fine man with erysipelas in his leg. On inquiring as to the treatment the "nurse" told us that he washed it for himself twice a day with Condy's fluid, but that otherwise no dressing was used. We could not but think what a pity it was that more vigorous measures were not tried, since by a speedy curing of the leg the rates would be relieved of that man's keep. He was too long for his bed.

There were eight patients in bed in all; in this part of the infirmary, including senile debility, rheumatism, paralysis, chest complaints, and old age, and several very infirm men and women up in the wards. We were shown a small ward with four beds in it, all occupied; it opened immediately from one of the yards, it was without a fireplace, and was lighted by one small window. This is the tramps' sick ward. We could not ascertain that any one person was responsible for attendance in this ward, and, if assistance was wanted in the night, the most able-bodied of the tramps would have to go some little distance before lie could obtain it, as there is no communication bell.

The sanitary appliances are quite rudimentary; there is no water laid on to the upper floors; the only conveniences for the wards are commodes, of which there are a few in each ward; one is placed outside on each landing, intended for use at night, that for the men being enclosed within a screen, that for the women being open. It can hardly be expected that these poor infirm folk will go outside the wards on a cold night, nor is it well that they should. The commodes in the wards are emptied after 6 in the morning. On going round the wards we saw some ordinary utensils about, some of which were unemptied. The closets are all outside; they are simply cesspools, and some were very unpleasant.

The water supply is ample, and is obtained from wells in the courts. The pumps in each court discharge over troughs down which the refuse water is emptied.

There is only one fixed bath, and that is in the tramps' room; it is a small one, sunk in the floor, with a tap to supply hot water, but the cold has to be carried in from the yard. We saw no baths which could be used for the sick, and, as every drop of water must be carried up or down, it is probable that bathing is not largely practised in this infirmary; indeed, the patients and their linen did not look particularly clean at the time of our visit.

The "nurse" is untrained; she is solely responsible for the care of the sick and of midwifery cases; there is no night nurse nor regular pauper help at night. On inquiring how the helpless patients were attended to during the night, we were informed that they had to obtain such assistance as they could from the more able-bodied paupers who slept in the ward. As we found that bedsores were recognised as one of the usual ailments in the infirmary, it can be imagined how much help these paupers are able to render to each other. We pictured to ourselves the sad condition of these helpless old people, passing the long hours of the dark nights on their comfortless beds, uncared for, uncleansed, unfed. We say "dark night" because we have ascertained that all lights were removed from the wards after the patients are in bed, nor did we see any appliances for lighting the staircases or passages.

The labour ward is for two beds; it has no separate offices, and all refuse must be carried downstairs.

There is no system of classification; we saw the imbeciles and "harmless lunatics" among the patients in the wards; one half-witted boy was busy serving the dinners. There were no lock cases in the infirmary, and we were informed that there were no isolation wards for offensive cases. The "harmless lunatics" appeared to be straying about where they pleased.

On our way round the house we passed through the "nursery," a large ill-furnished room, the floor laid down with paving stones; there was a large table, two benches, two wooden cradles, a few chairs, the latter round a fireplace which was most insufficient to warm the room in the winter. In this room the infants stay with their mothers until they are 2 years old. There was a baby in each cradle, one looking very ill; its mother thought it was "sickening for something." There was no rug, or even a bit of sacking on which the infants might crawl; a more dreary place to be called a nursery can hardly be imagined. Though not properly coming within the scope of this inquiry, we mention this room as indicating the lack of a kindly and sympathetic spirit on the part of those responsible for the management of the house.

The dinners were being served at the time of our visit. It was "broth day"; the broth, made of mutton and vegetables, both looked and smelt good, but it was served in wooden bowls which were black with age and grease. We tasted the bread and butter, both of which were good. We saw no bed cards in the wards, but the master informed us that the medical officer has a free hand in ordering extras, and that milk and beef tea are taken into the wards for the sick at night. As the last meal is given at 6 o'clock, and the first at 8 in the morning, it is necessary that the old, people should have something to take in the night.

The day room on the men's side is used for sleeping purposes; there were four beds in it; it is also the tailor's shop where the male clothing is looked over and mended. It is a very small room, with one window, and at the time of our visit the floor was piled with clothing, and the air of the room was quite unwholesome. On the women's side the day room is not used for a sleeping room; it had one large settle in it, but no comfortable chairs or anything to make it homely.

On passing through one of the courts we were shown the disinfecting apparatus. It is a small galvanised iron box, like a good-sized tank, the lid broken at the edges, and having underneath it a tray for the fire; this was standing in a shed close to the closets.

It seems hopeless to make any recommendation in the case of this infirmary. The building is unsuitable for its purpose, and the system on which it is worked is faulty in every particular.

Reading, Berkshire (1894)

This report from the *British Medical Journal* campaign to improve Poor Law nursing featured Reading workhouse.[60] Later becoming Battle Hospital, the site is now covered by modern housing.

READING.

Our request to visit and report on this infirmary met at once with a ready assent on the part of the Board, the Chairman (Mr. Apsley Smith) was waiting to act as cicerone on our arrival. It is a pleasure to turn from some of the squalid ill-found houses with which we have made acquaintance to a country union which is doing its best to meet the wants of the inmates and to bring itself abreast of the times, and as we went through its various departments we could see evidence of thoughtful consideration on the part of the guardians seconded by their officers.

We turned our steps to the infirmary which stands well apart from the house to the left hand after passing through the gates. It is a new building of two storeys in the form of the letter H, the administration block being in the middle connected with the male and female wings by an open covered causeway. The ground around the infirmary was still being turned up by the workmen, but it is intended that the recreation grounds for the patients shall be both in front of and behind the hospital. On entering the middle block we found the "sister's" quarters, the nurses' dining-room, waiting-room, and surgery, and the lying-in wards, the latter on the first floor. The nurses' quarters are not yet finished, for it was found that the plans had not provided sufficient accommodation for the nursing staff, the original estimate of staff not being adequate to the needs of the hospital.

The lying-in wards consist of three wards, the labour ward with two beds in direct communication with another ward, also with two beds, for the patients after the labour is over; a larger ward holding six beds for the convalescents. The women remain in this department for at least a month or longer if it is necessary. The sister, who is the midwife, informed us that the number of confinements was about 26 in the year. This department has its separate offices of modern construction, an ample supply of hot and cold water, and a bath. There were two convalescents in the large ward.

The wards form the two uprights of the letter, the entrance is in the middle with wards on each side on the ground floor and upstairs; on the female side each ward holds 16 beds, on the male side the wards hold 18 beds. The construction of the two sides is alike, oblong rooms with windows on each side, a bed between the windows, and windows at the end, one of which is a door opening on to the garden or a balcony on the first floor. At this far end of the ward are the sanitary arrangements located in turrets, the bath-room on the one hand the lavatories on the other; these latter comprise two closets and a slop sink, the latter is a useful detail that is often overlooked. The bath is white porcelain set out from the wall; the floor is tiled, the walls cemented; hot and cold water are laid on. On the landings at the other end of the wards there is a small kitchen common to both wards, store-rooms for linen and clothing, for ward stores and medicines; also a separation ward with 3 beds, and in one case we found that the small ward had a closet, and hot and cold water supply adjacent. These separation wards are on every landing. The landings are tiled, the staircases are of stone, fenced by low brick walls. The walls of the wards are cement, painted in two shades of terra-cotta. The windows appeared to us to be set rather too high in the walls; they are sash windows, and above the sash is a ventilating section that opens outward, with a regulating bar. The wards are warmed by a central stove, the flue passing under the floor, the fires facing two ways; supplementary to the stove are steam pipes that are carried round the ward at the skirting. We noticed small ventilators in the walls at the level of the cornice, but it was evident that the chief method of ventilation is by means of the windows.

The bedsteads, most of them fitted with spring and hair mattresses, struck us as rather narrow, — 2 feet 9 inches. This, we were informed, is the width recommended by the Local Government Board; we should have preferred another 3 inches for comfort. The mattresses were made in three sections, facilitating the removal of any section that may be soiled. This is a good plan, but we would suggest that, instead of being of equal size, the section at the head should be smaller, and that at the feet larger, when a restless patient would not so easily disarrange the bed. Some of the old bedsteads are still in use, a flock bed with a feather bed on the top. We also saw some open locker tables between the beds; they consisted of two shelves, divided by a partition, the top being wider to form a table. The various oddments of personal possessions were not tidy to the eye, but it is more cleanly to have the contents in view. Tables, benches, armchairs, and a merlin chair completed the ward furniture. There are no day rooms, nor separate wards for the children.

The sister informed us that the wards were exceptionally light for the time of year; the greater number of cases that we saw were old age and paralysis. We noted with pleasure that the incontinent cases were distributed in the wards — were not relegated to some out-building or back ward, treated as the pariahs of the workhouse. On talking this method over with the sister, she said that in her experience — and this extends over twelve years — such a practice was unnecessary and exceedingly unwholesome. A severe case of ulceration of the leg on the female side was being treated in a small ward; iodoform was the dressing. Cases of phthisis, heart disease, rheumatism, and paraplegia were in the general wards. On the male side, beside the usual cases, there was a man with aneurysm, another convalescent from pneumonia; the sister feared that he was developing phthisis. In a small ward there was a man dying of phthisis. In conversation with the medical officer, Mr. Guilding, he said that with the material at his disposal he would be able to undertake any operation in the infirmary or to carry through any treatment. We noticed the absence of bed-cards, but these are under consideration, the present medical officer having only just been appointed. One of the female wards is at present used by the female imbeciles, the separation wards for these cases being in the hands of the builder. The patients are not classified as medical and surgical, the latter bearing a small proportion to the former.

There are two isolation buildings. One of these is "the cottage," in which are placed the male and female lock cases, tramps, under treatment, and some cases of offensive ulcerated legs. This building holds 12 beds in two wards, and can be used as male and female isolation simultaneously — at the time of our visit the patients were all males; there is bath-room and lavatory accommodation, and, by an ingenious contrivance of approach, was available for the two wards. The wards are heated by steam pipes and an open fire, the pipes were in use, and it struck very warm on entering. In another part of the grounds we came upon the infectious hospital, a one-storeyed hut, having two wards for 4 beds each, kitchen, bath room, and small laundry. The water supply is heated in the kitchen boiler. This hut is for the intercurrent cases only, and some of its space is being utilised for the additional nurses; when required for its original purpose, the nurses would be housed elsewhere.

As the department that we have been describing is that for which the sister is responsible, it will be well to state the number and style of her assistants. The sister is head of the nursing department, under the master, but she rules in her own department; there are four assistant nurses and two probationers to nurse the 150 in the hospital and those patients who are in isolation; two of the staff are on night duty, taking one month on night and three months on day duty alternately. The "cottage" is under the charge of a wards-man, the dressings being attended to by the nurses; he is responsible at night, calling aid if required. All the nurses are trained, the probationers are there as pupils; they will be instructed in nursing by the sister, who will also teach them midwifery; they will also have the advantage of lectures by the courtesy of the authorities of the Royal Berkshire Hospital. The pauper inmates are kept to the cleaning and service of the wards, except that they must help the night nurses with the bed making, until the Board is in a position to give more help at night. The hospital is in telephonic communication with the master's office. and the doctor's house is connected by telephone with the office.

The food is prepared in the main kitchen, where it is divided into portions on plates, and sent to the hospital in covered tins; we were informed that it was quite hot when served out. The dieting of the sick is in the hands of the medical officer. On looking through the table of that which is given to the infirm, we see that it includes fresh cooked meat three days in the week. and on the other days there is hash, meat pie, or suet pudding, and broth. With the meat they have potato, or other vegetable; they also have butter and tea allowed to them. We saw the dinner being served, and it looked well cooked. The bread is made in the house; both it and the butter tasted of good quality. The sister informed us that any special diets that may be ordered for the sick are always nicely prepared. The kitchen is under a man cook.

There are about 60 certified lunatics under the care of the guardians, for whose accommodation alterations are being made in one of the detached buildings. These plans did not recommend themselves to us, for they only include the female patients, the male lunatics having been removed to the house with their male attendant. This arrangement seemed to us to be extravagant as duplicating all the service, and necessitating the appointment of an assistant for the female attendant unless she is to be always on duty, and unless the guardians are prepared to run the risk of a casualty. This block comprises the dayroom, dormitories, and attendant's rooms, with the bathrooms, lavatories, and padded room. We understand that the original plan included male and female quarters, with attendants' rooms in the middle block, an arrangement that sounds more complete. The place was in the hands of the workmen, so that we could hardly judge of its capabilities, but we were unfavourably impressed with the padded room. The floor of this is laid in padded sections screwed to the floor. In the event of excreta being on the sections it would flow between the interstices, and the floor could not be cleansed except by removing the pads. The window also appeared to be quite unprotected. We noticed the same defect in construction in the padded room on the male side.

The washing for the whole establishment, with the exception of that used in the infectious hut, is done in the one laundry. It is a large, well-lighted building, the steam for the coppers comes from the great heating boilers, which are beneath the ironing room, supplying warmth as well as steam, so that the only fire in the laundry is the ironing stove. All machinery is turned by hand. The soiled hospital sheets are at once put in a large sunk tank with Jeyes' fluid as a purifying agent, before they go through the washhouse. In this same shed there is the disinfecting oven, heated by steam; we noted that there appeared to be no pyrometer indicating the heat, it might be well to add this. The two large boilers heat the water, and send the steam for supplying warmth all over the building. In the winter the master thought it would be necessary to work both boilers.

In concluding this article, we note with satisfaction the steady progress that trained nursing has made in this union. The nurse who now holds the post of sister has worked in the old hospital for twelve years in the face of many difficulties, at first with a male nurse for the men, and then later on single-handed. It must be gratifying to all concerned to see the results, and we cordially re-echo the Chairman's words, that it is well to have seen the end of two such abuses as pauper nursing and the male nurse.

South Dublin, Ireland (1895)

One of the Irish reports from the *British Medical Journal* campaign to improve workhouse nursing came from the South Dublin union.[61] The site is now shared by St James' Hospital and Trinity College, with a few of the older buildings still surviving.

As the city of Dublin is divided by the river into north and south portions, it has two unions corresponding to these divisions; that in the south being the larger, and regarded by the authorities as somewhat of a model to other unions. The blocks are built of grey stone, which gives a prison-like aspect to the exterior, and the whole forms a large establishment capable of accommodating 3,000 inmates; these include able-bodied, infirm, sick, lunatics (that is, feeble-minded and idiots), and children.

The sick department is divided into "Catholic" and "Protestant" Hospitals, and there is a separate hospital for the children. The Roman Catholic patients are nursed by the nuns (Sisters of Mercy) and the Protestant by deaconesses, some of whom have been trained in the Tottenham Hospital, and formed part of the body under Dr. Lazeron. The nuns are untrained as nurses; they also nurse in the Children's Hospital.

The hospitals are supervised by a resident medical officer, who has 1,000 or more patients under his care, and there are three visiting doctors, each of whom has charge of one department. The matron who, in the absence of the master, kindly accompanied us round the building, gave us every facility for inspection. The wards gave us the impression of being overcrowded, an impression which a closer view confirmed. They are long, narrow rooms, not lofty, and as the windows are small, and not carried up to the cornice, the ventilation is imperfect; the beds are placed side by side, with only enough space between them to stand in, and that amount of space is not always possible; in some of the wards the rafters are unceiled, and on the top storeys the roofs are pitched. The walls have a smooth surface painted in two colours. As these wards are occupied by the patients without the relief of a day room, and as in winter they would be more crowded, with less ventilation than on a summer day, and with more artificial light, we felt convinced that the cubic allowance was insufficient. The ground plan of the hospitals forms three sides of a square, the Protestant Hospital taking one side, with the male patients on the top floor and the females on the two lower floors. The Children's

Hospital stands adjacent and accommodates over 100 patients; among these are the delicate children, and those who are unfit for school life.

The patients are classified as medical, surgical, and phthisical. A few female lock patients are kept apart and retained under treatment because they have children, but the bulk of these cases are sent to the Government Lock Hospital. Mild cases of epilepsy are treated in these wards; simple idiots are also brought into the wards for treatment. A small bed card was over each bed; it was the regulation card, giving no clinical information. We noticed also a few temperature charts. The cases are such as would be found in any general hospital except that there were more cases of hopeless paralysis and senility. We were glad to see that these sad cases were being nursed in the general wards. The special wards for phthisis (this disease being very prevalent and fatal in Ireland) are kept at a higher temperature.

Each patient was supplied with a small high table between the beds for food; there was a long table down the middle of the ward with benches, a few armchairs and ordinary chairs; a few commodes and lockers completed the furniture. The bedsteads are mostly of iron, with wire-wove and hair mattresses for special patients ; otherwise cocoa fibre and straw is in use, and the matron informed us that some wood-wool shavings had been sent for trial in the ticks. We did not observe that any of the beds were provided with pulls. This is a great omission, especially in a workhouse hospital where so many of the patients are helpless, and where the assistance is so scanty.

The nursing in the part under the nuns is carried on under the triple disadvantage of being done by an untrained staff, of the nursing of the male patients being confined to supervision only, and of the night nursing being in the hands of a different staff. We noticed at once the difference between the work of the trained and untrained nurses, though the nuns brought system and order into their wards, their work was just lacking in that attention to details of nursing which can only be learnt in a hospital. Pauper help is very largely used in nursing the sick; the supply of nuns or of deaconesses is about one to each large ward containing 45 to 50 beds, or to a group of smaller wards, so that too mush reliance is placed on the inmates, or "deputies" as they are called. These paupers receive extra rations, and have some privileges, besides such bribes in kind or money as they may receive from the patients. On the female side most of the deputies are women of indifferent character, retained in the house because of their children; on the male side we noticed some able-bodied deputies who ought to have been earning their living outside, and off the rates. We omitted to mention that there is a wardmaster — an officer responsible for the control of the ward under the nuns.

At night there is one nurse for the male side and one for the female side, assisted by a staff of deputies, one or more of whom sit up in each ward. By this arrangement a large and important hospital is practically nursed by paupers, especially at night.

The patients in the separation ward appeared to be looking after themselves, or at best were in charge of an inmate. It is hard to conceive a more dismal hole than that in which we found these cases — a small, dark ward, crowded with women and children of a very low type, dirty and untidy in their persons and clothing, the unfortunate infants uncared for except by their mothers; the whitewashed walls, dirty floor. and pitched roof, small windows, low wooden frames, and straw beds, presented a picture of official neglect which we shall not soon forget. The door is locked on these inmates from 7 p.m., and they are left to get through the night with such decency and cleanliness as can be obtained by the use of pails, etc., and under no vestige of control.

The Children's Hospital is a bright and cheerful spot among these dreary surroundings; the wards are large, walls painted in two colours, cots down the middle, and small bedsteads round the walls, with toys, pictures, and plants giving it a pleasant appearance. The boys' and girls' wards duplicate each other on the ground floor. There is also a good playground, but no dayroom to relieve the wards in bad weather. The children are treated here until the age of 14 or 15. The hospital is nursed by the nuns and the inmates. The cases include every variety — the chronic hip-joint, or spinal case, with cases requiring active surgical treatment, or of acute medical diseases; some convalescents were running about.

The nursery for healthy infants under 2 years occupies two floors, that for the day being on the ground floor, and above is the room where the mothers sleep with their infants. In the day nursery there was a large number of babies, some in wooden cradles or being nursed by their mothers. The cradles are filled with straw, covered by a sheet and blanket; some of the cots that we looked into had wet sheets and straw; in some the food had been upset and not cleansed; many of the infants were untidy and ill cared for, the whole nursery showing want of control and supervision. The atmosphere, in spite of cross ventilation, was very close; there was no sense of freshness, but a very powerful odour of uncleanness. There is an officer over the nursery, but she is much handicapped in her work by the ignorant mothers, who are very difficult to manage. The lavatory and bath room attached to this department was littered and untidy, and anything but wholesome.

Besides these two departments for children, there is a probationary ward for the detention of fresh admissions without their parents for ten or more days at the discretion of the medical officer before they are sent into the schools.

The aged and infirm, as is the case in all Irish workhouses, form a separate class, and are located in blocks quite away from the hospitals. That for women was one of the best parts of the house; they are in small huts which run three sides round a garden where are seats, flowers, and grass, all of easy access from the wards. The wards themselves had a bright, home-like appearance, the cross-lights and the distance from the high buildings allowing of plenty of sunshine. The old men are not so well placed; they are in one of the stone blocks, their wards are dark and low-pitched, are crowded, and altogether are destitute of the comfort that one looks for for the aged. Here we were introduced to the "harrow" bed, which is quite a feature in an Irish workhouse; it consists of five parallel wooden bars supported at the foot on an iron crossbar and two iron legs, and at the head it rests on a continuous rail fixed on iron uprights about 6 inches from the wall, or, failing the rail, its place is taken by two legs; there is no bed head, the tick and pillows resting against the wall, and there are no sides. The bed is 2 feet 3 inches wide, stands about a foot from the ground, and on this is placed the straw tick. A variation of this bed is two low trestles, supporting two or three planks.

These old people are under the care of inmates, themselves only one remove from the stage of infirmity; no one is supposed to be in these wards who requires any help during the night, and that is as well, taking into consideration that the infirm are locked in their wards at 7 p.m., with only such assistance as they can render each other; and also that the only sanitary appliances are the commodes or pails in the wards. We did not notice anything but benches for the old men, either in their day room or wards.

The lunacy wards are beyond these blocks, separated from them by locked gates. The wards are large, but very full, the beds being placed in double rows back to back down the middle of the ward, as well as down the sides, an arrangement that appeared to us to be an unusual one for that class of patient. Some of the more helpless cases were in crib or box beds filled with straw; the wards were distinctly overcrowded, for the ceiling was low-pitched and the windows small. Several of the inmates were in the court, but many were in bed. One recent admission, the victim of puerperal mania, was disturbing the whole ward by her cries, and arousing some of the patients to restlessness; this patient was restrained in bed by the usual lunatic's nightgown, and the matron was going to put on extra pauper assistants for the night. We were informed that there is no padded room, as violent cases are sent at once to the asylum; but in this case, the attack being recent, the doctor wished not to send the woman to the asylum. There is a great want all through the various departments of small wards for isolation. These wards are under the charge of officers, but they are not trained in lunacy work, and the number of patients under their care, amounting sometimes to 60 or more, makes it quite impossible for the attendants with only the help of the deputies to do more than keep these unfortunates in their places; indeed, it appeared to us that neither in their accommodation nor treatment was much done for these unhappy patients. The male lunatics are similarly circumstanced, if possible more crowded.

The maternity block is near the gate, and is a small self-contained house, accommodating 40 beds in four wards. On the ground floor there are two wards for the labour cases; the wards are used indiscriminately, there being no separate room for the confinement, and above are the wards for pregnant women. There is no day room. The walls are whitewashed, and there is a want of light, the block being overshadowed by taller buildings. The number of confinements varies from 80 to 100 per annum. The women are attended by a midwife, who at the time of our visit was incapacitated from duty by a poisoned hand; her place was taken by a midwife from outside.

We were surprised to learn that there are no sanitary appliances in this block. The matron showed us a privy at some little distance, to which everything has to be carried. There is no bath room, slop-sink, or any of these adjuncts to nursing; and as there appeared to be structural space for the addition of these offices, we are at a loss to discover the cause of their absence.

The wards are heated by open fireplaces; many of them are old-fashioned and wasteful of heat and coals. In the winter there are besides steam-pipes running round the skirting of the wards; these pipes are of very large diameter. The windows throughout the buildings are small, set in heavy frames, and they do not reach the cornice. Sometimes they open on a pivot, and otherwise the upper half of the sash falls inwards, on a toothed bar; as the frames are heavy, these are awkward to manage. Gas is used throughout the workhouse.

The sanitary system is in course of alteration, many new closets are being added to the wards, and additional bath rooms with hot and cold supply; these will be a great improvement. The new closets are fitted in the modern style with the flush, and they are on the landings near the wards; this situation appeared to us too near to be sanitary, as the space did not admit of an intercepting lobby. There are some closets outside the male wards that are flushed automatically. We were informed that the cistern discharges itself every four hours, but, whatever may be the interval, it is evidently insufficient, as the trough was full of filth, and the fittings, floor. etc., were in a dirty state. There also appeared to be a deficiency in the arrangements for the disposal of foul clothing, as we came across a soiled tick hung over the railing outside a ward, making the air quite insanitary; we were informed that it was on its way to the laundry.

The laundries and kitchens are attached to each hospital, and are under the control of the officers; some of them were well-appointed kitchens, with suitable appliances for expeditious and economical cooking. There are, besides, the main kitchen and laundry for general service. This union kills its own meat; we saw the victims in a paddock close to the building awaiting their turn of sacrifice. The bread also is baked in the house. The sick diet is in the hands of the medical staff; the children are largely fed on eggs and milk. The inmates were assembling for dinner at 2 o'clock; this is surely a long interval for the old and young, the breakfast hour being 8 o'clock.

Cootehill, County Cavan (1895)

> The second Irish report included from *British Medical Journal* campaign to improve workhouse nursing is that for the rural Cootehill Union in County Cavan.[62] The Cootehill workhouse building no longer exist.

We received a cordial welcome from Dr. Moorhead, medical officer of the workhouse, who very kindly took us round, giving us every help in his power. The house, a grey stone building, stands close to the railway station, but about a mile from the town, on rising ground, facing south and north. It is what is styled a "second class house," a term describing its capacity (about 800 inmates), but not referring to its efficiency.

Passing through the lodge and the body of the house we came to the infirmary. As we looked at the exterior we were struck by the small slit apertures in the wall which serve as windows; they are a relic of the time when the therapeutic value of light and air was not understood. On the ground floor is the surgery, a small room full of drugs, and intended for the use of the medical officer; to the back is a disused ward holding 8 beds, now used for operations, or for the isolation of any case; opposite is a stone paved room intended for a men's day-room when the infirmary is full; the corresponding room on the female side is used as the infirmary kitchen; its equipment is a wide open grate, over which was suspended a large cauldron, containing water, we believe, a large iron boiler containing the only water at hand for use, a dresser, some tin plates, mugs, a saucepan, and a frying pan. There is a close range in the nurse's kitchen upstairs.

It is almost impossible to convey to the reader the picture of squalor and wretchedness that greeted our eyes as we mounted the stairs to the first floor where the sick are; long narrow rooms, beds on each side, 6 on a side in the first ward, and about 4 on a side in the continuation ward; the beds close together, on one side (the north) square windows in heavy iron frames, and opposite to them the slit-like apertures already commented on, rough colour-washed walls, roof open to the slates, an old-fashioned grate at one end, more chimney than fire, a bench and a few wooden armchairs; a bucket, chair, and a small table at one end completed the furniture. The bedsteads, close together, were many of them of the hospital pattern, but we saw the "harrow" bed in use besides. On the spring beds Dr. Moorhead uses a pad of old blanketing, this being, in his

'Harrow' beds in a ward at Cootehill workhouse infirmary.

opinion, more sanitary than the hair mattress, as it can be washed, but on the "harrow" beds there was a tick filled with straw, and all the pillows are of straw. On the old bedsteads the tick and pillow are placed against the wall, which is sometimes damp. As the square windows are neither weather-tight nor air-proof, the lower section has been boarded up, as some of the beds are across them; the whole of the ventilation is by means of the windows, the upper section swings on a pivot regulated by a toothed bar, but the frames are so heavy that it is a trial of strength to open them; such other openings as were in the roof or cornice were evidently out of gear. There are four such wards, two on each side, and it must be observed that those at each end are over the lunatics' quarters.

The patients presented all the variety of ailment that is found in a general hospital, though the larger number are chronic cases; the wards were comparatively empty, as it was the summer; there were 22 patients in the wards, and 35 in all on the medical relief book. Several of these were in bed; a man with rheumatic arthritis, a severe case of pneumonia, a case of intestinal obstruction, ulceration of the leg, senile debility. and some good cases of recovery from operation; all surgical cases are dealt with here, as it is practically the hospital for the district. There is no lying-in ward, the women being confined in the general wards.

The nurse, a trained midwife, has acquired her general training under the medical officer; her wards were clean and showed that much can be done for the sick by a zealous nurse, even under such unpromising circumstances. She has the assistance of an inmate in each ward, and on the male side there is a paid wardsman, who works under the nurse, and who has been of much service in inducing habits of order and cleanliness (Dr. Moorhead's report). There is no night nurse. Dr. Moorhead selects the wardswomen from the older women, rejecting, if possible, those who are in the house with infants, the latter being likely to neglect the patients for the sake of their child. The nurse is responsible to the medical officer for the infirmary, and she also is held responsible for the custody of the lunatics. There are bells from the wards to the nurse's room.

The fever hospital, a two-storeyed building, stands at right angles to the main building. It was built later than the infirmary, and exhibits many improvements in its structure and arrangement; the walls have a smooth surface; the wards are larger and more lofty; the windows are of fair size and face each other; the ceilings are plastered; but the fireplaces are of bad construction, and there are no internal sanitary appliances. A nurse — untrained, but experienced — is in charge, with pauper help. At the time of our visit there were two patients, both convalescent, under her care; considering the decline of fever all over the country, the number of patients is never likely to be large, except in the event of an epidemic. Still, as the nurse has entire charge of the laundry and kitchen in the hospital her hands must be more than full when her patients are in the acute stage.

The lunatics were almost a sadder sight than the sick in the wards; they are in the two ends of the infirmary on the ground floor. Their quarters consist of the old cells disused by the medical officer, but not removed by the guardians, and the corridor and dayroom attached. In the corridor were 3 beds head to foot against the wall, and the other beds were in the day-room, no furniture but a bench and a table, rough whitewashed walls, a small window, and an old grate protected by bars. The recreation ground, a stone-walled grass-grown yard, having a deal board as a seat; the woman standing up, herself feeble-minded, is the caretaker, the previous one having been discharged by the doctor for beating the poor creatures. These unhappy wretches are confined to this section, where neither treatment nor alleviation is possible. On the male side the section is the same, but many of the men were employed about the place.

The airing courts attached to the infirmary are small grass-grown courts at the back of the building. In this house Dr. Moorhead has endeavoured to redeem the waste of desolation by laying them out somewhat like a garden, and placing a few seats for the old people, an act of kindness that has been much appreciated, the old people finding some relief to the monotony of their existence by the cultivation of the garden. The law of classification is so rigid that these poor people are practically imprisoned in the part of the house to which they are assigned. The rank grass that we saw in the lunatics' yard is anything but wholesome for the inmates.

We now turned our steps to the body of the house, where are the quarters for the aged men and women. These consist of long wards, low-pitched and unceiled, rough, whitewashed walls, windows at either end, and three at the side, a stove, harrow beds down each side, a few benches without backs, and a table at one end. The rooms were dirty, the patients were unkempt and unwashed, and as the only materials that we saw for the toilet were a tin basin and a dirty round towel this was not to be wondered at. This ward is approached through a concrete floored apartment called the dayroom, equally dirty and uninviting; most of the men were here, seated on a cross-bench in front of the comfortless grate; a long deal table, almost as black as the floor, was the only other furniture. On the female side most of the women were in the dormitory, many of them at needlework; their appearance was not quite so bad as that of the men, though the conditions in which they lived were the same. Both the men and women are in charge of an inmate, these caretakers themselves being old and infirm. In fine weather this class can sit under the sheds in the yard, but in the winter they are confined to their quarters. Before passing to the nursery we will describe the sanitary arrangements in these and the sick wards. It must be understood that there are no indoor conveniences, and that the privies are at some distance from the wards, and therefore unavailable in bad weather or at night; to meet this difficulty the old people are provided with open pails or buckets; in the sick wards these buckets are enclosed in a wooden chair. It must also be observed that the infirm wards are locked on the outside from 7 p.m. until 6.30 a.m. The greater part of that time the ward is in darkness, and the only assistance available is such as the inmates can render to each other. The pails remain unemptied until the morning in both the sick and the

222

infirm wards. We pictured to ourselves these wards locked up, the windows closed to husband the feeble warmth of the stove; the inmates on their narrow beds, from which they may slip to the floor in their weakness and there remain until the morning; the filthy-smelling buckets, some doubtless upset in the dark; no water to be had, no help available except in case of dire need; we turned away sick at heart that such things should be. In the sick wards the nurse is at hand, but there is no night nurse, and the excreta of the sick poison the air in those crowded wards. In the lunatic wards the same unsavoury method prevails, and the well-known dirty habits of the feeble-minded add to the foulness of the surroundings. The privies in this house are on the waggon system; a movable trough receives the soil, and when full is drawn out of a door at the back and wheeled on to the land. We noticed that the trough was neither cleansed or purified before being returned to the privy.

The nursery is close to the women's dayroom. It is a small room, having one window, rough walls, raftered ceiling, and an old grate set in the angle of the wall. We saw three infants in this nursery; one asleep in a wooden chair by the fire, its vomited food on its clothing and on the floor; another in a wooden cradle asleep; and the third sitting up, and roaring lustily for the attendant, who was not in the nursery. These infants were not clean or sweet; we were informed that their mothers were supposed to take care of them. We saw nothing suggestive of a nursery — no toys, amusements, or pictures. The room opens on to a yard.

There are no baths either in the infirmary, the fever hospital, or the infirm wards, nor is any water laid on to these departments, except to the laundry. The water for the infirmary is obtained from a tank in the body of the house, and that for the body of the house from a large well, from which it is pumped up by the inmates into the tank. The movable bath, having to be filled and emptied by hand, is now practically disused from lack of labour. The kitchen and the laundry remain as they were constructed when the house was built; in the former, three large boilers each, with its separate fire — one for the stirabout, one for potatoes, and one for holding cold water; in the laundry two old wash-tubs, a copper, and a box filled with stones on rollers serves as a mangle. Both these offices were very dirty — a dirty pauper was head cook, and two women were splashing dirty clothes about in dirty water in the laundry. The sole cooking utensils that we saw were two saucepans and a frying pan. It is no wonder that Dr. Moorhead pathetically remarks in his report that it is no use his ordering meat, for he has no one to cook it. Under these circumstances we were not surprised to find that the dietary was as elementary as the appliances, consisting principally of porridge, milk and bread for the able-bodied and old people, and for the sick such food as could be cooked in the small ill-found kitchen in the infirmary.

It has been our custom in concluding these reports to focus the results of the inspection; thus, we hope, giving some aid to the guardians in the work of reform; but in this case we find ourselves confronted with a building in all ways unsuitable for the work required of it, and, when the question of adaptation is considered, the cost of fitting it for the use of a modern hospital will be so large and the result so unsatisfactory that we hesitate to suggest it. As we considered the circumstances of the district and the proximity of workhouses quite in excess of the population, we saw a prospect of amalgamation leading to better classification and the more efficient treatment of the sick and infirm. The alternative is a new infirmary, which would be cheaper in the end than the attempt to patch and adapt an unadaptable building.

Ecclesall Bierlow, West Yorkshire (1896)

In August 1896, Mr Rutherfourd Pye-Smith, Emeritus Professor of Surgery at Sheffield University, toured the Ecclesall Bierlow union. His impressions and criticisms of the establishment, and that of the neighbouring Sheffield Union's workhouse at Fir Vale (or Firvale), were published in the form of a series of letters to a local newspaper.[63] The Ecclesall Bierlow workhouse site, later Nether Edge Hospital, has now been converted to residential use.

ECCLESALL UNION WORKHOUSE.

I arrived about eleven o'clock, and found the Board sitting. On requesting to be shown over (as already courteously promised by the Chairman), I was asked into the Board Room and told that one of the guardians would accompany me, as the Master was engaged. I found my guide well acquainted with all parts of the institution. He spends a day there once a week, I heard. Would that more members of the Visiting Committee did the same!

I was anxious first of all to see the casual quarters, and accordingly we went there at once. A superintendent and his wife reside on the premises, which are separate from the rest of the workhouse, to admit casual paupers of either sex any evening. On admission, each casual has to strip and bathe, and then has a dark woollen night dress given him and some rugs. He is then locked into small cell in which is a large plank that serves for his bed, with a raised boxlike end for a pillow There is no other furniture; this plank is his table, chair, and bed. A tiny inner cell opens out at the end, provided with iron grating of two-inch squares. In this inner cell the stone-breaking is done, and the broken stone has to be thrown out through the grating. Each cell is provided with a bell, to call the superintendent in case of need. Two casuals only were in the cells on the day of my visit, and they were both picking oakum. By Act of Parliament it is provided that every casual pauper shall perform a certain task in return for his night's lodging and board. Men sleeping (as is usual) two nights in the casual ward are required to break from 5 to 13cwt. of stone, or to pick 4lbs. of unbeaten oakum (or twice that quantity of beaten oakum), or to do nine hours' work digging, pumping, sawing, or grinding. Women are required to do half this amount of oakum picking, or else nine hours' work washing, scrubbing, or needlework. The Master the Workhouse, or the Superintendent of the Casual Ward, is required to keep hung, where casual paupers can see it, a printed copy of these regulations, with dietary, etc. I noticed that the copy displayed did not state the quantity of stone to be broken, and on examination I found that it had been out of date for fifteen years! an evidence, I fear, of some carelessness in this department, though, in justice, I must say that a more recent card, containing the present regulations, was found hanging in the hall of the main building, not, however, where it could be seen by the casual paupers. Of the two men present, one had got through about half his task in four hours. He had done such work before. The other was a poor little fellow, one of whose legs had been amputated some months ago at the Firvale Workhouse. He was anxious to get there again, as the stump was sore from the pressure of his artificial leg, which had been purchased for him, he said, by a collection among kind friends. He took the opportunity of our visit to ask leave for early discharge, in order that he might be in time to get an order for admission to the Firvale Workhouse Hospital that evening, and he was promised that his application should be reported. Two pauper inmates were assisting in the casualty department. One had been there nine months, and was asked by my guide if he was allowed tobacco. He replied in the negative, but (doubtless emboldened by the query, and, perhaps, also the fact that my guide was enjoying a cigarette) said had meant to ask if might not have a little. He, too, was promised that the Master's consent should asked. The number of casuals admitted through the year amounts to over 5,000, giving a weekly average of about 100, or over a dozen every day. The night-dresses and rugs are stoved once a week and washed "less often!" The amount of stone given to be broken is the maximum allowed by law when it is limestone, but is reduced to 10cwt. when it is ganister. The dietary on which this work has to done is as follows:— At 6 a.m., breakfast, 6oz. of bread and a pint of gruel; at noon, dinner, 8oz. of bread and 1½oz. cheese; at 6 p.m., supper, the same as breakfast.

It was a relief to turn from the prison-like casual cells to the recently-erected wood shed. Stone-breaking and oakum-picking seem unremunerative to all concerned, but the sawing and chopping up old railway sleepers for fire-wood is a respectable trade, and in this shed a dozen or twenty men were busily engaged, under the eye of task-master, earning their own living, and thus helping to reduce the rates. Some, indeed, were casuals, who would get nothing in return for their work beyond two nights' lodging, and the meals I have mentioned. Some were inmates, glad to be thus occupied. Others were outworkers, technically paupers, but sleeping at their own homes, bringing their own meals with them, and free to take home on Saturday evening their meagre and hard-earned wages. I spoke to an honest-looking Irishman, who was getting through his work more rapidly than most, and found that he had been working there for 18 months. He is paid 1s. 10½d. on the four days that he works full time, and 1s. 6d. on Mondays and Saturdays. Out of this weekly wage of 10s. 6d. he has to support himself and a sick wife! Pauper women working in the laundry get 2s. a day for four days in the week, and their meals.

It was now nearly noon, and I was anxious to get the dinner served to the inmates, who number, all told, nearly 600. It was a meat-dinner day, and I was allowed to see and taste the huge legs of boiled beef that were being rapidly cut up in thick slices, weighed, and distributed to the company, who were ranged, as if for a lecture, at long narrow tables facing the kitchen. It was certainly the coarsest meat I have ever come across. Potatoes and liquor from the meat were served with it, and bread

226

was supplied to each person. A large tin mug of water to drink out of, and a small bowl of salt, did common duty at each table. The kitchens, bakehouse, and pantry were then visited. The bread, admittedly unsatisfactory till a few months ago, is now considered very good. Black beetles are still a difficulty, but they are being much reduced by traps, and do not find their way into the bread and other victuals anything like so frequently as they used! The "butter," which appears on the dietary for the aged and sick, is in reality margarine, and, made up into little half-ounce pats, is a good imitation. The subject of the paupers' diet is so important and so large that I shall reserve general criticism for separate letter.

Our next visit was to the lunatic wards. There is accommodation here for 27 of each sex, but the present number are greatly in excess of this, and about 30 lunatics have to sleep the main building. Their recreation consists in the use of a bagatelle board, and a few books, and walking exercise in a dreary asphalted yard; no other occupation, and music, to break the dull monotony of their daily existence. Once a year only, at Christmastide, are they enlivened with some entertainment.

We had now arrived at the Hospital block, where 180 patients are under treatment, and have the advantages of the enlivening influences of the bright faces and dresses of the nurses, the doctor's daily visit, and some little decoration of the wards. There are four day nurses and two night nurses, so that each day nurse has about 45 patients under her charge, distributed, in some cases, in many as five different wards. When it is remembered that a large portion of her time is occupied keeping in order the patients' clothing and bed linen, it is obvious that the nurse has little time to devote to the nursing of her numerous charge. Wardswomen, from among the female inmates, assist the nurses, and in return get a meat dinner every day. One pauper woman, sixty years of age, has entire charge of six chronic cases, who require more than usual attention. I was told she liked the work, and did it extremely well. If so, she surely deserves to be treated no longer as a pauper. One wonders, however, and shudders to fancy what was the state of the wards, of the patients, of their bed linen and clothing, previous to the introduction of trained nursing only two years ago! No wonder if the death-rate then was markedly higher than it is at present.

Passing next through the dismal-looking chapel, we arrived the quarters of the old married couples. The arrangement by which chronic infirm inmates have a separate apartment for husband and wife is more than 15 years old. At present ten such apartments are occupied. "You will find them very happy and contented," my guide foretold, and I was quite prepared to do so. The first couple we visited were not very communicative, and I was disappointed at finding nothing so very different from the general aspect of things in the workhouse. One tiny room serves the old people for all purposes. They fetch their meals from the kitchen, but have the privilege of brewing their own tea. The ordinary workhouse garb stamps their fate, though they may have been respectable ratepayers in the parish as long as their strength held out. We went to the next room, that of a couple nearly 70 years of age, who had been there many years. "Well," my guide asked them, "are you comfortable? Have you anything to complain of?" A short pause, and then the man replied, "That's a hard question to answer."

My guide showed evident pleasure in turning from forlorn age to hopeful youth, and he soon brought me to the school, where 32 boys and a similar number of girls are brought up under the care of a schoolmaster and schoolmistress, assisted by a staff of pauper inmates! The boys were at their lessons, and I counted 33 in the room, and, on inquiring, found that four imbecile boys are brought in to follow the scholastic course with them! At my guide's request, the schoolmaster kindly broke off his lesson to set them to sing. I could not but be saddened as I felt the depressing effect presented to the eye by the general lack of child-like and intelligent brightness in the aspect of the poor lads, clothed their corduroy uniforms, as they sang, accompanied by the harmonium, the sweet music and words, "Beautiful stream, so pure and free, flow on." Six of the girls were going out to tea, by a lady's kind invitation, and we met them, dressed in a by no means unbecoming uniform of blue serge, with straw hats. Asked to let us hear their voices, they pathetically sang, "Feed this young and tender plant." I had no difficulty in believing my guide's testimony to their good behaviour; the only doubt I felt was as to whether children brought up in the midst of such surroundings, and circumstanced they must know they are, can evince spirit enough to behave badly.

We had to see the largest department of the institution, the infirm block, that is, the part where inmates over 60 years of age pass their existence. They are divided into two classes, the "middle-aged," between 60 and 70, and the "old," between 70 and 103, which last was stated to be the age of one cheery old man, who took advantage of his years, and insisted in wandering about the grounds, and enjoying, in a modified way, the sweets of liberty. May the hand of authority continue to deal leniently with his whims, and press but lightly on his fast declining days. The dormitories for these old people seemed to me much too crowded. Their day-rooms are also crowded and very dull. In the day-room for those under 70 there is no open fireplace, and there are only forms to sit on. One luxury they do get, and it is highly appreciated. Every man over 60 years of age is allowed an ounce of tobacco per week. What strikes one most sadly, in passing through their day-rooms, is the helpless condition of inactivity which pervades the inmates. We found among them one poor fellow only 38 years of age, nearly blind, and with no occupation whereby to pass the live-long days.

True to his promises, my indefatigable guide now took me back the casual wards, the Master of the Workhouse accompanying us. The poor cripple was found to have got through scarcely half his task of oakum picking (a tedious and by means easy job), but after explaining his case to the Master, and being put through cross-questioning, he was allowed to leave. The assisting inmate was then interceded for, and he ultimately received a promise of a weekly allowance tobacco.

I now took leave of the Guardian who had so kindly shown me over the whole institution, of the Master, and of the Clerk to the Board of Guardians, who courteously gave me some valuable statistical information, and I went home, to experience a sleep-disturbed night, in which the familiar moan of Alexander Selkirk seemed to shape itself to the occasion —

> O Workhouses, where are the charms
> That Guardians have found your faces?
> Better dwell in the midst of alarms,
> Than be kept in these horrible places!

I must not close this letter without gratefully acknowledging the courtesy and assistance received from the chairman and other members of the Board of Guardians, and from the various officers, in my investigations, nor without testifying to the vast improvements which have evidently been recently made in many parts of the institution, and to the awakening to present shortcomings which is evidenced by the numerous schemes now on hand. Within the last two years a revolution has been effected by the introduction of trained nursing and all that it has brought in its wake, and by the replacement of nearly all the old baths, middens, etc., by sanitary appliances of modern type. At present, I understand that a new meat and milk storehouse is about to he erected, that a new hospital, costing about £10,000, is to be built, as well as a new maternity ward and a new reception-house for children; that a nurses' home, with exercise grounds, has been purchased, and that a library for the inmates is to be formed.

> As was often the case with such reports, Mr Pye-Smith's account was challenged by those who felt stung by its criticisms. A lengthy rebuttal of many of his complaints, signed 'Arcturus', subsequently appeared in the newspaper's letters columns, a flavour of which is included below.[64]

Sir, Dr. Pye-Smith's fretful querulousness on the subject of that "dismal" and "dreary," that "horrible place," the Poor House in Ecclesall, was in such strange contrast my vivid remembrance of its admirably ordered, its delightfully clean, and brightly cheerful look when I went through it some years ago that I decided, in the interests of truth and justice, to revisit it, to verify my impressions, before putting pen to paper on the subject. Mine was surprise visit. At half-past two in the afternoon, I telephoned asking if it would be convenient for me to see through the house, and at three, I drove up to it, thereby leaving no time for smartening up the vast establishment, where they keep no more cats than can catch mice.

I saw better baths, and more up-to-date, than are common in gentlemen's houses which have cost from eight to eighteen thousand pounds, and I was told that there were four score of them fixed on the premises. I saw, in the infant school, children all fat and fair and chubby that, if Dr. Pye-Smith will get up a prize show of children, I will back the Ecclesall ones, weight for age, to take the chief prizes. Those rosy cherubs have baths, pure as pearl, night and morning. I saw trained nurses, all looking smart and bright and nice, moving about wards immaculately clean, where one of their duties was to serve ailing paupers with fresh eggs — eggs occasionally at the rate of six per day — and the best of beef tea. I saw young girls going out for the afternoon, arrayed in blue serge and neat straw hate, as smart as so many little aristocrats going a yachting. I saw a bakehouse as irreproachable in its walls of fluxed white enamel as the Duke of Portland's famous dairy, and in that bakehouse loaves white and good as heart could wish for or eyes ever hope to see. I was assured one of the sprightly nurses that at neither of our great public hospitals are the wards quite equal in condition to the sick wards of the Poor House at Ecclesall. I found that even the casuals — 75 per cent, of whom are of the professional "unemployed" — can, by touching an electric button, summon the attendant, also that those parts of the house which are not show places, but little-frequented passages, were more innocent of the slightest stain or speck than the like out-of-sight places in England's Ducal Palaces. The "huge legs of boiled beef" I did not see, for dinner was over, and out of the way, but I take it that there are thousands poor families in Sheffield whose eyes would glisten if they could behold a few such mountains of beef — beef as good as any provided for our soldiers — coming their way. Unlike Dr. Pye-Smith, I have not been in the habit of regarding tea as better than new milk, uncreamed from the cow; I don't believe it one bit, nor do the medical profession. To good, sweet oatmeal, served in the shape of milk porridge, I have no objection. Milk porridge asked for at the best hotels in London, on the breakfast-tables of the homes of the nobility, and to all who may sneer at it. I commend Dr. Samuel Johnson's reply to the Cockney who said:— "In London oats are the food of horses, in Scotland they are the food of men." The Doctor promptly answered: "And where do you see such men as in Scotland, or horses in London?"

The self-constituted Censor of the Board deplores the absence of cricket fields in connection with the Workhouse. He is wrong. Cricket and football both are played by the boys on the Workhouse estate. He reports that there is but one musical instrument in all the building. Wrong again. There are four harmoniums, one organ, one musical-box, with ten tunes, and one violin. He deplores the lack of periodicals in the library. Wrong once more. There is a good library, and as for periodicals, they inundated with them, and among these is a liberal supply from the office of your journal. He suggests that the children and such of the adults as are of defective intellect are not taken out. Still wrong, undeviatingly wrong. Weather permitting they are taken for long walks; they go to flower shows and galas, parks, picture galleries, museums, they accept invitations to the private houses and grounds of ladies and gentlemen interested in their welfare. He would have the boys and girls attired as smartly when indoors as when dressed for a pleasant walk. Unerringly wrong once more. Out of doors the boys are attired in good blue serge, as are also the girls, but in the house and its play-grounds, the lads will climb walls, or be down on their knees playing marbles, and their out-door respectability is too good for that. He says:— "One woman of sixty years of age has entire charge of six chronic cases, who require more than usual attention. Still incorrect. This "one pauper woman" works under the supervision of a trained nurse. He regrets that in connection with the House there is no Brabazon scheme. Persistently wrong. The Brabazon scheme is at work there, and ladies, whose intelligence is equal to their benevolence—ladies whom I could name—work the scheme. He is pathetic on the subject of the wood choppers and their pay. Obstinately in error. The work is light, the average earnings twelve shillings per week, the maximum earnings sixteen shillings per week, and the people outside who do a trade in firewood don't pay more. What would Dr. Pye-Smith have? There is, it is true, no piano in the woodshed to inspirit the workers. Would he have the workers chop-chop to the music of — Chopin? It seems to that Dr. Smith's "facts" have slipped out of the pigeon-hole of his memory, and got mixed up together as thoroughly as if he had been in a railway collision, and had rolled over an embankment, until his memoranda had all turned upside down. He affirms that the inmates never had ROAST meat except at Christmas. Will he never deviate into correctness? There is roast meat every Friday. He says there is lack of intelligence. inside the House, and he proves that there is also, some lack outside it. On this theme his cranium is a museum of mistakes.

Sheffield, West Yorkshire (1896)

The other institution visited by Mr Pye-Smith was the Sheffield union workhouse, located to the north of the city at Fir Vale (or Firvale).[65] Now the city's Northern General Hospital, a number of buildings from the workhouse era are still in use.

FIR VALE WORKHOUSE.

It was a bright morning, and the beautiful situation of the establishment, and its long avenues of poplars, bright with nasturtium borders, and the well-timbered wood beyond, were quite refreshing. A few men were at work, wheeling earth, in the field, where were also a crop of oats and large quantities of vegetables. But then the "Great House!" a block of buildings close on a quarter of a mile long, with isolated blocks springing up all over. The date on the foundation stone is September, 1878. It has accommodation for 1,748 inmates.

On asking to see the Master, I found that he was away, but the Matron very kindly offered to take me over the institution. In a bright-looking grass-yard a few old women were walking about, their ugly uniform spoiling what might otherwise have been a pleasant picture. The first room we entered was the sewing room, where some 60 or more old women were busily engaged making the same ugly garments that they are forced to wear. Passing through one of the day-rooms, where a few books seemed to be the only source of recreation, we came to the Nursery, where in their quaint little cage-like cradles, infants were being attended by infirm old women. How unlike the bright young nursemaids one sees in ordinary life! We have recently been told why the babies are considerately removed from such influences when they arrive at three years of age! The poor little mites have only a dreary asphalted yard to take their out-door exercise in.

The next was, indeed, a dismal room, but happily it was empty. It is for able-bodied women who misconduct themselves in the house, or who are constantly returning after their discharge. On an average there are half-a-dozen here every day. They sit here, with no outlook through the windows, and pick two pounds of unbeaten oakum a day. The work makes their fingers sore at first, but not to the extent of blistering them.

We then passed through several dormitories, on the doors of which is marked the cubic space of each room, and the number of occupants. About 440 cubic feet of air per person seems to be generally allowed. It is none too much, though well over the minimum allowed by the Local Government Board.

I was glad to find that the pauper wards-women have no authority over the inmates, their duties being cleaning only. The doors of the dormitories are locked from outside at night, and, indeed, locked doors during the day time seem almost universal throughout the building, but, inside a glass case, which can be broken in case of fire or other need, a key hangs near the door in almost every room.

The next department seen was the laundry, where about 20,000 articles are washed every week! A dozen women, out-workers, get 1s. 6d. a day and their three meals for working here. Besides these, about 30 of the able-bodied inmates assist the two paid laundry women. In other parts of the house out-workers receive 1s. 3d. a day and their meals for scrubbing.

These are women without children. The extra 3d. a day earned by the women in the laundry is for the support of their children! There is apparently plenty of work in the house to occupy all the able-bodied women. It is with the able-bodied men, in times of bad trade, and when most outside work is stopped by frost, that the Guardians seem to experience the greatest difficulty.

After a glance at the dining hall, where, but for the addition of pepper pots, the scene presented much the same appearance as at Ecclesall, we went to the kitchen, and I was invited to taste the dinner of the day, which happened to be soup. I was rash enough to take a breakfast cupful, with a piece of their excellent bread, and I paid the penalty of a severe attack of indigestion. A professional cook and five bakers are employed here, and have half-a-dozen inmates to assist them. Black beetles, as at Ecclesall, are a great nuisance, and occasionally get into the food, but vigorous steps are being taken to decimate them.

In the stores I saw specimens of the milk, which is tested daily, and is on the whole very satisfactory, 145 gallons are consumed every day! It might be well to have the margarine and other provisions analysed occasionally. Large quantities of clothing were seen in another part of the stores. Exactly the same articles of underclothing are given to every inmate according to sex and age — an arrangement I have known to act harshly and injuriously in individual instances.

The Lunatic Asylum was next visited. Both male and female day rooms are provided with a piano, which, when a good performer is obtainable, must exercise a most beneficial influence. In the male ward, a poor old Scripture reader was pathetically singing hymns to the tune of "Auld Lang Syne"!

The hospital wards are, most of them, very bright, the decoration of the walls and the fine show of flowers giving an aspect of cheerfulness which forms a pleasing contrast to the rest of the institution.

Previous to the introduction of trained nursing, six years ago, the nursing, I was told, was done by a staff of seven untrained women. Now, there are as many as 36 nurses. Much of their time is, however, occupied in attending to the bed-linen and clothing of the patients.

Passing through the dispensary and operation room, we were shown the manufacture of aerated waters, which, by means of a machine lately purchased, are supplied to the hospital and other parts of the institution at a surprisingly cheap and rapid rate.

The married people's quarters were not on view, in consequence of classification alterations. There are at present four such couples in the institution, but provision is being made for nine old couples near the old site, and for about 20 more at Goddard Hall. They are to have a day-room and a bath-room to every nine persons.

Taking leave of the matron, who had so courteously devoted three or four hours to showing me over the main building, and finding that I should not have time to visit the Children's Homes, I was now conducted to the casuals' quarters.

The general plan of the casual block is similar to that at Ecclesall, but the Tramp Master has two paid assistants under him. The porter's wife looks after the women and children. The numbers of late have considerably exceeded 6,000 a year, giving a weekly average of 120. No stone-breaking has been done here for the last three months, the Corporation not requiring it; 13 cwt. of granite is the quantity given for a day's task. The casuals present at the time of my visit were all engaged in cutting wood. I was told that, perhaps, three-quarters of the casuals are chronic tramps, and that drink is the main cause of their falling out of the ranks of honest labour, into which their very appearance must make it impossible for them ever again to enter.

I went home, wondering that we citizens of Sheffield should be so apathetic to the final lot of many who have helped to build our city's reputation, and to create the wealth that abounds in its suburbs, that those who undertake the work of dealing with the destitute seem so blind to the evils inseparable from pauper palaces, and that practical Christianity at the end of the nineteenth century has found no better way than this for meeting the needs of the poor; and I felt, with Wordsworth —

> Have I not reason to lament?
> What man has made of man?

Whilst admitting to the full the great improvements effected of late by the Guardians in the working of the Poor-Laws, the removal of the children from the workhouse being the most conspicuous, the most valuable, and the most hopeful, and whilst gladly admitting, from personal inspection, that the Fir Vale workhouse appears to be generally well and carefully managed as an institution, there are as yet, I think, many occasions for criticism. The vast size of the building must make it impossible for anyone to know all that goes on within its walls, and the enormous number of inmates must render it utterly impracticable for anyone to show personal interest in each one. On the same account the hateful system of locking every door is perhaps almost inevitable, since it must be a question between the paupers being locked or lost! The same lack of suitable occupation for the old and infirm is noticeable, as at Ecclesall, with the same absence of interest and hope in almost every face. The common rooms of the able-bodied are, I think, disgracefully lacking in the smallest attempt at anything comfortable or elevating. The conditions of the casual and of the outworker are very similar to those found at Ecclesall, and are open to similar criticism. The evils of pauper superintendence, though not entirely absent, are much less apparent than at Ecclesall, owing to the greater proportion of paid assistants in the various departments. The numbers of the medical staff and of the nursing staff, in proportion to the number of patients approach much more nearly than at Ecclesall to those usual at charitable hospitals. The sick wards are bright, and a piano has recently been purchased for use in various parts of the institution. The uniform of the women is in every respect about as bad as it can be. Why should it be uniform at all? Surely the numbers dealt with would render variety as easily attainable as uniformity. A workhouse badge is as repulsive to adults as it is harmful to children. The regulations for visiting and leave of absence are, I think, unnecessarily restricted, in spite of the occasional luxury of a stroll in the wood. The diet, which I propose to discuss more fully in another letter, is in many respects extremely unsatisfactory. The entire absence of tea from the dietary of all under 60 years of age, women as well as men, is a great mistake, and is on a par with the great restriction in the allowance of tobacco to the old men, not a quarter of whom seem to get it. What will the wives of the Guardians say when they hear that the women who work hard at Fir Vale all day never get a taste of tea? This brings me to my last criticism. A great deal might be done here, as at Ecclesall, by the appointment of a Ladies' Visiting Committee.

Finally, I must repeat my conviction that, if the Guardians would look at the questions which must constantly be presenting themselves to them "from the point of view and feeling of the helpless poor," that is, if they would put themselves in their place, the conclusions arrived at would be more satisfactory than they have often been.

Oundle, Northamptonshire (1896)

> 'A Month in an English Poorhouse' is by Max Bennett Thrasher, the establishment in question being the Oundle union workhouse. The author, an American friend of a relative of the matron, stayed there the summer of 1894, his portrait of the institution appearing in the *New England Magazine* in 1896.[66] The workhouse site later became Glapthorne Road Hospital. The infirmary, chapel and lodge/boardroom survive, the latter now home to Oundle library.

The usual name in England for what we term a poorhouse is "The Union"; and certain parishes combine for the support of a common refuge for their poor, just as in this country the towns of a county unite to support a common county house or farm. I think that, as a general thing, the Union serves a much smaller territory than the county house; and is not used as a place for the confinement of minor criminals, but merely as a retreat for the helpless and homeless. Modern methods for the treatment of the pauper element have wrought many reforms in the management of the Unions since Dickens turned the electric light of his scorching descriptions upon them, and every year sees new efforts made by earnest philanthropists to improve their condition. In size and management the Unions vary greatly in different parts of the kingdom, ranging from the huge establishment which accommodates a thousand inmates to the smallest, which shelters but a very few.

The Union which I visited is situated just outside a small town in Northamptonshire, surrounded by fields and lanes and roads, beautiful as only the English country can be. The low, rambling old house, built nearly a century ago, is of stone, and the passing of the years has colored it with the soft gray tones which time alone can give. Two long wings at the rear, three stories high, lead out from an octagonal central tower. In front of these, long, low wings surround two large courtyards, divided by the main hall of the building, the gable end of which fronts the street and forms the main entrance to the house. It had always been one of the cherished desires of my heart to sleep in a stone tower, into which I should ascend by winding flights of stone steps; and it was my lot to have my wish gratified in this English poorhouse, for my room was in the very top of the octagon, in shape like no other room in the world, I am convinced. I went up to it by three winding flights of stone stairs, over which so many feet had trod that many of the steps were worn deeply; it had even been necessary to repair them by setting in new pieces of stone. The walls of the house are covered in many places with masses of rich, green English ivy, while in others our own Virginia creeper forms a blanket no less beautiful. The grounds and gardens which surround the house are exquisitely kept, and are so extensive that one can wander about the walks for hours. In front of the house, long, box-bordered beds are filled, as the season advances, with a succession of brilliant blossoms. When I first went up the broad, gravel walk, which leads from the street or, more properly, the country road, to the entrance, the whole place was gorgeous with the orange and gold of gillyflowers. A little later, roses held full sway; and later still, an army of pure white lilies, numbered by hundreds, marched in stately array down both sides of the long walk.

At the sides, and behind the house, the more material factors were considered. Huge beds of strawberries, patches of new potatoes, peas, beans, asparagus and lettuce were as carefully tended as the flowers. Many of the walks were bordered with lines of currant bushes, red, white and black, while carefully trained raspberry and gooseberry bushes were loaded down with fruit. In one corner, but by no means crowded, were the beds of mint, thyme, parsley and other savory herbs, which are considered such a necessary adjunct to every English kitchen. A hedge of apple trees, trained upon frames, in the set English fashion, together with some fine old box and yew trees, clipped for years into rigid shapes, add much to the picturesque beauty of the place. Behind the house a screen of trees makes a delicate green background for the gray walls of the old building. In front of it the ground slopes gently down to the valley of the river Nene, thence rising to a range of beautiful hills beyond. Just in the foreground stands a huge old stone windmill with wooden sails damaged by time, which still, however, gather strength enough when a strong wind blows to propel the antiquated corn-grinding machinery which yet remains inside.

All matters which pertain to the government and management of a Union are in the hands of a board of guardians, consisting of at least one member from each parish represented, and as many more as the population of the parish justifies. All the Unions in the kingdom are under the jurisdiction of the national Local Government Board, established about twenty years ago. Their accounts are audited by a government auditor, and every institution is liable at any time to receive a visit of investigation from the government inspector. The O— Union represents thirty-nine parishes, and there are forty-two members on the board. Meetings of this body are held in the board room at the Union every two weeks, presided over by the president of the board, who is chosen annually from among the members. The time required for these meetings and for the other duties devolving upon a guardian is not inconsiderable; but neither the president nor the members of the board receive any pay for their services. All clerical work connected with the institution, the keeping of accounts, etc., is performed by an officer known as the clerk of the board, who is paid £200 a year. Each Union also retains what is known as "the relieving officer," whose salary, in the case of this Union, was the same as that of the clerk. The salaries of the clerk and the relieving officer are net, and they live outside of the building. The remaining paid officials are the master, matron, nurse and porter, who are paid smaller sums and boarded and lodged in the house.

All applications for regular admission to the Union must be made through the relieving officer, and although the inmates can go out at any time they choose, they cannot return without a new certificate of admission. Any one who wishes to be taken into the house makes application to the relieving officer, stating his or her needs. If the officer is satisfied that he is justified in doing so, he grants admission until the next meeting of the board of guardians, retention after that depending upon the decision of the board. At the meetings of the board all cases come up for consideration, and if they are decided to be deserving, permanent residence is granted or an arrangement made for "outdoor relief." The horror of going to the workhouse leads many to prefer to remain outside, to get along with the scanty assistance furnished them, in more independence, but probably much less comfort, than they would have if in the house. The maximum allowance for out-door relief for a married couple is four shillings and sixpence ($1.12) weekly, and for a widow, three shillings (75c). Until recently this dole was, in the quaint old English fashion, "half a crown and two loaves."

The number of inmates at O— Union averages about seventy. At the time I happened to make inquiry, there were thirty-nine men, twenty-three women and eleven children. Formerly there were many more children, so many that a separate school for them was maintained in the house, and a competent schoolmistress retained on the staff; but during late years the practice has obtained of getting as many as possible of the children homes outside, where they can work for their board and go to school. The few remaining in the house, of school age, attend the regular schools in the town. The total expenses of this Union were, in round numbers, £3600 for the year ending last "Lady Day," the 25th of March, which is in England the closing day of the fiscal year. From a quarter to a third of this was probably devoted to out-door relief, the rest representing the running expenses of the house. This provides, as I have said, for the poor of thirty-nine parishes; but the English parish varies so much in size that a better idea of the territory covered can be gained from the fact that the nearest Union on one side is seventeen miles distant, and on the other, thirteen. Whether the present system of caring for the poor best combines efficiency and economy is one of the public questions which is being much discussed in England to-day.

The inmates of the Union are generally old people, cripples, feeble-minded persons, and young children. Very few of these, however, will be absolutely helpless, and all who are able are expected and encouraged to do such light work as they can towards keeping up the establishment. The men take all the care of the grounds and gardens. The matron is allowed a capable maid, hired outside, for her own assistance, but she is the only paid servant about the place. Those who are best able to act as nurses care for the more helpless. By a recent law, every Union is obliged to retain a capable trained nurse to oversee this work and care for those who are seriously ill. Special rooms, large, light and airy, filled with fresh, clean beds, furnish ample accommodation for those who are ill or helpless. A part of one of the front wings is fitted up as a laundry, and all the work for the house is done here, much of it by women who are strong physically but feeble in mind. One of the prettiest places about the grounds is the clothes yard, where, shut in by a hawthorn hedge, there is a big expanse of green turf, soft as plush, on which the wash is spread to whiten or above which it hangs to dry. It rarely happens that there are not enough able-bodied and capable women in the Union to do the cooking and all the other necessary work of the house. These are usually homeless women with children, often illegitimate, so young that the mothers are temporarily unable to go out to service, to which, as soon as their children get old enough, they return.

In no case did it seem to me that the amount of work required was unreasonable. Many of the more infirm old men do nothing except stroll about the walks in the grounds or sit on a bench in the sun. One confined to a wheeled chair was wheeled out each day by his more fortunate companions. One courtyard is reserved for the men, the other for the women. The old women have a comfortable sitting-room which they use in common, and in this room those who can walk about spend most of the daylight hours. Opening out of this room, on the back side of the women's wing of the building, and shut in by a high wall, is "the old ladies' garden," one of the brightest spots about the place. Here the female inmates are at liberty to wander at will; and a pleasanter place, with its soft green grass, roses and other flowers, quaint old yew trees, and comfortable benches, it would be hard to find. I secured a snap shot at a group of women who had clustered in the door of the sitting room one day to wonder what I was about. When they saw the picture afterwards, and learned that I was going to take it home with me, one old woman who was in the extreme background raised a prodigious wail of disgust and dissatisfaction that she had not been brought more fully into view, declaring that she didn't see any reason why she "shouldn't go over the water just as well as the rest of them hussies." This "going over the water" I found was almost invariably the way in which the lower classes of people all over England speak of going to America. For them there is but one body of water and one destination.

Back of the women's garden is a playground for the girls, also with a high wall, now little used, since there are so few children; and back of the men's ward is a large yard for the boys, to which they have access at almost all hours, and in which I watched many a game of cricket.

The rules of the house are few, but those few are enforced. At six at night all must be in the house or in their courtyards, and the gates are locked. At a later hour all are locked into their respective sleeping wards. No visitors come or go without being recorded in a book kept by the porter; and the main gates of the grounds are locked at nine every night. None of the inmates are allowed to leave the grounds without permission, unless they take it upon themselves to leave permanently, in which case they cannot return if, as often happens, they wish to, without a new certificate of admission from the relieving officer. Men who wish to go out get permission from the master, women from the matron. Unless there is some reason why they should not go, as a disposition to drink on the part of some men, they are allowed to make frequent excursions into the town, while many make visits of from a day to two or three weeks upon relatives in the surrounding country, who are glad to welcome them for a short time but are unable to furnish them a permanent home.

While in the Union all inmates wear the special dress provided them. In the case of the men, this is a stout brown corduroy suit. The women have gowns of dark blue, with neat shawls and bonnets for street wear and Sundays. The clothes worn by persons when they enter the Union are preserved, and if at any time they wish to leave they must take off the Union suit and wear out their own. Many of the inmates have good suits or dresses, which they have been able to procure in one way or another, and which they keep carefully to wear when they go out to visit.

The hours for meals, in the summer, were: breakfast at half-past six, dinner at twelve, and supper at half-past five. All who are able to walk eat in one large dining hall. I do not remember the bills of fare, which change from day to day, or the allowance per person, both established by law; but the impression I received was that the food was good and the supply ample. The staples were oatmeal porridge, bread and butter, cheese, meat and potatoes, with tea for drink. The good judgment of the master and the ingenuity and kind heart of the matron result in adding much to the palatableness of the fare. I used to wonder why so much ground was devoted to growing rhubarb, a plot in front of the "tramp house" as large as four ordinary gardens being covered with the big leaves of that plant, until one day I happened to be in the kitchen just as the matron was overseeing the making of rhubarb pudding for that day's dinner. A huge earthen crock as big as a bushel basket, containing several gallons of stewed rhubarb, stood in the middle of the floor, and into this she was dishing big ladles of sugar to make it eatable. The pastry to be served with it was steaming, at the time, in two immense coppers as large as old-fashioned wash kettles.

A special diet, nourishing, is prescribed for the weak, the aged and the ill; and here again the hand of the matron is seen, bearing bowls of broth and delicacies of her own making to tempt dull appetites. In addition to this, there are frequent treats of tea, sugar and cakes, for the old women, when all share alike. These come from the more charitable of the surrounding country gentry, from interested visitors, often from the matron herself, who takes a special interest in "my old ladies." The old men, it is almost needless to say, prefer tobacco to tea, and practical British philanthropy frequently gratifies them. Lady L— , the wife of a nobleman who lives near, is perhaps the most thoughtful patroness of the establishment. Twice every year she visits the Union to give each woman there a quarter of a pound of tea, with sugar and cakes, and every old man a quarter of a pound of tobacco. Nor is this all, for frequent supplies of game and other good things come over from L— Hall. Last Christmas the preserves there sent fifty fat rabbits to make the Union boarders a holiday dinner. Every old woman in the establishment has her own teapot and its accessories, her own safe corner where all these personal properties can be kept, and in one way and another each manages so that the caddy is rarely empty. Many have friends outside who send them small sums occasionally, — a sixpence is richness, — the remittances being usually in postage stamps, which are brought to the matron to be changed for money. Some earn small amounts by sewing or knitting articles which are purchased by charitably disposed visitors; and every Saturday afternoon a messenger goes to town to shop, charged with a long list composed of such weighty items as "tuppence worth of tea for Peters," "hapenny worth of sugar for Brown."

The administration of the Union provides for various committees, chosen from among the members of the board of guardians. Among these are committees on finance, sanitation, reading, chapel, etc., and, most important of all, a visiting committee of three, any one of whom has the right unexpectedly to demand admission to any part of the house at any hour of the day or night for the purpose of inspecting the details of management. Every Union is obliged, by the law of the kingdom, to provide a doctor and a chaplain. The doctor at O— is paid £30 a year. He is required to come to the house twice a week regularly, and as much oftener as any patient may require. It is also stipulated that at the price paid he is to furnish his own medicine. Provision must be made for religious services at least twice a week. Some Unions have a resident chaplain, some hire a man, and others by alternating two or more men get a supply for nothing. The O— Union pays £50 a year to the vicar of the parish, who has his two curates do the work and divides the pay between them. Two services are held on Sunday and one on Wednesday afternoon. At least one visit a week is made also to drill the people in the form of service or the children in singing. Service was formerly held in a hall in the building proper, but recently a handsome stone chapel has been built on the outskirts of the garden. Attendance upon service is not obligatory, but every one is expected to attend unless there is some good reason why they should not. I used often to go; and, sitting in a seat near the door where I could survey the whole congregation, it seemed to me to be the most pathetic sight I had ever seen. Except for the children, who sat together near the door as a choir, their fresh young voices led by a cottage organ which the master played — except for these, and for a vacant face here and there which bespoke the feeble mind behind it, all were old, gray, bent with the toil of a lifetime, shaking with the palsy of advancing years. Life, which in too many cases had brought little of happiness to them, held nothing in the future but the end. It made me think of Herkomer's "Last Muster"; but that, with its wealth of color, is infinitely more cheerful than this could ever be. It is hard for a clergyman to adjust a sermon so as to meet the minds and wants of such a congregation as this. One can hardly preach the beauty of self sacrifice and generosity to those who have nothing to give, or the blessedness of loving one's neighbors to men and women whom no one loves. One curate, a young man with a strong, earnest face, seemed to realize this, and, leaning over the little reading desk, he would forget to preach, in his desire to speak such words as he could of comfort and encouragement.

The chapel, which cost about £1000, was built wholly by charitable contributions, the work being superintended by the vicar of the parish. The day it was formally opened was a great day for the Union, as the bishop of the diocese and other great people were to be present. Naturally all of the inmates were out in full force, new suits and dresses making them look a highly respectable congregation. One little incident impressed me, as showing an unusual amount of thoughtfulness in the treatment of these people. As there had been a considerable debt incurred in the building of the chapel, and as most of the gentry from the surrounding parishes would be present at the services, it was decided that this would be a favorable time for taking up a collection. It occurred to one person, however, that when this was done there would be one large part of the congregation, the inmates of the Union, who, since they had nothing, would have nothing to give. Fortunately, in this case a well filled purse was behind a warm heart, and from it came a generous supply of silver, divided equally among the inmates, so that, when the box was passed, each dropped in a sixpence with as much pride as their titled neighbors did a sovereign. The social magnates of the county look upon the building of a workhouse chapel like this as one of the legitimate charities which they are bound to support, and they take a thoroughly practical interest in it.

One of the principal offices of the parish Union is the sheltering of the floating vagrant population. By the present poor law of the kingdom, those who may make application at the Union, declaring that they are without the means of procuring food and shelter, are fed and lodged for at least one night, being required to do a stated amount of work the next day in return. In the case of men, this means cutting wood or breaking stone for a certain number of hours, while the women pick oakum. The number of persons who make such application is considerable. I do not think that there was ever a night, during the month that I was at the Union, that the "tramp house," as it was called, was empty, while sometimes there would be as many as a dozen seeking shelter. Among these there would occasionally be an intelligent, self-respecting person, whom misfortune of some kind, illness or lack of work, had reduced to this strait; but usually the applicants belonged to the true vagrant class, whose life is practically spent in tramping from one end of Great Britain to the other, claiming shelter and food in this way when they cannot be obtained otherwise more easily. The vagrant department is wholly separated from the rest of the Union, so far that a prominent notice beside the great iron gates which give access to the broad walk which leads up to the house reads, "Vagrants admitted only at the boarded gates." These are further down the street, at the extreme corner of the grounds, and from them a walk leads to the "tramp house," a solid, low stone building, with barred windows, standing by itself in a corner of the garden. Comfortable sleeping accommodations are furnished here, with a separate ward for such few women as may come in; and the ample but plain supply of food — porridge, bread and water — which the law allows, is brought out here. The institution effects one desirable result, at least, for one room is fitted with a bath tub and a plentiful supply of hot water, and every applicant is obliged to take a thorough bath before being allowed to go to bed. As this rule is rigidly enforced at all Unions, it follows that the habitual vagrant who spends life wandering from workhouse to workhouse acquires at least the merit of cleanliness. Each applicant is required to empty his pockets of all they contain before he is granted shelter, the very miscellaneous contents being made up into a bundle for which he is given a check. This is to ascertain if the wanderers are really without money, having which they are obliged to go out and get lodging for themselves at some public house. Experienced vagrants become very expert in concealing what small amount of money they may happen to have, to the extent sometimes of burying it outside the grounds, under the hedges, before they come in.

Haslingden, Lancashire (1898)

The following uncredited newspaper article describes a visit to the Haslingden union workhouse situated at Higher Pikelaw, between Haslingden and Rawtenstall.[67] The site later became the Rossendale General Hospital but is now covered by a modern housing estate.

THE UNION WORKHOUSE.

There are 326 inmates within the Workhouse walls, made up of old men and women; young men and women, and boys and girls. One hundred lie on the sick beds of the Infirmary; 72 are imbeciles or idiots, of whom 48 are females; 29 are boys, and 24 are girls, with five infants under two years of age. There are fathers and mothers here; grandfathers and grandmothers, and even great grandfathers and great grandmothers.

Since Mr. and Mrs. Robert Brown were appointed the master, and matron in 1893 I have only visited the house twice, my last inspection, being one afternoon last week, and which happened to be under very pleasing circumstances. Mr. Brown has seen the workhouse grow, having come to it as a carpenter in 1868, and a better selection to succeed Mr. Hay, and Miss Hay (who became matron on the death of Mrs. Hay) could not have been made. I have seen enough to lead me to the conclusion that Mr. Brown is respected, and even loved from the youngest child to the oldest inmate, and his intelligent and considerate care for the poor unfortunates is shared in by his wife and daughter, Miss Brown, a very able assistant.

A remark of Mrs. Brown as an old woman walked up the yard that "Old Sarah" had been in the house the longest, having been an inmate of the old workhouse at Haslingden, carried my memory back to that very primitive workhouse, and to the times when, "Old Sammy" Spencer, like a ministering angel, distributed tobacco and snuff and small coins at 'Xmas time, and, when Mr. R. Munn was chairman of the Board. The difference between the old workhouse and the new is almost as great as between the old one-storeyed cottage and a palace. In the early sixties, I think, there were only about seventy inmates, and these were, huddled into some small rooms, near the Haslingden Parish Church, which were formerly used as handloom weaving shops. There were all sorts of cases, very stuffy, rooms, bad ventilation, and next to no classification. Baxter's brewery now stands on the site of the old workhouse.

The new workhouse at Pike Law, which was opened in 1870, is a fine architectural structure, elevated on the west side of the Rossendale Valley, of which it commands a full view. It is built of stone, with a couple of minarets or bell-like domes on the summit, and forms a conspicuous attraction to passengers on the railway, the tramway, or on foot. The boardroom, the porter's room, and relief rooms are erected on the north side of the house, and the infirmary is on the south side, so that the house itself stands back in the quadrangle, the fourth part of which is composed of grass plots, front yards, and the carriage drive and boundary wall, the space between the boundary wall and carriage drive being planted with trees and well grassed. The main entrance to the workhouse is by a flight of stone steps leading into the entrance hall, which has a very agreeable appearance, the walls being painted and decorated with pictures. A few steps lead into the main aisle, which runs from end to end of the building, and the different rooms for the inmates are on each, side. A similar corridor divides the bedrooms in the second storey. Two or three steps more lead into another corridor, branching from which are the master and matron's private room, the kitchen, and the, dining hall, a spacious room, which is lighted by a row of windows at the west end and all along the north end.

When visiting [the workhouse] last week the afternoon was fine, but very much overcast, and the inmates received quite an unexpected and to them marvellous treat. Mr. John Duckworth, one of the now Accrington Guardians, and his wife, and Mr. and Mrs. Fawbert, also of Accrington, were on a tour of inspection. Mr Duckworth had brought with him his phonograph, and I attached, myself to hint to see how the inmates received an entertainment from Edison's wonderful invention. It was Mr. Duckworth's idea to give an entertainment in every room, but I suggested the advisability of trying the instrument in the dining room so that if acted the inmates in bulk, young and old, could have the entertainment after tea, or supper, as they call it, which is served at a quarter to six. We went into the room to try the experiment, and placed the phonograph on the harmonium. There were two old men in the room, one placing the broad, another who seemed to be deafish, doing ditto with spoons, and knives. On Mr. Duckworth starting the machine the man with the bread, who was about the middle of the room, stopped short, with astonishment, and seemed for a moment literally transfixed with the slice of bread in his hand. As the song proceeded I went towards him, and was astonished to find that the phonograph was heard to better advantage than I had ever heard the instrument in any other place. The sound was even better at the far end of the room, and Mr Duckworth was greatly pleased. I asked the old man what he thought of it, and he replied, "Do you want to mek all the lunies leet?" (Do you want to make all the lunatics light in their heads). Jack and I laughed, and the old man asked whose invention is was. When he was told Edison, the American, he remarked that those Americans were wonderfully sharp fellows. This old man said he had been in the house seven years, as he was unable longer to work in a cotton mill.

More than pleased will the experiment the instrument was conveyed to the old women's room which overlooks the front grounds, and is well lighted, with numerous windows, each containing flowering plants or shrubs, grown in the workhouse greenhouses. As you enter here you cannot fail to be struck with the neatness of everything. The floor, are as well scrubbed as a kitchen table top; the twelve cots are neatly tucked up, with a blue coverlet on the top with the name of the Haslingden Union and year thrown up in white. There were eleven old women here, and as the little instrument was carried into the room and placed on a table near the fireplace, curiosity was aroused. Some wanted to know if it was a new-fangled clock, and when the funnel cane to view, they said it was suggestive of beer brewing, and spiced ale at 'Xmas time. When the funnel was fixed on the phonograph, one said it was a coffee mill. A band selection happened to be on the roller, and the sensation it caused the old people is not likely to be soon forgotten by those who witnessed it. The old lady, who was darning stockings in the other corner of the room put them down, and the eleven old women in the adjoining room also came trouping in to learn where the music was coming from. One was reading, but dropped her book. How they all smiled and laughed and wondered. Some even said they could dance to it. Next came a comic song; and then a song with a chorus "Waste not, want not," seemed to please immensely. One old lady pointed out to me as the oldest in the room, and who had been sitting on her chair, and chucklingly right merrily to herself, now rose and examined the "thing," as they called it, and pronounced it wonderful. Another old lady pulled off her white cap and bent her ear over the trumpet to catch every sound. The old woman comes from Accrington, and is 86, and the youngest in this room was 64. If this group could only have been photographed in the positions they assumed the

248

photo would have been worth treasuring. "Nothing too good for the Irish" brought a clapping of hands by an Irish woman, and "Shure it's moighty wonderful." Later on when this woman had returned to the other room, and Mr. Brown and his lady visitors entered she showed with pride the rosary of chain and beads which Father Dillon had given her, and assured him that she prayed for him and everyone of them "Ivery blessed day." These old women seemed quite content, and looked very neat in their striped gowns, which were not all of one pattern, white caps, and grey woollen shoulder shawls. Inquiring from one of them as to the vacant bed I learned that there had been a death the previous week. The old women were very profuse in their thanks to Mr. Duckworth for his treat. Miss Ormerod, Accrington, has charge of these rooms.

The children's room was next visited, and only about a dozen of the younger girls and infant boys were present. When the little ones heard the instrument they grouped themselves round the table, and stared with childlike wonder and awe at the phonograph. Soma of them looked under the table, and round the instrument and down the trumpet to see if they could find the comic singer. I noticed that the lady visitors had preceded us for each child had a penny, several of which kept being dropped while the phonograph was going, and a large box of sweets had been left with the nurse. This room contains small rocking chairs and a rocking horse, and the children ail looked healthy and content. Some of them, Mr. Brown informs me, were mere waifs of skin and bone when they came at first, and the nursing and codling of them up seems to endear the little things to all about them. I noticed that there was a cupboard with a glass door full of toys and dolls. Those latter struck me as if they were dressed for ornament and were but little played with. The little girls that I have known always like dolls that they can knock about, soothe their imagined woes, or smack them or put them in their little cots. I hope Nurse Ormerod will not be afraid of letting those girls play with the dolls, and that ladies who replenish the stock will send some more serviceably dressed, and suited for this class of children.

The women's imbecile ward was to me one of the most affecting. It is a long room, lighted, by a row of windows on the left, which overlooks the back of the workhouse, the furthest end terminating with a greenhouse. Outside each window is a covered glass case filled with flowers, so that it is made as light as possible. There are no fewer than forty-eight females in this room, varying from one about fourteen to some about sixty, or

249

perhaps even older, in various stages of imbecility. Some read and others sew, while others are listless and do nothing. A Government Inspector has remarked on the lack of suitable literature in this room, and I would recommend friends to send illustrated papers of any kind, even to the halfpenny comics, which would be sure to interest some of them in their dull and monotonous lives. I learned from Nurse Bolton, a very pleasing and patient young lady who has charge of this great number of imbeciles, that none of them were sufficiently bad to go to the county asylum, and that none of them were very violent, though at times they were peculiar. One woman when the phonograph was going felt inclined to sing and talk. She had been a member of the Salvation Army, and often was seized with the singing mania. The saner part of these women were very much interested with the phonograph, and the younger portion laughed and giggled with glee, making comments to each other. In the nurse's ante-room, the "aristocratic" lady, a tall, gaunt woman, with a beard on the chin end, had a recital to herself; but she seemed more interested in inquiring about the hay crops, and some lost property which she lays claim to, and money, than with the instrument, and this was the only person with whom the phonograph was a failure. This once-clever woman was very much at home with the lady visitors, and shook hands and received them most lady-like. She said she thought she had seen them before, and she told Mr. Duckworth he had better bank the cheque which he showed to her.

Leaving this room and entering another, you will find the boys' room. On my previous visit they were "at home" for the holidays, and three of them were busy making kites, the younger interestedly looking on. They had made four square kites out, of various coloured papers, and they were very well made, too. The bats and balls were lying on one side of the room, and in reply to Mr. Brown the boys said they would rather be outside playing cricket, if the weather had permitted. These lads got to hear the phonograph later on in the general dining room. The instrument was introduced to the inmates in this room immediately after tea.

The phonograph was placed on the pulpit, and the wonder, laughing of the old and young as George Emms's comic song, "I'm a funny little man" broke on their ears, and the clapping of hands of the boys and girls, showed what a success the "marvel" was going tobe with them. Mr. Duckworth changed about a dozen tunes, and then having two new cylinders there was a roar as "John Henry," a very comic looking lad was called to sing into the trumpet. He sang most comically the sang "One more polka," and then a little girl piped in a clear soprano voice song about "Gathering shells on the seashore." A whistler was asked for but none was forthcoming, and then "John Henry" was in requisition again. A sheet of music was handed to him, which he rolled up for a trumpet and performed a singular melody which they called "Ding-dong." His singing was so funny that he was asked to repeat it, with his usual accompaniment of a few steps. The lad bends both knees together, and throws out his legs as if skating, and dances his steps on the edge of his clogs. A whistler was now forthcoming in a boy named Forrest, who whistled "I'll stick to the ship lad" very nicely. When Mr. Duckworth reproduced these songs the joy of the inmates was very great and they applauded heartily, evidently convinced that there were "no boggarts or witches of Pendle," as one old woman remarked. Mr. Brown briefly and plainly explained how the sounds of the lads and lasses' voices produced impressions on the wax cylinder so fine that he could not see them, and then when the instrument was set going it reproduced the tones of the voice. He expressed his own gratification and those of the nurses and inmates for what had been to them all a marvellous treat, and his call on them to give three hearty cheers for Mr. Duckworth, was responded to with huzzahs which showed that they were very heartfelt and came from some good lungs. Mr. Duckworth responded with a few suitable remarks, and promised that he would bring them some singers, and give them a concert on some future occasion, an announcement which brought forth more cheering. The inmates were then dismissed.

Whitechapel, London (1902)

> In the summer of 1902, the American writer Jack London visited England and, disguised in old clothes, spent time among the poor in the capital's East End, including a night in the Whitechapel workhouse casual ward, on what is now Fulbourne Street.[68]

After my two unsuccessful attempts to penetrate the Whitechapel casual ward, I started early, and joined the desolate line before three o'clock in the afternoon. They did not 'let in' till six, but at that early hour I was number 20, while the news had gone forth that only twenty-two were to be admitted. By four o'clock there were thirty-four in line, the last ten hanging on in the slender hope of getting in by some kind of a miracle. Many more came, looked at the line, and went away, wise to the bitter fact that the spike would be 'full up.'

At six o'clock the line moved up, and we were admitted in groups of three. Name, age, occupation, place of birth, condition of destitution, and the previous night's 'doss,' were taken with lightning-like rapidity by the superintendent; and as I turned I was startled by a man's thrusting into my hand something that felt like a brick, and shouting into my ear, 'Any knives, matches, or tobacco?' 'No, sir,' I lied, as lied every man who entered. As I passed downstairs to the cellar, I looked at the brick in my hand, and saw that by doing violence to the language it might be called 'bread.' By its weight and hardness it certainly must have been unleavened.

The light was very dim down in the cellar, and before I knew it some other man had thrust a pannikin into my other hand. Then I stumbled on to a still darker room, where were benches and tables and men. The place smelled vilely, and the sombre gloom, and the mumble of voices from out of the obscurity, made it seem more like some anteroom to the infernal regions.

Most of the men were suffering from tired feet, and they prefaced the meal by removing their shoes and unbinding the filthy rags with which their feet were wrapped. This added to the general noisomeness, while it took away from my appetite.

I had eaten a hearty dinner five hours before, and to have done justice to the fare before me I should have fasted for a couple of days. The pannikin contained skilly, three-quarters of a pint, a mixture of Indian corn and hot water. The men were dipping their bread into heaps of salt scattered over the dirty tables. I attempted the same, but the bread seemed to stick in my mouth, and I remembered the words of the Carpenter: 'You need a pint of water to eat the bread nicely.'[69]

I went over into a dark corner where I had observed other men going, and found the water. Then I returned and attacked the skilly. It was coarse of texture, unseasoned, gross, and bitter. This bitterness which lingered persistently in the mouth after the skilly had passed on, I found especially repulsive. I struggled manfully, but was mastered by my qualms, and half a dozen mouthfuls of skilly and bread was the measure of my success.

The man beside me ate his own share, and mine to boot, scraped the pannikins, and looked hungrily for more.

"I met a "towny," and he stood me too good a dinner," I explained.

"An' I 'aven't 'ad a bite since yesterday mornin'," he replied.

"How about tobacco?" I asked. "Will the bloke bother with a fellow now?"

"Oh, no," he answered me. "No bloody fear. This is the easiest spike goin'. Y'oughto see some of them. Search you to the skin."

The pannikins scraped clean, conversation began to spring up. "This super'tendent 'ere is always writin' to the papers 'bout us mugs," said a man on the other side of me.

"What does he say?" I asked.

"Oh, 'e sez we're no good, a lot o' blackguards an' scoundrels as won't work. Tells all the ole tricks I've bin 'earin' for twenty years an' w'ich I never seen a mug ever do. Las' thing of 'is I see, 'e was tellin' 'ow a mug gets out o' the spike, wi' a crust in 'is pockit. An' w'en 'e sees a nice ole gentleman comin' along the street 'e chucks the crust into the drain, an' borrows the old gent's stick to poke it out. An' then the ole gent gi'es 'im a tanner".[70]

The majority of these men, nay, all of them, I found, do not like the spike, and only come to it when driven in. After the 'rest up' they are good for two or three days and nights on the streets, when they are driven in again for another rest. This continuous hardship quickly breaks their constitutions, and they realize it, though only in a vague way; while it is so much the common run of things that they do not worry about it.

'On the doss,' they call vagabondage here, which corresponds to 'on the road' in the United States. The agreement is that kipping, or dossing, or sleeping, is the hardest problem they have to face, harder even than that of food. The inclement weather and the harsh laws are mainly responsible for this, while the men themselves ascribe their homelessness to foreign immigration, especially of Polish and Russian Jews, who take their places at lower wages and establish the sweating system.

By seven o'clock we were called away to bathe and go to bed. We stripped our clothes, wrapping them up in our coats and buckling our belts about them, and deposited them in a heaped rack and on the floor — a beautiful scheme for the spread of vermin. Then, two by two, we entered the bathroom. There were two ordinary tubs, and this I know: the two men preceding had washed in that water, we washed in the same water, and it was not changed for the two men that followed us. This I know; but I am quite certain that the twenty-two of us washed in the same water.

I did no more than make a show of splashing some of this dubious liquid at myself, while I hastily brushed it off with a towel wet from the bodies of other men. My equanimity was not restored by seeing the back of one poor wretch a mass of blood from attacks of vermin and retaliatory scratching.

A shirt was handed me — which I could not help but wonder how many other men had worn; and with a couple of blankets under my arm I trudged off to the sleeping apartment. This was a long, narrow room, traversed by two low iron rails. Between these rails were stretched, not hammocks, but pieces of canvas, six feet long and less than two feet wide. These were the beds, and they were six inches apart and about eight inches above the floor. The chief difficulty was that the head was somewhat higher than the feet, which caused the body constantly to slip down. Being slung to the same rails, when one man moved, no matter how slightly, the rest were set rocking; and whenever I dozed somebody was sure to struggle back to the position from which he had slipped, and arouse me again.

Many hours passed before I won to sleep. It was only seven in the evening, and the voices of children, in shrill outcry, playing in the street, continued till nearly midnight. The smell was frightful and sickening, while my imagination broke loose, and my skin crept and crawled till I was nearly frantic. Grunting, groaning, and snoring arose like the sounds emitted by some sea monster, and several times, afflicted by nightmare, one or another, by his shrieks and yells, aroused the lot of us. Toward morning I was awakened by a rat or some similar animal on my breast. In the quick transition from sleep to waking, before I was completely myself, I raised a shout to wake the dead. At any rate, I woke the living, and they cursed me roundly for my lack of manners.

But morning came, with a six o'clock breakfast of bread and skilly, which I gave away; and we were told off to our various tasks. Some were set to scrubbing and cleaning, others to picking oakum, and eight of us were convoyed across the street to the Whitechapel Infirmary, where we were set at scavenger work. This was the method by which we paid for our skilly and canvas, and I, for one, know that I paid in full many times over.

Though we had most revolting tasks to perform, our allotment was considered the best, and the other men deemed themselves lucky in being chosen to perform it.

"Don't touch it, mate, the nurse sez it's deadly," warned my working partner, as I held open a sack into which he was emptying a garbage can.

It came from the sick wards, and I told him that I purposed neither to touch it, nor to allow it to touch me. Nevertheless, I had to carry the sack, and other sacks, down five flights of stairs and empty them in a receptacle where the corruption was speedily sprinkled with strong disinfectant.

Perhaps there is a wise mercy in all this. These men of the spike, the peg, and the street, are encumbrances. Broken by hardship, ill fed, and worse nourished, they are always the first to be struck down by disease, as they are likewise the quickest to die.

We were sprinkling disinfectant by the mortuary, when the dead wagon drove up and five bodies were packed into it. The conversation turned to the 'white potion' and 'black jack,' and I found they were all agreed that the poor person, man or woman, who in the Infirmary gave too much trouble or was in a bad way, was 'polished off.' That is to say, the incurables and the obstreperous were given a dose of 'black jack' or the 'white potion,' and sent over the divide. It does not matter in the least whether this be actually so or not. The point is, they have the feeling that it is so, and they have created the language with which to express that feeling — 'black jack,' 'white potion,' 'polishing off.'

At eight o'clock we went down into a cellar under the Infirmary, where tea was brought to us, and the hospital scraps. These were heaped high on a huge platter in an indescribable mess — pieces of bread, chunks of grease and fat pork, the burnt skin from the outside of roasted joints, bones, in short, all the leavings from the fingers and mouths of the sick ones suffering from all manner of diseases. Into this mess the men plunged their hands, digging, pawing, turning over, examining, rejecting, and scrambling for. It wasn't pretty. Pigs couldn't have done worse. But the poor devils were hungry, and they ate ravenously of the swill, and when they could eat no more they bundled what was left into their handkerchiefs and thrust it inside their shirts.

It is the rule of the casual ward that a man who enters must stay two nights and a day; but I had seen sufficient for my purpose, had paid for my skilly and canvas, and was preparing to run for it.

"Come on, let's sling it," I said to one of my mates, pointing toward the open gate through which the dead wagon had come.

"An' get fourteen days?"

"No; get away."

"Aw, I come 'ere for a rest,' he said complacently. 'An' another night's kip won't 'urt me none."

They were all of this opinion, so I was forced to 'sling it' alone.

"You cawn't ever come back 'ere again for a doss," they warned me.

"No bloody fear," said I, with an enthusiasm they could not comprehend; and, dodging out the gate, I sped down the street.

Dewsbury, West Yorkshire (1904)

> Mary Higgs was born in 1854 in Devizes, Wiltshire, the daughter of Congregational minister. In 1879, she married the Rev. Thomas Higgs, later settling in Oldham, Lancashire. After becoming Secretary of the Ladies Committee visiting the Oldham union workhouse, an interest in vagrancy reform led her to discover first-hand what conditions were like, particularly for women, in accommodation such as casual wards. In 1903, she and a friend, dressed in old clothes, braved the Dewsbury workhouse casual ward.[71]

A FIRST NIGHT IN THE WORKHOUSE TRAMP WARD.

We arrived, alone, a few minutes before six, at the workhouse lodge, which stood all by itself down a long lane which ended in iron gates. This lodge was very small, and was occupied by a man, the workhouse buildings being a little way off. There were a good many trees around, and it was a pretty spot, but lonely. The man was a male pauper, and no one else was in sight. We had to enter his hut to answer questions, which he recorded in a book, and we were then out of sight of the house. The nearest building was the tramp ward, the door of which stood open; but there was no one in it, as we afterwards found. A single woman would be completely at the mercy of this man. If our pilgrimage has had no other result, I shall be glad to be able to expose the positive wrong of allowing a male pauper, in a lonely office, to admit the female tramps. When we first arrived at the gate he told us to wait a few minutes, as we were before time. Some male tramps came up, and we saw him send away one poor, utterly ragged man, who begged pitifully to be admitted. The lodge-keeper told him he could not claim because he had been in that workhouse within the month. So he limped away. He could not possibly reach another workhouse that night. The man admitted three others, and sent them on to the male quarters. He let us in at five minutes to six. We thought this was kind, as he might have kept us waiting, and it had begun to rain. He took my friend's name, occupation, age, where she came from, and her destination, and then sent her on, rather imperatively, to the tramp ward. She stood at the door, some way off, waiting for me. He kept me inside his lodge, and began to take the details. He talked to me in what I suppose he thought a very agreeable manner, telling me he wished I had come alone earlier, and he would have given me a cup of tea. I thanked him, wondering if this was usual, and then he took my age, and finding I was a married woman (I must use his exact words), he said, "Just the right age for a bit of funning; come down to me later in the evening." I was too horror-struck to reply; besides, I was in his power, with no one within call but my friend, and all the conditions unknown and strange. Probably silence was best; he took it for consent, and, as other tramps were coming, let me pass on. I made a mental vow to expose him before I left the place. He took my bundle, and asked if I had any money. I gave him my last penny. I received a wooden token for the bundle. I then joined my friend, and told her she had better give up her umbrella and her penny. She went to do so after some tramps had passed, and though I stood and waited, and she was only gone a moment, he tried to kiss her as she gave him the things!

When she joined me, very indignant, we went forward into an oblong room containing six bedsteads with wire mattresses and filthy straw pillows. A wooden table and bench and "Regulations for Tramps" were the remaining articles of furniture. There were big, rather low, windows on three sides; the bottom panes were frosted, except one, which had been broken and mended with plain glass, and overlooked the yard where the male tramps worked. Presently our wayfaring friend arrived, and we all three sat and waited a considerable time. A solitary woman might have been at the mercy of the man at the gate some time. No one was in sight, or came near us, till at last a motherly-looking woman entered by a door leading to a room beyond. She asked us if we were clean. Our fellow-traveller (whose garments were at any rate *not* clean) was let off, as she had spent the last night in a workhouse tramp ward. We said we should like a bath, and were shown into a bath-room and allowed to bathe ourselves. Our clothes were taken from us, and we were given blue nightgowns. These looked fairly clean, but had been worn before. They were dirty round the neck, and stained in places; we *hoped* they had been stoved! The old woman dressed in one without bathing. We found in the morning that both blankets and nightgowns were folded up and put away on shelves, just as we found them, apparently, and left for new comers. We were told that the blankets were "often stoved," but I have since ascertained that they are not stoved at all workhouses every day. All kinds of personal vermin might be left in them by a tramp who went straight out of dirty clothes to bed, and even a bath might leave them open to suspicion. We saw several bugs on the ceiling in this ward. Perhaps the using of others' dirty nightgowns was the most revolting feature in our tramp. At neither workhouse were the garments handed to us *clean*. We found afterwards that by Government regulation clean bath water and a clean garment can be *demanded*, but this we did not know. It should be *supplied*. After the bath we were each given four blankets and told to make our beds and get into them. The art of bed-making on a wire mattress, without any other mattress to cover it, is a difficult one, even with four blankets. The regulation number is two, and with these I fancy the best plan would be to roll yourself round and lie on the mattress. For the wire abstracts beat from the body, and *one* is an insufficient protection. Even with one spread all over and another doubled under the body and two above I woke many times cold. In winter the ward is warmed by hot-water pipes, but the blankets are the same. A plank bed, such as is given in some workhouses, would probably be warmer, though harder. Put to bed, like babies, at about half-past six, the kind woman in charge brought us our food. We felt rather more cheerful after our bath, with the large, airy room, instead of the foul, common lodging-house; only one thing had exercised my mind — "What did that pauper mean by my going to him later?" However, I told the portress all about what he said. She was very indignant, and said I must tell the superintendent of the tramp ward next morning, that she had to leave us, but would take good care to lock us in, and I need not be afraid, he could not get at us. We were very hungry, having had nothing to eat since about twelve o'clock. Anything eatable would be welcome, and we were also thirsty. We were given a small lading-can three parts full of hot gruel and a thick crust of bread. The latter we were *quite* hungry enough to eat, but when we tasted the gruel it was *perfectly saltless*. A salt-box on the table, into which many fingers had been dipped was brought us; the old woman said we were "lucky to get that." But we had no *spoons*; it was impossible to mix the salt properly into the ocean of nauseous food. I am fond of gruel, and in my hunger and thirst could easily have taken it if fairly palatable. But I could only cast in a few grains of salt and drink a little to moisten the dry bread; my companion could not stomach it at all, and the old woman, being accustomed to workhouse ways, had a little tea in her pocket, and got the kind attendant to pour the gruel down the w.c. and infuse her tea with hot water from the bath tap. We were then left locked in alone, at eight o'clock, when no more tramps would be admitted. The bath-room, containing our clothes, was locked; the closet was left unlocked; a pail was also given us for sanitary purposes. We had no means of assuaging the thirst which grew upon us as the night went on; for dry bread, even if washed down with thin gruel, is very provocative of thirst. I no longer wonder that tramps beg twopence for a drink and make for the nearest public-house. Left alone, we could hear outside the voice of the porter. I wondered if he expected us to open a window. However, we stayed quiet, but had one "scare." Suddenly a door at the end of the room was unlocked, and a *man* put his head in! He only asked," how many?" and when we answered "Three," he locked us in speedily. I could not, however, get to sleep for a long time after finding that a *man* had the key of our room, especially as our elderly friend had told us of another workhouse where the portress left the care of the female tramps to a man almost entirely, and she added that "he did what he liked with them." I expressed horror at such a state of things, but she assured me it was so, and warned us not on any account to go into that workhouse. She said, however, that it was some time since she had been there, and "things might be different."

At last my companions slept the sleep of weariness. Sounds outside had ceased; within, my friend coughed and the old woman groaned and shifted. The trees waved without the windows, and two bugs slowly crawled on the ceiling. I measured distances with my eye. They would not drop on my bed! I pity the tramp who has only two blankets on a wire mattress. I could not get thoroughly warm with four; some part of me seemed constantly to feel the cold wire meshes through the thin covering. The floor would be preferable. I have been told since at one workhouse, with considerable surprise on the part of the portress, that the male tramps prefer the floor to their plank bed! I do not wonder. The pillow was too dirty to put one's face on, so I covered it with a blanket.

In this workhouse the management was lax — too lax to ensure cleanliness; clothes and towels appeared to have been used, and blankets were probably unstoved. As our own clothes are taken away and locked up, it would be impossible for a tramp to wash any article of personal clothing. Consequently she must tramp on, growing day by day more dirty, in spite of baths, especially as really dirty work is required of her in return for "board and lodging!" There was no comb for the hair; fortunately we had one in our pocket. In the morning we were roused about seven o'clock and told to dress. Our clothes were in the bath-room. We had the luxury of a morning wash. Our garments had been left on the floor just as we took them off, and so were our companion's, which looked decidedly unclean by daylight. The kind attendant said she had to go, but waited till I had told the portress (who arrived to set us our task) the conduct of the man at the gate, and I claimed her protection, as I should have to pass him when going out. Both exclaimed when I told his words, and one said, "Plenty of cups of tea I expect he's given, the villain!" The portress assured me she would watch me out, and that I need not fear him, as he daren't touch me when she was there, and she said that after I had gone she should report him.

Before this happened, however, we had our breakfast given us, which was exactly a repetition of supper — saltless gruel and dry bread. We ate as much as we could and were very thirsty. I had drunk some water with my hand from the bath-room tap as soon as I got up. We put what bread we could not eat into our pocket as a supply for the day, and were told to empty the rest of our gruel down the w.c. It thus disappeared; but what waste! A mug of coffee or tea would at least have washed down the dry bread; or a quarter of the quantity of gruel, properly made, would have been acceptable, with a mug of cold water for a proper drink.

The portress told us when we had done our work we might go out at eleven o'clock. We thanked her — we had expected to stay another night, and perhaps pick oakum, but we should have almost starved on the food, as our sugar was in our bundle, so we were relieved to find we had only to clean the tramp ward and go. We were told to "sweep the ward and make all clean." We did not think of scrubbing the room, which, as it was large, would have been a big task, but the portress afterwards scolded us for not doing so. It was not dirty, so we swept it, cleaned the taps, bath, and wash-basins, washed up the pots, dusted, and, having made all, we waited for release. We sat on the form, and when the portress came in and saw us sitting down she spoke to us very sharply. I suppose she did not like to see us idle. We told her we would have scrubbed the floor if we had known we ought; but we did not know, as we had never been in a workhouse before. She was somewhat mollified, and let us off with a mild scolding some time before eleven o'clock. She stood at the door and watched us receive our things from the male pauper and leave the gates. He hastened to give us them without a word, and also restored our two pennies.

Tynemouth, Durham (1909)

As part of its investigations, the 1905 Royal Commission on the Poor Laws visited a large number of workhouses and other establishments across Great Britain and Ireland. Accounts of these visits were included among the voluminous appendices to the Commission's report, published in 1909. Although the institutions involved were anonymised (using asterisks), many can be identified from the incidental detail that they included. Here is the Commission's description of the Tynemouth union workhouse.[72]

We visited the workhouse which is built, upon open ground about a mile from the central part of * * [North Shields]. The Union comprises the County Borough of * * [Tynemouth], the Borough of * * [Wallsend], and several rural parishes.

The master said the matron was ill, and we were, therefore, unable to see her. (I was told afterwards by a guardian that the matron had been addicted to drink, but was supposed to have been cured by a dream.)

There were 713 persons in the workhouse, including 409 men, 175 women, and 129 children.

The staff consists of the master and matron (who are man and wife), the assistant matron and the porter (who are also man and wife), seamstress, laundress, cook, and baker. There are a male attendant in the convalescent ward, a female attendant in the old men's ward, two female industrial trainers (one of whom is married to one of the master's clerks),

261

for the children, a tailor, shoemaker, and engineer or handy man. The master has two clerks, one of whom takes charge of the children out of school hours.

The hospital staff consists of a superintendent, three charge nurses, eight probationers, a day attendant, and a night attendant.

Church of England and Catholic services are held.

Separate accommodation is available for married couples who wish to be together. Only one couple was in occupation though there was also an old woman who had only recently lost her husband. There is a steam laundry and a swimming bath. The water for the workhouse is obtained from wells in the grounds.

Stick-chopping is provided for the men able to work, the hours being from about 7.30 a.m. to 4 p.m. Potatoes grown in nearly sufficient quantities for the requirements of the workhouse. The women's clothes are made by the inmates, but the men's clothes are bought.

Male vagrants are detained two days, but women only one day unless they wish to stay longer. There are eleven cells and some association wards.

The general impression of the workhouse was not unfavourable., There is plenty of ground, including a field where the children appeared to play football, etc. It was a sunny morning, and nearly all the rooms seemed to have a good share of the sunshine. They were generally clean, and the paint on the passage walls was in good condition. The stores were tidy, and clean, and the articles seemed good. The beds were also clean, and each had three blankets which were doubled to make five thicknesses. The gas fittings were well polished, and looked as if they had only been fixed a short time, but the master said they had been there since the house was opened, seventeen years ago. In the men's day-rooms notices with regard to swearing were hung up, though probably they wore not always obeyed. The boys are in the swimming bath nearly every day, and about twenty of them can swim.

On the other hand, the children's lavatory was not at all satisfactory. There were no basins, and the children had to wash in the water as it flowed from the pipe. They had no tooth brushes, and no special attention seemed to be given to their teeth. There were only two or three hairbrushes,

The aged women's day-room was rather crowded and no books or periodicals are provided, though a few are occasionally given by persons interested in the inmates. The phthisis ward was stuffy, although nearly all the windows were slightly open. They might, however, have been opened wider.

The infants' quarters in the workhouse itself were empty, the whole of the children (twenty-six) having taken the measles and been sent to the infirmary attached to the workhouse.

There is a separate lying-in ward for three or four cases, but the accommodation for nurses is so insufficient that the labour ward off it is used for a nurse's room, and confinements take place in the general ward.

Whilst there is room for improvement in this workhouse in regard to the points mentioned, and others, the general appearance is probably above the average.

New buildings are being erected, and when these are completed, the accommodation, both inside and outside, will be sufficient for all present requirements. The workhouse could, with capable management and a few structural alterations, be made efficient in all departments.

Guildford, Surrey (1909)

> The 1905 Royal Commission's report includes this visit to the Guildford union workhouse.[73] The workhouse casual ward, now home to the Spike Museum, is a rare survivor of such a building.

Visited the workhouse first; the central block built about 18— , with stone stairs, small wards, etc.; additions on all sides about eleven years old. It is too small for present needs, and in the winter beds for men are put in the chapel and in the children's building. The Guardians are making their additions piecemeal, and have difficulties with the Local Government Board, which is pressing them to take all the children out of the workhouses. The latest additions are the new tramp wards and the married couples' quarters. The former are nearly all on the solitary cell system; there is a superintendent in charge, and his wife looks after the female side. There were 188 vagrants in the last, fortnight, as against 130 the previous year; about eight women. Only a few in to-day; all gone to * * for the hop-picking. All are kept for the two nights, no distinction being made in favour of the genuine working man, though the superintendent thinks he gets a few of these. The tasks are sawing wood, and pounding flints, and picking oakum, the latter being reserved for the worst cases. Sometimes, however, they prefer the oakum, when they are used to it. The superintendent and his wife much wish for powers to take the children, who are learning nothing but evil. No disinfecting done here unless the tramps ask for it; then their clothes are sent over to The House. *The soup copper is in the washhouse.*

The married couples' quarters are exceedingly nice; accommodation for six couples, only two there at present, the surplus rooms being used for nurses. The old people there were very "superior," pension standard by appearance. They have a common room for meals, which are sent in from the House.

The workhouse itself has the advantage of the old buildings, that the small wards admit of variety and classification, reading room, workroom, etc. One night ward on the ground floor so that the most infirm need not go upstairs. Signs of consideration were not wanting, and yet the place was more melancholy than any I have visited yet. The Guardians do not allow the Brabazon scheme, on the ground that those paupers who can work at all should be profitably employed. A great deal of firewood is sold; and there is a garden in-which the paupers work. No separate accommodation for epileptics and imbeciles, but there are only slew of these, about five epileptic and eight imbeciles. A good many girls come in to be confined; there is no Committee for looking after these, but a lady interests herself in them and is allowed to come in when she likes. Inmates are allowed out once in three months upon application to the Board; they go to stay with friends. Visiting days twice a week, and on Sundays if they bring a card from a Guardian. The men go out to work in the summer to a certain extent.

The infirmary is in the same block of buildings as the workhouse, and under the master. No resident doctor. Nine nurses. These mostly live in the building. I only saw the men's side: small wards, and I was struck by the isolation of the patients. At least four or five cases of only one in a ward, and I saw no nurses about.

(About 10.30 nearly every pauper I met was munching; it was explained that this was lunch,[74] which they eat over their work.)

The most unsatisfactory feature would seem to be the children. The Guardians are much, divided as to the best way of dealing with them. Sixty are in "scattered homes"; about twelve in the workhouse; five have been returned from the homes for bad behaviour or otherwise. The working men on the Board seem strongly opposed to the homes, and in favour of keeping the children in the workhouse; and opinion, against the homes seems strengthening. I should judge that the type of foster mother is not quite good enough for the work. I saw one, who seemed hardly up to the mark. On the other hand the children in the House are not satisfactory. There seems also need of more systematic training; the girls are sent to service at fourteen, having picked up what they could in the homes; them is no training at all for the boys; a few are sent to the * * the others are "found places for" with farmers and others. Of one I heard that he was sent to a farmer, put to sleep alone in an out-house, ran away, and is now dying of consumption.

The board is a large one, 43; two lady members. The Chairman is a gentleman and there are some others, several clergymen, but the majority seem to be of the small tradesman class. A group of three or four working men from * * — railway porter, saddler etc. — whose only interest appeared to be in making difficulties and saying disagreeable things. They were really of a most disappointing type, incapable of keeping to the subject in hand, and full of jealousies because they were not on certain Committees.

New applications for relief are taken by the whole Board. Two of these. Those decisions seemed wise, but little consideration was shown in the manner of treating the applicants by many of the Board, I should judge by the tradesman element; Chairman was quite courteous, and a clergyman undertook to help one of the men refused to make his own arrangements. Medical orders confirmed as a matter of course.

For old cases the Board divides into two Committees. 'The Guardians do not seem to take much interest in this work, many of them leaving. The scale of relief seems to be about 3s. for a single person. I did not hear how often cases are revised, but gathered from cases six weeks. Relieving officers' advice is taken; perhaps the decision is left almost too much to them; there are four of them. One difficult case of an old decrepit woman living in a remote cottage under bad conditions, whom they wished to bring into the house but could not.

Coventry, Warwickshire (1909)

> The 1905 Royal Commission rated the Coventry union workhouse, on London Road, as 'the worst that we have yet seen'.[75] Later used as a Salvation Army hostel, the building incorporated the remains of the old Whitefriars monastery, one section of which still survives.

This institution is on the site of a religious house belonging in pre-Reformation days to the Carmelites, having been founded in the 14th century. The cloister still stands, and is now used as a dining-hall for the inmates. Two adjacent cells, dating from the same period, are used as bath rooms; they are dark, ill-ventilated, and, of course, quite unsuited to their present purpose. Other buildings for the able-bodied, for the aged and infirm, for the children, for officers' quarters, etc. have been erected during the last 200 years. For the most part they are below the standard of modern requirements. They are grouped, or rather packed, round the and there is little or no free circulation of air.

The Whitefriars monastery forming part of the Coventry workhouse.

The most recently erected blocks are two pavilions for the sick. In one provision is made for about seventy beds, of which sixty-one were occupied on the occasion of our visit. They were for the most part acute cases. The nursing staff consists of one trained nurse and one probationer, with the help of three able-bodied paupers as ward-women.

The second pavilion contains seventy-two beds, of which sixty-four were occupied. The patients are for the most part chronic cases: The nursing staff consists of one trained nurse, one probationer, assisted by three female and four male paupers from the house. In addition, a good many of the chronic sick were muddling and fussing about the wards, and gave an impression of inadequate discipline, if not of general confusion. The superintendent nurse was trained in the infirmary from the age of sixteen, and she has had no other experience. She is now about forty years of age. It seemed to us that the lack of order, discipline, etc., might be due to her lack of training. She knows no standard but that of the Infirmary. And no doubt the present pavilions are palatial when compared with the old sick wards which now form part of the workhouse. That so imperfectly trained an officer should be in charge seems unfair to the patients, and almost to preclude hope of improved 'administration. The imbecile wards are also under her control. There are thirty-eight female imbeciles and sane epileptics, of whom two paid attendants are in charge, assisted by-one pauper inmate. There are thirty-eight male imbeciles and sane epileptics with one male attendant assisted by two male paupers. On night duty there is one female attendant assisted by a male pauper for both male and female wards.

The children (thirty-nine girls and twenty-three boys) are housed in the Workhouse under the care of a male and a female industrial trainer, but they are not kept separate from the adult inmates. Indeed, the children's wards left on our minds a marked impression of confusion and defective administration. But the accommodation is so unsatisfactory that no higher standard is to be anticipated. For example, the baths are so insufficient that many of the children have to use the baths provided for the adult paupers adjacent to the cloister. The lavatories, both in construction and arrangement, are such, as to prevent the officials teaching the children cleanly and tidy habits. The matron (a not very efficient officer) complained (and quite rightly as we thought) that she could not do her duty by the children in such inadequate accommodation; but she could not get the Guardians to move. In appearance the children were dirty untidy, ill-kept, and almost neglected. Their clothes might be described with very little exaggeration as ragged, and when the Inspector told a group of children to take off their right boots large holes were displayed in six stockings out of thirteen: The eyes of some of the children seemed suspiciously "weak," and in two or three cases to be suffering from some serious inflammation. We were told that there had been several "eye cases" lately and that two had been transferred to the infirmary. The children's sleeping accommodation seemed most unsatisfactory — the girls sleep two in a bed; those who have mothers in the house sleep with them in the adult wards. Small children who need attention at night sleep with an adult inmate. The babies, we were told, were similarly provided with a foster mother.

The whole condition of the workhouse reflects great discredit on the Board of Guardians, it is overcrowded and ill-managed, and the staff is inadequate. Indeed, the detailed administration seemed so incompetent as to be almost cruel. For example, we came, across a boy, aged sixteen, so crippled that his legs are practically useless, and he has to move with the help of his hands. He can neither read nor write, but does a little work in the tailor's shop, and spends most of his time playing marbles in a paved yard. He has been an inmate for two years. The Guardians have never considered whether any method of training and education could be provided for him.

We asked why the children were still kept in the workhouse, and we were informed. "that the question of children's accommodation had been under consideration for many years, and that unhappily it had become a Party question; the Unionists were in the majority and were opposed to any expenditure involved in the provision of proper accommodation." The Vice-Chairman (a Liberal) hinted that the Unionists would lose the election on this question. But the Chairman. (who we were told controlled the Board) could not agree with the Vice-Chairman. The only question at issue is the cost, and rate of 1d. in the £ produces £1,260 per annum. It is to be regretted that the infirmary pavilions were erected before the children removed. Speaking generally, we may say that this workhouse is the worst that we have yet seen.

Bradford, West Yorkshire (1909)

> The 1905 Royal Commission visited the Bradford union's Homes for the Aged and Deserving Poor, one of the few instances of such accommodation.[76] The homes, at Daisy Hill, are still used by the city's social services.

The Homes for the Aged and. Deserving Poor may be described as adequately supported almshouses, under disciplinary conditions, such as obtain and are enforced among the passengers of a mail steamer. Each room accommodates either husband and wife, or two aged persons, male or female, who, before leaving the workhouse, decided that they could and would like to live together. The rooms are comfortably furnished, well lighted and warmed, and the occupants have on the walls, etc., the little possessions, pictures, etc., which originally found a place in their old homes. They have their meals in their own rooms. The materials for breakfast and tea are served out weekly; and the inmates have these meals when they think fit Within reason they get up when they like, and go to bed when they like. Dinner is cooked in a common kitchen by the wife of the superintendent, and properly served in each room. There is a kind of common room, where religious services, concerts, etc., are: provided. The swing gate of the institution is always open. The inmates go out when they please, but we understood that they seldom go beyond the garden: they prefer that their friends should come and see them, and we were told, not a few look in for a "cup of tea." The old folk dust and tidy their own rooms, but the rougher work is done by some sane epileptic young men, who have been transferred from the house, in order that they may be made as comfortable as possible, having regard to the malady which has blasted their lives. We have only three criticisms:—

(i.) As far as we could judge the fundamental principle of the Report of 1834 is violated — the lot of these aged inmates seemed distinctly more eligible than that of the independent labourer outside. But the workhouse test is applied, for admission is through the house.

(ii.) The success of the scheme depends on the very careful selection of the highest type of workhouse inmate. If such are not in the workhouse, the Guardians may not be willing to let the houses remain empty; and if a lower type is admitted, then all manner of restrictions will have to be introduced, and the houses will lose their character and charm.

(iii.) One old lady whom we saw at the Out-Relief Committee informed the Chairman that she hoped she might be eligible for relief in one "of the new houses" when she was a little older.

Birmingham, Warwickshire (1909)

The 1905 Royal Commission visited the Birmingham workhouse and infirmary which shared a site at Dudley Road, Winson Green.[77] Now the City Hospital, most of the old workhouse buildings have been demolished although the 1880s infirmary largely survives.

We visited the workhouse and infirmary. The former is a large and rambling mass of buildings, the earlier parts being erected some fifty years back and additions casually added from time to time to meet any special wants. The master, though intelligent seemed inert, and he' was in addition very deaf. His deafness was caused by an assault upon him with a knife by an able-bodied pauper.

The whole management was loose and old-fashioned. The work for the able-bodied was light and not properly supervised, and loafing seemed to be very prevalent. There has been a very rapid increase of indoor relief in recent years in the Union; so much so that the Local Government Board have recently specially directed the attention of the Guardians to the increase, no doubt largely due to this cause. The Inspector fully admitted the want of systematic control in the establishment, and he proposes to give special attention towards improving the administration.

On the women's side of the workhouse, things were no better. The matron hardly seemed up to the task of managing so large an establishment, and the assistant matron, who had recently been brought from * * , was open-mouthed in her condemnation of the administration. She seemed energetic and capable, and although she had effected some improvement she was desirous of leaving the place as soon as she could. She took us into the infirm ward, which was full of bedridden old women, many of whom had been in bed for months. She asserted that they were not properly taken care of, and were dirty and some of them with bed sores.

The laundry was an untidy old-fashioned shed entirely worked by manual pauper labour, under the superintendence of one outside washerwoman.

Until quite recently the pauper women scrubbed and cleaned the men quarters; now the latter clean one floor.

The feeble-minded women do much of this cleaning and scrubbing, and consequently are more in contact with the men than is advisable.

All venereal cases are dealt with by the workhouse medical men and treated in that quarter, to which arrangement the matron of the infirmary strongly objected.

As regards the paupers themselves, the master, matron and assistant matron commented on the poor physique of the paupers, the latter asserting that, so far as women are concerned, it was very inferior to the physique of the * * pauper.

The master and matron both contended that the paupers had greatly deteriorated, especially the men, in the locality during the last twenty years, and that, though they were now more easy to manage, they had not the grit or muscle of their predecessors. The master considered syphilis as a great contributing factor to pauperism.

Subsequently we visited the infirmary. This was also a huge building — the corridor from the lodge to the nurses' quarters being of a mile. In its order and management this institution was the antithesis of the other. There are 1,300 beds, 1,100 of Which are filled on the average.

The matron, a lady of great capacity and vitality, dominated the whole establishment. She had 120 nurses under her, and everything seemed to be in excellent order and working smoothly. This is the more noteworthy as a special arrangement is in force, which at first sight Would seem calculated to lead to friction and want of uniformity. The infirmary is divided into four sections, each under the control of a consulting doctor, not being on the premises, but who has under him a resident doctor.

There is a steward, who undertakes what he calls the commercial business of the infirmary, and the matron who has entire control of the nursing.

Leith, Midlothian (1909)

The 1905 Royal Commission included Scotland in its remit and visited a number of poorhouses (Scotland's equivalent to workhouses) including two at Leith, to the north of Edinburgh.[78] None of the buildings survive.

The poorhouse is an old structure, being built in 18—. As a poorhouse for * * [South Leith], it is now used for all classes of indoor poor, except sick patients; these are provided for in the * * [North Leith] Poorhouse, * * [North Leith] and * * [South Leith] now being one parish. These two institutions are under the management of the * * [Leith] Parish Council.

Both institutions are overcrowded. A new institution is in course of erection on another site, to accommodate all classes of inmates. The two poorhouses are now advertised for sale.

The * * [South Leith] Poorhouse was the first visited by us. It is a very undesirable institution. The buildings are in a bad state of repair, and the arrangements of the wards are such as to make proper supervision of the wards very difficult. The children's quarters are very cheerless. The whole of the wards are very untidy — we may lay, without hesitation, dirty. The tables in the dining-hall would be much better for a thorough scrubbing, which they do not seem to have had for years. Every room in the buildings seems to be under the immediate charge of an inmate or inmates.

There is a sort of classification of inmates made by the governor on character prior to admission, yet no information is given to the governor by the inspectors as to previous mode of life, and the pauper's record is not consulted.

The usual method is the governor questions the inmates who are likely to be fit subjects for the classification wards. The Parish Councillors usually recommend the cases as being suitable. The governor, of course, places great weight upon the opinion of Councillors. Inmates are divided into four classes:—

1st. Those over 60 years of age, of good character before admission.
2nd. Those of any age, of good character in the house.
3rd. Those who are left out of the two other classes.
4th. Children.

Epileptics and mentally deficients are mixed up with the ordinary inmates. One blind youth under 20 was in the second-class men's ward. The governor did not know what was to become of him; he had no suggestion to make.

There are 27 children, ranging from 2 weeks to 14 years of age. 9 boys and girls attend school, and have their meals with the adult inmates in the dining-hall. One girl of 14 is very dull, and suffers from deafness. She is not attending school. Her future is — so far as one can see — that of a permanent pauper for life.

The midday meal on the day of our visit was Scotch broth, bread and cold meat. The allowance of bread seemed excessive; it is not distributed according to appetite.

Special diet is given, at the discretion of the governor, to those performing useful work. Three male inmates were having very good Irish stew.

The total number of inmates was 306, and the staff consisted of the governor, a matron, assistant matron, cook, children's nurse, sewing-maid, laundry-maid, male clerk, labour master, and porter; total staff, 10. The male inmates who are able to do any work are employed in chopping firewood, the women in laundry work and cleaning.

The governor told us that he admits urgent cases on his own responsibility, but always calls in the Medical Officer to examine and certify on the same day, however late. He also draws the attention of the Medical Officer to all cases ready for discharge. There is no regular systematic medical examination of the inmates with that object. The governor does not consider any man or woman over 60 years of age as suitable for discharge, to earn their own living; therefore no person over 60 is brought under the notice of the Medical Officer for the purpose of discharge.

The * * [North Leith] Poorhouse, now used as an hospital, is in marked contrast with the one described. The grounds are neat, clean, and well looked after. The wards are also in good order, and the patients seemed well cared for. There are 155 patients in at present, nearly all of whom were in bed. Provision is made for the outdoor treatment of male consumptives. The Medical Officer, however, said there was not much satisfaction in treating them; very few, indeed, came in early enough. It was, he said, difficult to maintain proper discipline. If pressure was brought to bear, they took their discharge, only to come in again later in a much worse condition,

There are four trained nurses in all, assisted by 27 pauper wardsmen, wardswomen, and cleaners.

Headington and Oxford, Oxfordshire (1931)

> In 1931, former Oxford MP Frank Gray published an account of his experiences in the casual wards of Oxfordshire workhouses, which he had visited disguised as a tramp. He contrasted the dire conditions in the Headington 'spike' with its much more well-appointed neighbour, located just two miles away in Oxford. However, Headington was still popular with tramps because there was virtually no supervision during their stay.[79]

I reach the gates of Headington; so do about twenty others. We loaf around the gates. Two boys in a milk float jeer at us as they pass. A casual snarls: "You — —, your turn may come!" Another says: "Why do the — — exhibit us out here?"

The doors open, the "tramp major" in charge lets us in; we push to get front places, to answer questions hurriedly, and snatch our piece of bread. Then we go into the casual ward without any suggestion of a search or a bath, or indeed a wash. We are locked and bolted in. How curious it is that any one should be afraid that we may abscond from the hospitality given us!

The ward is a narrow building, perhaps eleven feet wide and eighteen yards long, four feet of the width being passageway till this stone passage becomes sleeping accommodation under pressure for space. On the right, as you enter, is a sloping platform, starting nine inches from the stone floor and rising to a height of eighteen inches against the wall. This platform is broken up by nine-inch upright boards, fourteen inches apart.

It looks in the gloom like a row of coffins, and each tramp who is quick enough to get in claims one. He thinks himself lucky in getting it. Every one else sleeps on the floor, under this erection or in the passageway.

At the end of this ward — a cold outbuilding — and only partly partitioned off, is a foul lavatory and bath, unused and unusable for washing. This was all we were given at Headington, however great or small the number requiring accommodation.

Nobody has to sleep under the raised boards to-night, in the dirty, high-windowed, elongated cell, with the almost uncovered combination of bath and cesspool at the end. The young tramp and I sleep in our clothes, for there is neither search, baths, nor handing over of raiment in this hell, where all men are at last equal.

In society we all believe we have our inferiors, if not our superiors. This first belief fades in the Headington casual ward. Reproduce this casual ward in any gaol in England and the nation would cry "Shame!"

There is one candle to light the fifteen yards of humanity, and two Irish tramps arriving late and in drink quarrel with the rest of us locked in this cell as to the exact position where this candle shall stand. Why do we quarrel in this black hole — in this horror of filth and indecency? Why, in truth, do we want this candle at all to cast shadows in this hole of shame?

Morning has come; the dirt-laden grills of our cell say so. There is a shout from the porter for the production of unemployment cards by those who can produce them. There is not one, for none of us here is a genuine worker. Had we cards we should produce them, for by doing so we gain our immediate release, without task or work. Like the rest I have no card, so I perforce do three hours' sawing.

The task is over. I am again on the "open road," on the outskirts of Oxford, and less than two miles from the Oxford workhouse, where I intend to stay to-night. I have passed through Headington Union. I might have passed in an advanced stage of carrying smallpox, at death's door, or mad, and yet have remained uncared for and unnoticed.

*   *   *

I reach the grounds of the Oxford workhouse, pass through the long foregrounds, and track out the casual ward. I sit on the ground outside. The concourse of tramps here gathers by twos and threes.

It must want many minutes to six o'clock when a permanent inmate passes and says: "Why don't you go in? It's been open for a long while." We enter a brightly lighted room with spotlessly clean tables and forms, and to these are brought bread, margarine, and cocoa, before any inquisition, search, or inquiry is held; for this is an institution which has not lost its soul.

"Dad"[80] is of the gathering. He sits next to me. He pours a little sugar into my mug of cocoa — the widow's mite — a much greater act from a tramp to a tramp than it may appear.

* * *

The meal at the Oxford casual ward is over. The porter calls first for those who have come from Woodstock. A lot get up — so do I — and the porter says: "You are as deaf as I am." In a later class I get up again. I am searched. How well I know the porter and how well he knows me! But he does not recognize me. I am passed on to a permanent inmate, who is lending a hand — and he superintends me while I strip with others, pile my bundle of rags on theirs, and take my bath. There is certainly more ceremonial about the bath at Oxford, and no man is entitled to complain if he uses the water after another — some use it without complaining. You see this consideration becomes a mere unnoticeable detail in the general horror of life as a tramp.

I get a workhouse shirt, go into a spacious, healthy, and clean department, and, best of all, to a spring bedstead, straw mattress, and straw pillow. There is sufficient space, too, between the bedsteads. We are treated like decent men.

Some of us are, and all have got a great deal of good in them. If men's hearts could be searched it would be found that this better treatment has more than once stirred that latent better spirit to rise from the level of the tramp and the outcast.

And so to sleep.

On the morrow my task before release is to scrub the floors of two large outhouse dormitories, apparently overflow casual wards.

* * *

We are now about to parade for our departure. I see "Dad" at the parade. I watch a young official go up to him and hear him say: "Why don't you stop here with us, Dad? You are too old for this game now. You will be getting knocked down on the road." At this act of kindness a tear comes to the old man's eye — he is still capable of responding — and then he passes out, passes out to pick up the trail of death.

Bibliography

⌐mous. (1888). *A Walk through the Public Institutions of Macclesfield.* Macclesfield Courier and Herald.

Bedford, P., & Howard, D. (1985). *St. James's University Hospital, Leeds – a Pictorial History.*

Craven, C. W. (1887). A Night in the Workhouse. In *The 'Keighley' Series of Poems, Tales and Sketches, No. 1.*

Gray, F. (1931). *The Tramp: his Meaning and Being.*

Greenwood, J. (1866, January 12-15). A Night in a Workhouse. *Pall Mall Gazette.*

Higginbotham, P. (2008). *The Workhouse Cookbook.*

Higginbotham, P. (2012). *The Workhouse Encyclopedia.*

Higgs, M. (1904). *Five Days and Five Nights as a Tramp Among Tramps — Social Investigation by a Lady.*

Kohl, J. G. (1844). *Travels in Ireland.*

London, J. (1903). *The People of the Abyss.*

Orange, J. (1840). *History and Antiquities of Nottingham.*

British Parliamentary Papers

PP. (1777). *Report on the Returns made by the Overseers of the Poor.*

PP. (1834). *Report into the Administration and Practical Operation of the Poor Laws.*

PP. (1834a). *Report into the Administration and Practical Operation of the Poor Laws: Appendix A (Reports).*

PP. (1835). *First Annual Report of the Poor Law Commissioners.*

PP. (1909a). *Royal Commission on the Poor Laws and Relief of Distress, Majority Report.*

PP. (1909b). *Royal Commission on the Poor Laws and Relief of Distress, Minoriry Report.*

PP. (1909c). *Royal Commission on the Poor Laws and Relief of Distress. Appendix 28: Reports of Site Visits.*

Notes and Sou

PP indicates an item in British Parliamentary P

1. PP, 1777.
2. Higginbotham, 2012, p. 305.
3. *ibid.*
4. PP, 1834.
5. Bedford & Howard, 1985, pp. 18-19.
6. Personal recollection to author from Mr Laurie Liddiard.
7. PP, 1834a, pp. 531-3A.
8. Higginbotham, 2008, p. 35.
9. PP, 1834a, p. 170A.
10. PP, 1835, pp. 132-3.
11. *ibid.* pp.108-9.
12. *Kent Gazette*, 27 February 1838.
13. Orange, 1840, pp. 905-9.
14. Kohl, 1844, pp. 287-91.
15. *Household Words*, 13 July 1850, pp.361-4.
16. *All the Year Round*, 18 February 1860, pp. 392-6.
17. 'Sairey' Gamp is a dissolute nurse in Dickens' novel *Martin Chuzzlewit*.
18. *The Lancet*, 9 September 1865, pp. 296-8.
19. *The Lancet*, 26 August 1865, pp. 242-3.
20. Greenwood, 1866.
21. *All the Year* Round, 28 April 1866, pp. 37`-2.
22. *All the Year Round*, 14 December 1867, pp. 16-20.
23. Miss Miggs is a character in Dickens' novel *Barnaby Rudge*.
24. *The Lancet*, 19 October 1867, pp. 496-7.
25. A condition of the skin or scalp characterized by scales or crusts.
26. A character in Dante's *Divine Comedy*, sentenced to death by starvation.
27. *All the Year Round*, 30 November 1867, pp. 541-5.
28. John Wemmick is a character in Dickens' novel *Great Expectations*.
29. *All the Year Round*, 7 December 1867, pp. 558-64.
30. Smike is a character in Dickens' novel *Nicholas Nickleby*.
31. Daly was an Irish navvy who died from gross neglect in the Holborn workhouse in December 1864.
32. Gibson died from neglect and ill-treatment in the St Giles' workhouse infirmary in February 1865.
33. Scolly died in the Bethnal Green casual ward in January 1866.
34. Mr Tulliver is a character in George Elliot's novel *The Mill on the Floss*.
35. *The Sphinx*, 15 April 1871, pp. 115-6, and 29 April 1871, pp. 122-3.
36. Craven, 1887.
37. Anonymous, 1888.
38. A reference to James Greenwood's 'A Night in a Workhouse'.
39. *The Englishwoman's Review (New Series)* 15 February 1889, pp.49-58.

...*iver*, July 1889, pp. 643-6.
The Sunday at Home, 17 August 1889, pp. 524-6, and 24 August, pp. 541-3.
42. *The Sunday at Home*, 21 September 1889, pp. 604-7.
43. A bar gallon contains 16 pints.
44. *The Sunday at Home*, 26 October 1889, pp. 681-4.
45. *The Sunday at Home*, 30 November 1889, pp. 74-7.
46. 'Sairey' Gamp is a dissolute nurse in Dickens' novel *Martin Chuzzlewit*.
47. A hospital previously reported on by Mrs Brewer.
48. *The Sunday at Home*, 15 March 1890, pp. 316-9.
49. An annual exhibition in which health and science prominently featured.
50. *The Sunday at Home*, 31 May 1890, pp. 488-92.
51. In the original article, the location was erroneously referred to as 'Chorley'.
52. Manchester's other workhouse was at Crumpsall.
53. *The Sunday at Home*, 26 July 1890, pp. 617-20.
54. The Kirkdale industrial schools.
55. *The Sunday at Home*, 9 August 1890, pp. 652-3.
56. *ibid.*, pp. 653-4.
57. *The Sunday at Home*, 20 September 1890, pp. 747-8.
58. *ibid.*, pp. 748-750.
59. *British Medical Journal*, 30 June 1894, pp. 1422-3.
60. *British Medical Journal*, 8 December 1894, pp. 1317-8.
61. *British Medical Journal*, 28 September 1895, pp. 795-7.
62. *British Medical Journal*, 12 October 1895, pp. 923-5.
63. *Sheffield Daily Telegraph*, 2 September 1896.
64. *Sheffield Daily Telegraph*, 12 September 1896.
65. *Sheffield Daily Telegraph*, 4 September 1896.
66. *New England Magazine*, June 1896, pp 452-460.
67. *Rossendale Divisional Gazette*, 25 June 1898.
68. London, 1903, pp. 91-114.
69. 'The Carpenter' was a man previously encountered by London.
70. A 'tanner' was a colloquial name for a sixpence in pre-decimal UK coinage.
71. Higgs, 1904, pp. 16-22.
72. PP, 1909c, pp. 90-1.
73. *ibid.*, pp. 213-4.
74. 'Lunch' was a mid-morning snack rather than a midday meal.
75. PP, 1909c, pp. 69-71.
76. *ibid.*, p. 48.
77. *ibid.*, pp. 52-53.
78. *ibid.*, p. 261.
79. Gray, 1931.
80. 'Dad' was an elderly tramp previously encountered by Gray.

Location

Berkshire
  Reading, 208
  Wallingford, 26
Cheshire
  Macclesfield, 124
Durham
  Tynemouth, 261
Essex
  Billericay, 73
  Romford, 72
Flintshire
  Hawarden, 25
Gloucestershire
  Cirencester, 193
  Gloucester, 196
Hampshire
  Basingstoke, 74
  Hursley, 89
Ireland
  Cootehill, 219
  North Dublin, 38
  South Dublin, 213
Kent
  Blean, 29
Lancashire
  Chorlton, 110, 179
  Haslingden, 246
  Liverpool, 185
  Manchester (Swinton), 41
London
  Islington, 159
  Lambeth, 62, 173
  Lewisham, 58
  Shoreditch, 166
  St Martin in the Fields, 54
  St Marylebone, 143, 152
  St Pancras, 133

Ste
Wan
Whitec
Midlothian
  Leith, 272
Northamptonshire
  Oundle, 237
Nottinghamshire
  Nottingham, 32
Oxfordshire
  Headington, 274
  Oxford, 275
Pembrokeshire
  Haverfordwest, 204
Staffordshire
  Leek, 97
Suffolk
  Bulcamp, 27
Surrey
  Farnham, 83
  Guildford, 263
Sussex
  Brighton, 22
  Newhaven, 201
Warwickshire
  Birmingham, 270
  Coventry, 266
Wiltshire
  Swindon, 198
Yorkshire, West
  Bradford, 269
  Dewsbury, 256
  Ecclesall Bierlow, 224
  Keighley, 118
  Sheffield, 232

Printed in Poland
by Amazon Fulfillment
Poland Sp. z o.o., Wrocław

57245719R00159